The Settl

for the U.S. Virgin Islands

St. Croix, St. John, St. Thomas

17th Edition

**For those of you who are
considering settling in this
part of the tropics, or for
those already here,
this *handbook* provides
an objective look at living,
working, or investing in the
United States Virgin Islands.
For the visitor, this book
should help you get better
acquainted with these islands,
and explore them with a
greater awareness.**

On the cover:
Kids take a flying leap into the warm, inviting
waters off Buck Island, U.S. Virgin Islands.

*Cover photo by Wendy Carpenter Garth
Special thanks to Ivan Minarik
and other photo contributors to this edition.*

Library of Congress Control Number
(reverts to Serial #)
ISSN 1554-9739

The Settler's Handbook
17th Edition
is published by
Chey'nanigans, Corp.
1524 Acorn Way, #1G
Solvang, Ca 93643
(888) 867-5979/ (340)277-6994
Publisher: Cheyenne Harty
Editor/Production Manager: Cheyenne Harty/Sandra Harty Gutierrez
Layout: Cheyenne Harty
Sales Manager: Sandra Harty Gutierrez
info@cheynanigans.com/info@pinkelephantpromotions.com
www.visettlershandbook.com
© 2013 copyright Chey'nanigansCorp. All rights reserved.
Additional copies of this Handbook can be obtained from
Pink Elephant Promotions at P.O. Box 477, C'sted, St. Croix 00821
Quantity prices on request.
The current owner / publisher has revised the book in:
January 2013

Acknowledgements

Much appreciation and foresight to those who started this wonderful concept of a publication in the early 1970s. It's a fine idea that has continuously blossomed. This publisher hopes to continue this tradition, and that others who follow will too. Special acknowledgements to previous publishers: Doug Burns, Gloria Bourne, Judy Megnin, and Linda Bruton for growing this book.

Consultation thanks to consultant, Historian, William Cissell, plus various government agency personnel too numerous to mention. Many thanks to all, past and present who added a fact or clarification. Your assistance was greatly appreciated.

The Settler's Handbook
for the U.S. Virgin Islands
17th Edition
TABLE of CONTENTS

11/19/2012 "I used the Settler's Handbook to evaluate my move to Paradise and found the information provided to be both useful and accurate. My move to Paradise was a huge success, and it is now a distinct privilege for me to come full circle and advertise my business in this book. If you are looking to buy your own piece of America's Paradise come on down; the lifestyle and the water are both warm and inviting".
Scot F. McChain

11/13/12 "The VI Settler's Handbook is a must-have for anyone interested in relocating to the Virgin Islands. It is an invaluable resource for how to ship your goods and offers choices of shipping companies. It also walks soon-to-be locals through the steps of moving, including car registration, insurance and any required documentation. The book educates the reader on local customs and holidays – something which could take years to learn without this handy resource. I highly recommend the VI Settler's Handbook!
Fran Geocaris, Marketing Manager Divi Carina Bay Casino – 11 years, St. Croix Chamber of Commerce Board of Directors – 6 years

9/10 "The Settlers Handbook" has been part of our relocation package for decades. We send it to all our buyers from off-island! It answers all those important questions like: How do I ship my car, personals. Will I be allowed to relocate my dog. How to build a home. What to expect.
Julie San Martin, Team San Martin, ReMax, St.Croix

9/10 We've watched this book grow in popularity since Linda's first revision in 2002. The SHB is a tremendous resource for anyone in the process of moving to the USVI, contemplating, or planning to. It contains extremely valuable information applicable to individuals, families or businesses.
Tom Yaegel, VisitTheVI.com

The Settler's Handbook
for the U.S. Virgin Islands

Introduction

Ahhh, the Caribbean… visions of azure waters, swaying palm trees, and rum punches; truly a dreamer's vacation, but imagine living here. Some people make those dreams a reality. The Settler's Handbook is for those who are vacationing here, contemplating moving here, investing here, or for those who have just moved here. It is for those who are lured to the tropics, for the Virgin Islands charmed not only Christopher Columbus, but millions of others who have since landed on their shores.

How do you identify those who live here? For one thing, check out those bumper stickers that say, "Not all of us here are on vacation!" What's it like to live here? What can you expect? Read on.

The Settler's Handbook, 17th Edition, hopes to enlighten you on island living, whether you are a prospective settler, a vacationer, or a new business person. While each of the three islands, St. Croix, St. John and St. Thomas, has a unique style, they all share the charms and flavors of the Caribbean and the protection of the Stars and Stripes. In this up-dated 17th edition of The Handbook, we present the latest facts, figures, trends, pros and cons, about visiting, living and working in our islands. We hope this information will make your relocation, your vacation, or your investment, more successful.

Location of the
United States Virgin Islands

Florida

Bahamas

Cuba

Cayman
Islands

ATLANTIC   OCEAN

Greater Antilles

Longitude: 65 degrees

Jamaica

Dominican
Republic

Haiti

British
Virgin Islands

Puerto Rico

CARIBBEAN   SEA

U.S.Virgin Islands

Latitude: 15 degrees

South America

Lesser Antilles

*The physical location and relationship of the United States Virgin Islands
(see inset) between the North and South American continents, United States
Mainland, the Atlantic Ocean and the other islands of the Caribbean.*

i

Settler's Handbook Chapter 1

An Overview

The United States Virgin Islands, geologically formed of sedimentary rock and undersea lava flows, are located in the beautiful waters of the northern Caribbean, within the chain of all the Antilles, just west of the Atlantic Ocean. Surrounding the three Virgin Islands of St. Croix, St. John, St. Thomas—are 50 small, mostly uninhabited offshore islands and cays.

St. Croix, St. John and St. Thomas lie approximately 1,100 miles southeast of Miami and 1,650 miles south and east of New York City. Puerto Rico, a U.S. Commonwealth, is west and a little north about ninety miles away.The islands are in the Atlantic Time Zone, one hour ahead of New York and Florida,but on the same time during Daylight Savings Time. St. Croix's latitude is a little over 17 degrees, while St. Thomas and St. John are at approximately 18 degrees. That means if you fly a direct path, east to west around the earth, you also fly over Mexico City, Hawaii and Bombay, India. The longitude at 64 degrees aligns with the Canadian province of Nova Scotia to the north, and the South American country of Venezuela to the south.

St. Croix, the southernmost island, is nearly forty miles south of St. Thomas and St. John. The "big island" is almost 84 square miles and has approximately two-thirds of the total land mass of the Virgins. It is almost twenty-four miles from end to end, with a width of just over five miles at its widest point. The highest point is Mount Eagle, which rises 1,165 feet above sea level. The two main towns are Christiansted, mid-island on the north shore, and Frederiksted, on the west end. Both retain their names from the Danish period on St. Croix. St. Croix sounds like St. Croy, and its residents refer to themselves as Crucians; pronounced Crew'-shuns. St. Croix, is the only one of the three Virgins completely surrounded by the Caribbean Sea; St. Thomas and St. John are bounded by the Atlantic on the north.

St. John, the smallest island, is nine miles long and four miles wide, about twenty square miles of land. The highest point is Bordeaux Mountain at 1,277 feet. Cruz Bay at its west end is the main town and population center, and Coral Bay at the island's eastern end is a rapidly growing area. The island's residents are called St. Joe'-ne'ans. About two-thirds of St. John is a natural preservation, bequeathed by Laurance Rockefeller. Notable sites include historic ruins of Annaberg Plantation, a natural campsite at Maho Bay Campground and the famous Trunk Bay beach.

St. Thomas, thirteen miles long and three miles wide, has a total area of just over thirty-one square miles. Crown Mountain, at 1,550 feet and near the center of the island, is the highest point. Charlotte Amalie (pronounced (A'-mal-yah), the territorial capital of the U.S. Virgin Islands, is also the largest population center on St. Thomas. Growing population areas include the Tutu (mid-isle), and Red Hook sections (east end). Residents are called St. To'-me-ans.

Population

The territory of the Virgin Islands boomed during the 1960s when the population almost doubled. This was due to tourism, immigration work permits, an influx of retirees and federal aid. Unfortunately, the '70s saw the same economic recession that affected the U.S. mainland and the population in the islands declined. The U.S. census estimated the total population of the Virgin Islands in the '80s to be around 95,000 people. According to 2010 Census reports, the population of the islands was about 106,000, with about 50, 600 on St. Croix, 4,170 on St. John and 51,600 on St. Thomas. (what was available at press time (January 2013).

The inhabitants of the U.S. Virgin Islands are a unique collection of natives and peoples from the United States, various islands of the Caribbean, as well as Europe, the Middle East and South America. This has created a diversity in culture, giving the islands an extraordinary quality and personality.

Weather

The Virgin Islands proximity to the equator means that year-round, the length of the days are fairly consistent and the weather tropical. Residents lament the "cold" temperatures in January and February when the thermometer can dip to below 70 degrees F in the evening or early morning hours. That's long-sleeved shirt or sweater weather for those who are acclimatized. In the winter mid-day temperatures range from the high 70s to the mid-80s. In the summer, it's hot with a mid day range in the mid-80s to mid-90s. The record low is 57 and the record high 99. The year round 80 percent humidity is mitigated by the near-constant tradewinds. The annual average rainfall is about 43 inches. While statistics show September-October and May-June as the rainiest months, downpours can occur any \e. One year may be extremely wet and the next very dry. The western ₹ of the islands get the most rain. One obvious indication is the scrub and cactus on the eastern end of St. Croix and the so-called rain forest near Frederiksted in the west. In 1994, only 26 inches of rain fell, 17 inches less than the average. The drought caused hardships for all the islands residents who depend on rainfall to meet their agricultural, personal and household needs.A day-long downpour, however, can fill the water-saving cisterns. One or two day's worth of such rain can turn the brown hillsides to an emerald green. Hurricane season lasts from June 1 till November 30. Of the island weather it is often said, "if you don't like the weather, wait 10 minutes and it will change!

A Brief History

One hundred and fifty million years ago, when reptiles ruled the earth, there was neither a Caribbean Sea nor an Atlantic Ocean. The world's dry land mass (Pangaea) gradually split and spread to form the continents as we know them today (Continental Drift Theory). Even now the geological spreading continues and, where the great blocks of the earth's crust meet or diverge, titanic forces construct mountain chains or open deep ocean trenches which lead to rumbling volcanoes or shifting earthquakes. Cuba, Hispaniola, Puerto Rico, St. Thomas, St. John and the British Virgin Islands share a single large submerged bank which is part of the North American Plate. St. Croix, separated from her northern sisters by a two-mile deep ocean trench called the Virgin Islands Trench, is aligned along the northern edge of the Caribbean Plate on a mass called the Aves Ridge. To the south of the Caribbean Plate is the landmass of the South American Plate. The only active area as far as geologists can see is located in the Cayman Trough which runs in a line east-west, north of St. Croix, including Puerto Rico, St. Thomas, and other nearby islands. Other than minor tremors, no major activity has occurred in the area. Geologically, the islands are a conglomeration of ancient undersea lava flows, sedimentary and igneous rock formed under water from volcanic ash and layers of sand, and marine animals laid down by ocean currents. There was a major undersea earthquake along with tidal waves in 1867.Volcanic eruptions such as Montserrat in 1995 and the earthquake that submerged Port Royal, Jamaica three centuries ago, are reminders that the earth is in constant change.

The northern island chain in this part of the Caribbean, running east-west, is called the Greater Antilles. This includes: Hispaniola, Cuba and Puerto Rico. Southeast, including the Virgin Islands and extending in an arc toward the South American continent, are the Lesser Antilles. The island chains are the geophysical dividing line between the Atlantic and the Caribbean.

The First Settlers

Archaeological finds on St. Croix reveal artifacts that proved man was present in the Virgin Islands around 2500 B.C. Discoveries on St. Thomas at the Krum Bay site, under the location of the Water and Power Authority, show that a pre-ceramic tribe dates back to 2050 B.C. Other than the preceramic tribe, there have been three known pottery-making tribes who inhabited the islands: the Igneri or Ancient Ones from approximately A.D. 50 to A.D.650; the Taino or Arawak from A.D.650 to A.D.1425; and the Caribs from A.D.1425 to the late 17th century. Scientists believe the original inhabitants of the islands migrated up the Lesser Antilles from the South American coast. A ceremonial ball court or religious cultural center from the Taino era was discovered in the Salt River Bay area on St. Croix. That ceremonial site is the only one of its kind that has been discovered in the Lesser Antilles.

Explorers and Colonizers

Christopher Columbus and his crew were the first Europeans to visit the area known now as the Virgin Islands. While sailing north in 1493 along the Lesser Antilles chain, toward the community he'd established in Hispaniola (now Haiti and the Dominican Republic), Columbus sighted an island. The fleet decided to anchor near a bay (Salt River) in hopes of finding fresh water. The bay, called "AyAy" (The River) by the Tainos and "Cibuguiera" (Stony Land) by the Caribs, was to be named "Santa Cruz" by Columbus. The French would later keep the Holy Cross designation and call it "Ste. Croix."

Soldiers were dispatched in a longboat toward an Indian village for information. This landing party attacked some Caribs who approached in a canoe. A confrontation ensued, with at least one Spaniard and one Carib dying. Columbus, as a memorial to the dead Spaniard, named the site of the skirmish Cabo de las Flechas (Cape of the Arrows). Later, the Caribs would so harass the Spanish in Puerto Rico that they became a target for destruction and eventually retreated to other Carib communities on Dominica and Guadeloupe.

Columbus' fleet turned north to explore the islands on the horizon. They sailed past Anegada and Virgin Gorda (the eastern-most of what are now the British Virgin Islands), past St. Thomas and St. John. The explorer was so impressed by the number of islands that he named them in honor of St. Ursula and her legendary 11,000 martyred virgin companions. He resisted the temptation to anchor, continued westward and finally landed along Puerto Rico's west coast.

Though Spain claimed the Caribbean islands through Columbus' explorations, she made little effort to colonize the Lesser Antilles because they had no mineral wealth. During the two centuries that followed, the Greater and Lesser Antilles were the scenes of battles between English, Dutch and French admirals, pirates and privateers, all attracted first by rumor of Spanish treasure and later by the region's highly profitable products of cotton, sugar, rum, indigo and spices.

In the early 1640s, England and Holland were sparring over St. Croix. The English, farmers from the more settled island of St. Kitts, established a settlement around 1641 in the Salt River area of St. Croix. They would build a triangular earthwork structure to fortify their foothold. The structure, completed by the Dutch later, was called Fort Flamand (the Flemish fort) by the French. The Dutch West India Company also settled on the island around 1642. The English governor was killed and his settlers retaliated by killing the Dutch governor. The Dutch won, but allowed the English to remain. A few years later, the Dutch were forced out, leaving the English in control. In 1650, Spain would defeat and drive out the English. In 1650, the French surprised and defeated the Spanish garrison. The first French settlement was at Salt River; a later settlement was at the natural harbor on the north side of the island at present day Christiansted. They called it "Bassin." From 1655 to 1665, the French Crown leased the islands to the French Chapter of the Knights of Malta. During that time, the island continued to produce cotton, indigo, tobacco, sugar and tropical foods. In the late 17th century, the French were forced to abandon the island. Then, all but deserted, the island was occasionally visited by pirates and smugglers. French war ships arrived periodically to maintain title for the crown. When the French abandoned St. Croix, English woodcutters from Tortola moved in and engaged in lumbering.

France sold St. Croix to the Danish West India and Guinea Company in 1733. Denmark took over as a Crown Colony in 1755. This struggle for control of the islands, St. Croix in particular, demonstrates how the Caribbean would ebb and flow, matching the battles that existed in Europe in the 17th and 18th centuries. Blackbeard and other infamous pirates used St. Thomas to sell their plunder. St. Thomas continued to be the main port, and goods from the islands were shipped in and out by both legitimate companies and by smugglers and pirates. The coves and inlets of the islands proved to be havens for the smuggling of goods. By this period, sugar plantations and small farms had been established on St. John. With Charlotte Amalie's superb harbor, St. Thomas soon found its destiny as a trading center. In 1764 the island was proclaimed a free port. Many of the present-day Charlotte Amalie shops were once merchant warehouses with back doors facing the beaches and the harbor.

The Danes had become interested in sugar cultivation; the Danish West India and Guinea Company was chartered to expand the sugar plantations and control the African slave trade. Plantation agriculture began on St.

Thomas, using Danish indentured servants as laborers. The first shipments of African slaves arrived in 1673. In 1717, the Danes added St. John to their territory.When the French sold the island of St. Croix, Danish settlers from the plantations on St. Thomas sailed to St. John to farm. In 1733, a violent slave rebellion on St. John dislodged the Europeans for six months.

The Danish Era

On St. Croix, the Danes established the towns of Christiansted (named for King Christian VI of Denmark) in 1735, and Frederiksted (named for King Frederik V) in 1752. Friederich Moth, governor of the West India Company, designed the town layout for Christiansted and had the island of St. Croix surveyed into 150-acre estates. Moth encouraged settlers, who came from throughout the Caribbean, by offering tax benefits and reasonable land prices. Danish tolerance of ethnicity and religion also helped make the Virgin islands a melting pot, in which English eventually became the common language and Danish the language of the courts. Also spoken was a creole blend of Dutch, African, and later an English dialect, through which slaves and their owners communicated.

The rules and regulations put forth by the West India Company proved so rigid that the monarchy had to dissolve the company before economic growth could begin.The Danish crown purchased the charter from the West India Company in 1754 and moved the capital from Charlotte Amalie in St. Thomas to Christiansted in St. Croix. Prosperity peaked in the second half of the 18th century with exports of sugar and molasses, rum, hardwoods and cotton. At one point, due to its prodigious agricultural output, St. Croix

A Christiansted gallery

was called the "garden of the West Indies."

Danish West Indian architecture is emulated in the territory's elegant, sturdy, neo-classical buildings that are customized for West Indian weather. The second stories of these structures overhang sidewalks and create shady walkways called "galleries," which provide cover from both sun and rain. Windows, doors and open spacious rooms take advantage of the tradewinds, and Gutter systems on roofs help catch precious rainwater. The Danes established and rigidly enforced a strict building code for fire protection.

For building materials, Danes and black workers who had purchased their freedom made use of what was available. Yellow bricks from Danish ship ballasts were incorporated in much construction. And plantations were built mostly with coral quarried from the sea.

The islands of the West Indies played a significant role in the development of North America. Alexander Hamilton, the first Secretary of the U.S. Treasury, who wrote the *Federalist Papers*, began his career on St. Croix in a shipping firm owned by a New Yorker. The wealth and social status achieved by prominent island families appealed to colonial families in Philadelphia, New York and Charleston. Close family connections and trade would eventually help develop a natural friendship between the islands and the continent. And during the American Revolution the neutrality and freeport status of the Danish Virgins were important financial assets to the rebellious thirteen colonies. It is hence not surprising that the first salute from foreign soil to American independence was fired from Fort Frederik, St. Croix in 1776. Perhaps it is only fitting that the Virgin Islands now rest under America's Stars and Stripes.

Decline of Prosperity

In the early 19th century, the bright economic picture in the Danish Virgins dimmed. In 1803, as newly invented processing of beet sugar cut into the cane sugar market, Denmark formally ended the slave trade. Though the slave trade was over, slavery was not until those in captivity took action decades later. In 1848, dissatisfied Crucian slaves marched in Frederiksted demanding emancipation, and on July 3 Governor General Peter von Scholten, a man sympathetic to their cause, emancipated them. The governor's actions were considered illegal by the Danish government, and von Scholten was tried in Denmark for dereliction of duty. Labor was hence regulated by a colonial labor law that was deemed oppressive; 30 years later, in 1878, it culminated in a riot that led to the burning and destruction of homes and plantations. Denmark attempted to remedy the problems, but never again would the island achieve the prosperity and glory of the "golden age of sugar."As a result of economic decline, the population of the islands fell from 32,000 in 1829 to 14,600 in 1917. The capital city of the Danish West Indies alternated every six months between Charlotte Amalie, St. Thomas and Christiansted, St. Croix, till 1917, when Charlotte Amalie was appointed the permanent capital.

The U.S. Buys the Islands

U.S. efforts to buy the islands began in 1871 but were not successful until World War I, when the United States became concerned about German threats to the Panama Canal. The threat brought diplomats back to the negotiating table, and on March 31, 1917, the United States purchased the Virgin Islands for $25 million. The free port status of the islands was retained and is still in effect.

The islands were first administered by the U.S. Navy, with the

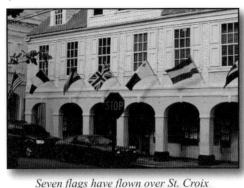

Seven flags have flown over St. Croix

Department of the Interior assuming jurisdiction in 1931.The Organic Act, passed by the United States Congress, provided local government in 1936. A 1954 revision of the Organic Act provided a three-branch territorial government. The first popularly elected governor of the Virgin Islands, Melvin H. Evans, took office in 1970.

The New VI Economy

The last sugar factory on St. Croix closed in 1966. Since then, the island's economy has been based on light and heavy industry, immigration, and tourism.St.Croix's industrial history is dynamic, and its changing nature is evidenced in the shining steel labyrinths dotting the south shore. On the western end of St.Croix's industrial landscape is the site of a former aluminum facility, which was first established in 1965 as Harvey Alumina. Over the years, the property has been owned by several aluminum companies, including Martin Marietta, Virgin Islands Alumina Corporation (VIALCO), and finally, Alcoa World Aluminum Corporation (ALCOA). Following a steady decline in the global aluminum market, ALCOA sold the site to St. Croix Renaissance Group, which has transformed the former aluminum plant into an industrial park. Renaissance Group touts the location's deep ports, desalinization plant and coal-fired power plant as amenities to attract tenants, which today includes Diageo, makers of Captain Morgan's rum.

West of the Renaissance park is HOVENSA, the company that has had the most impact on the island's recent economic history. Hess Oil Refinery of the Virgin Islands (HOVIC) began operations in 1966 and gradually increased its production to 650,000, making it the largest oil refinery in the world until 1974. In 1998 Hess Oil entered into a partial merger with Venezuelan oil company Petroleos de Venezuela and is now called HOVENSA. In January 2012, citing hemorrhaging finances, a weak global economy, and anemic projections for the refinery industry, HOVENSA announced intentions to pull the plug on its refinery operations, a move that led to layoffs for most of the company's approximately 2,000 employees. As of press time, the closure continues to have ripple effects on the local economy and has led to contention between the VI Government and HOVENSA over how to move forward. HOVENSA has expressed interest in continuing on as an oil storage facility.

Historically, oil and aluminum have been a catalyst for immigration. Labor needs in the last two decades have been satisfied by heavy immigration from Puerto Rico (continuing a century-old trend), from the United States mainland, and other parts of the Caribbean. The territory's population rebounded to 32,099 in 1960, and nearly tripled that figure by the early 1970s due mainly to new settlers and slower emigration. A 1969 study estimated that nearly a third of the territory's population was born in the Virgin Islands. Another third was born in the United States mainland, Europe and Puerto Rico. The final third were residents, bonded, and/or illegal aliens, almost exclusively from other islands in the Caribbean. As a result of unofficial immigration, the hard figures on population breakdowns are nearly non-existent. The United States Coast Guard, and the United States Border Patrol continue to battle the illegal immigration problem.

By 1977, when the territory's population was over 89,000, the portion of non-citizens had declined to less than a quarter of the population, with half of that number as permanent residents and the proportion of bonded workers or aliens dropping steadily. These figures don't necessarily represent the real number of people moving in or out, as categories change when residents become U.S. citizens and aliens achieve permanent status or return to home islands. Some bonded "temporary" workers have been in the Virgin Islands for two decades.

In 1982, the Congress of the United States passed the Virgin Islands Non Immigrant Alien Adjustment Act in order "to eliminate the uncertainty and insecurity of aliens who: a) legally entered the Virgin Islands of the United States as non immigrants for employment under the temporary alien labor program; b) have continued to reside in the Virgin Islands for long periods and, as a result, c) have contributed to the economic, social and cultural development of the Virgin Islands and have become an integral part of the society of the Virgin Islands."

Those who fell in this category and had lived within the territory since June 30, 1975 were given one year to comply with residency prerequisites (inspection and admission to the Virgin Islands as non-immigrant alien workers, their spouses, or their minor children). In the late 1980s many illegal aliens who had complied with the earlier requirements were granted permanent status under a United States Immigration Service Amnesty program. This new status often brought access to healthcare, education, housing, and the opportunity to eventually apply for citizenship.

The Puerto Rican community has a large segment on St. Croix where 45% of the population is Spanish speaking. St. Thomas has two French communities from St. Barths and the Dominican Republic. Settlers to the

Virgin Islands have come from the British Virgin Islands, Denmark, Germany, Spain, Portugal, India, Philippines, the Lesser and Greater Antilles, the Caribbean in general, the Arab nations, and the Far East. The United States Virgin Islands is a mini-United Nations where the "melting pot" bubbles to a calypso beat.

Recent Economic Development

Economic growth in the territory is in some aspects tied to the people it attracts. In this regard, there are some promising signs. In 2011 visitor arrivals to the three main islands totaled 2,687,952. A majority, 2,008,991, were cruise ship tourists, but the territory also welcomed 678,961 air arrivals. St. Thomas and St. John reported 1,287,096 cruise ship visitors, and St. Croix reported 158,196. While St.Croix, which has more shallow ports than St. Thomas, strives to increase cruise ship calls, the "big island" has experienced an increase in air visitors, showing significant hikes during the first quarter of 2012. St. Thomas is also attracting non-cruise visitors via an insurgence of condos and timeshares, one being the 220-unit Frenchmen's Cove. For updates on visitor arrivals, contact the VI Bureau of Economic Research at http://www.usviber.org.

Other developments may increase visitation and immigration. These include a new cancer center on St. Thomas and cardiac center on St. Croix, major condo construction on St. John, and three planned hotel casino resorts for St. Croix. There are also two Crucian marina projects pending. Developers have earned Coastal Zone Management approval for a new Frederiksted marina; and in Christansted a revamping of the Gallows Bay marina is expected to attract megayachts. Furthermore, some on St. Croix seek to cope with losses resulting from the HOVENSA refinery shut down by opening a cultural theme park, for which the VI Legislature passed a call for proposals in 2012.

St. Croix's rum industry is also on the rise. In January 2010, Diageo, the world's largest beer, wine and spirits company, opened a St. Croix distillery for Captain Morgan's, the world's second largest rum provider. Diageo's 30-year commitment to the territory will provide a major economic stimulus in the form of excise taxes and employment. The distillery has the capacity to distill up to 20 million proof gallons of Captain Morgan rum per year, supplies all rum used to make Captain Morgan-branded products in the nation, and is expected to generate an estimated $130 million in new tax revenue for the Virgin Islands government. Located in the St. Croix Renaissance park, the facility features a state-of-the-art, eco-friendly visitor's center, and is mostly run by locals, as at least 80 percent of full-time distillery employees are from the territory.

Settler's Handbook Chapter 2

Getting Acquainted...

AROUND the UNITED STATES VIRGIN ISLANDS

Even though the three islands, St. Croix, St. John and St. Thomas, have many similarities with their neighbors in the Caribbean, their differences are considerable. St. Croix's terrain encouraged agricultural development and a general spreading of the population throughout the island. St. John's size and natural beauty led to preservation of a national park on the island. And St. Thomas, with her steep inclines and a natural deep harbor, became a world-class port. So each island is different due to terrain, beneficial intervention and surrounding water, developing delightful and individual personalities and styles. As a result, the three sister islands of the United States Virgin Islands are beautiful examples of life in the Caribbean. They share qualities of the quintessential American paradise, but, like sisters in many families, they are strikingly unique, fiercely independent, usually squabbling, yet quite loyal to each other should outsiders ask.

AROUND the ISLANDS - St. Croix

The island of St. Croix has two charming towns, Christiansted and Frederiksted, with three other major shopping areas (Gallows Bay, Sunny Isle, and Sunshine Mall), marvelous beaches, scenic drives, outstanding watersport activities, three golf courses, some tennis courts, all spread out across the island's almost 84 sq. miles.

Christiansted

Our round-the-island tour begins with the historic city of Christiansted. Several blocks of the wharf area have been designated a National Historic Site by the National Park Service. The town features narrow streets and sturdy architecture similar to the style of the 18th century neo-classical. The strict requirements of the Danish building code, established in 1747 for fire and hurricane, spared the town from the dangers that have destroyed many historic areas elsewhere.

Among the most striking of these Danish structures is **Fort Christianvaern**, which currently serves as headquarters for the National Park Service and is a perfect place to begin an architectural tour of the town. This bright yellow fort overlooks **Christiansted Harbor, Protestant Cay** (home to Hotel on the Cay and once a burial ground for Protestants barred from the island cemetery by the French Catholic administration), scores of yachts, St. Thomas, and St. John. A prime example of colonial military architecture, the fort contains posted descriptions of the town's historic buildings. These include, the **Danish Customs House**, the **Scalehouse, Government House, Danish West India & Guinea Company Warehouse**, and the **Steeple Building**, which all date from the earliest period.

Fort Christiansvaern and the Steeple Building are open to the Public. The fort is open seven days a week from 8 a.m. to 4:45 p.m. on weekdays and 9 a.m. to 4:45 p.m. on the weekends. The Steeple Building is open weekdays from 9 a.m. to 4 p.m. Call 773-1460 for more information.

Frederiksted

Our island tour continues with St. Croix's other major town, Frederiksted, also known as "Freedom City." If you should arrive by cruise ship, you will dock at the new pier in Frederiksted where much of the town has been named an historic area. This turn-of-the-century town charms visitors with wide tree-shaded streets, a lovely waterfront, and several blocks of arcaded sidewalks. As a National Historic District, the city features such structures as the Old Customs House, the Fleming Building constructed of bricks from destroyed sugar mill chimneys, St. Paul's Anglican Church, dating from 1812, and the restored Fort Frederik located just to the left of the pier as you disembark. Built in the mid 1700s, the Fort has been in continuous use for military and other government purposes. The Fort is now a venue for cultural events as well as a Museum specializing in the history and architecture of Frederiksted, with rotating exhibits of local artists and craftspeople. Their open hours are: 8:30 a.m. to 4:00 p.m. Monday through Friday. Closed on holidays. Admission fee: $3.00 for adults, children under 16 are free (including school groups). For further information call: 772-2021 (fees and hours subject to change). Wherever you drive, you will find remnants of sugar mills in the landscape of the island. At the height of the plantation era, in the 1700s, St.Croix had 114 wind mills,14 ox-mills and was divided into 275 plantations, or estates. The island was once considered the premier sugar-producing area and the "bread basket" of the Caribbean. Most areas still carry the plantation or estate names that reflect the owner's thinking. Check a map, or, on your drive through the island, look for names like: Good Hope, Judith's Fancy, Lower and Upper Love, Barren Spot, Humbug, or William's Delight.

While St. Croix offers many variations in topography, the East End with Point Udall, the easternmost point of land in the United States, offers breath-taking sea vistas, gentle hills dotted with cactus and an unob-structed view of Buck Island, just six miles away. To get to **Point Udall**,

12

follow Route 82 past Cramer Park, past the **National Radio Astronomy Observatory**, and east along a newly paved road to the very tip, where you will find a monument at this point. As you stare out on the vast ocean, remember that the next major piece of land is Africa!

The **Buck Island Reef National Monument** features snorkeling, swimming, beautiful waters, sandy beaches, good hiking, and is a frequent stop— not only for the day-charter boats, but also the locals on weekends. Note that signs on occasion may be posted closing some of the walking trails for nesting turtles and wild bird or endangered animal protection. Most boats stop first at the sheltered sandy beach along the island's west shore, where you can practice snorkeling.

Cutural Tidbit

An author, folklorist and educator, Dr. George Franklin is well known for his witty and incisive look into Virgin Islands culture. Here are a few poignant pearls of local wisdom with Dr. Franklin's cachet.

• Between the Sand, Sea and Shore, we all Share the Same Surf. In other words, there are no private beaches in the Virgin Islands. All beaches must be accessible to all visitors and residence alike. NJoy

• Dress for Success. Beach clothing is for the beach. It is against custom and civil law to walk the streets in your bikinis. Decorum dictates. We may be paradise but we've changes the rule since after the time of Adam and Eve with their Fig Leaves Fashion.

•Good Friday ain't so good if you are searching for a drink at a bar or restaurant between the hours of 9:00am and 4:00 pm. It is against the law to serve alcohol on that day. Yep, it sucks like sweet lime.

A few minutes sail to the east end puts you at the famed underwater trail. Put your mask, fins and snorkel on, then splash into a dream world of beautiful coral and fish. Also note that there are only a few moorings placed at this end and you cannot drop anchor any other place here. These moorings were strategically placed to protect the coral and the underwater park. Only a few charter boats have their license to moor in this vicinity. If you can't swim, guides can tow you with a float. If you don't want to get wet, take a glass-bottomed boat for a glimpse of the island's superb marine life.The coral reef, lying just under the surface of the water, is a great mass of elkhorn coral extending like a horseshoe around the eastern side of the

island. Within its protection are thousands of hard and soft coral formations in an astonishing range of sizes, shapes and colors identified by underwater markers and an equally dazzling array of fish. All this is at a depth of only about 13 ft.

There is no fishing or "take" whatsoever inside the park boundaries. Possession of firearms, fishing, hunting gear, and spear guns are prohibited. You must stay off the fragile coral, and while on the shores and beaches, you must not collect any souvenirs. This is a nationally protected island on land and underwater.Also, before anchoring anywhere along the shores of St. Croix, look for mooring balls, put there for boats to tie up to and not drop their own anchor. Do not mistake fishermen's markers for fish pots for mooring balls.

St. Croix's mid-island area has many special sites to visit. On Queen Mary Highway, Route 70 on the map, look for the **St. George Village Botanical Garden** sign, a right turn off Queen Mary when you are heading west. You can spend as little as an hour or as long as a morning wandering around its lush gardens, tropical rain forest and restored village buildings.The Garden is open daily from 9-5 except for Christmas (692-2874). Recently added is their new visitor's Center and Museum Store. (Small admissions fee.)

History comes alive at **Whim Plantation Museum** (also on Rt. 70) as you walk among the historic 18th century buildings of this former sugar estate. The stately, authentically furnished Greathouse welcomes you with gracious guides waiting to tell you stories of past inhabitants and the reality of plantation life. Managed by the St. Croix Landmarks Society, this 12 acre site features a fully restored windmill, sugar factory ruins, cookhouse, tropical tress and a small sugarcane field. The Museum Store offers a tempting array of Caribbean crafts, artwork, books, prints and whimsical whatnots. Hours are 10am-4pm Monday through Saturday; small admission fee. Call 340-772-0598 or visit www.stcroixlandmarks.org for more information.

Nestled in the tranquil, tropical valley of Estate Little LaGrange (on Rt.

76) is **Lawaetz Family Museum**, a traditional homestead museum. This Danish West Indian house, with its rambling gardens, orchards and authentic furnishings, was the home of the Lawaetz family for more than one hundred years. Under the management of the St. Croix Landmarks Society, guided tours now introduce visitors to the traditions and values of a farming family living and working on St. Croix. Hours are 10am-4pm on Tuesdays, Thursdays and Saturdays; small admission fee. Call 340-772- 0598 or visit www.stcroixlandmarks.org for more information. St. Croix Landmarks Society's preservation efforts also extend to the **Apothecary Hall** exhibit, a nineteenth-century Danish colonial pharmacy museum on Queen Cross Street in Christiansted, and the **St. Croix Heritage Trail**. The nationally recognized Heritage Trail is a 72-mile driving tour that connects St. Croix's historic sites, attractions and natural areas.Watch for the brown and white sugar mill symbol road signs and visit http://heritagetrails.stcroixlandmarks.org for more information. Take Midland Road, Route 72 on the maps, to **Friedensfeld Moravian Church**. This intricate structure was prefabricated in Germany and carried to the islands in the mid-1800s. This is just one of the many historic churches on St. Croix.

For an intimate historical experience, one might want to pay **Sprat Hall** a visit. The territory's oldest plantation home, Sprat Hall dates back to the 17th century French occupation. Joyce Hurd, Spratt Hall's current owner, will provide prescheduled visits of her home, while her daughter Jill offers the opportunity to tour Frederiksted's beaches, historial ruins and rain forrest on horseback. For a tour of Sprat Hall contact Joyce Hurd at 719-1186. For a historical, pleasure filled horseback ride contact Paul and Jill's Equestrian Stable at 772-2880.

Cruzan Viril Ltd., located in Estate Diamond, off Queen Mary Highway and left on Route 64, or West Airport Road, is home of the famous **Cruzan Rum**. The rum factory traces its origin back to 1760, symbolizes longevity in the rum category, and embodies the real "spirit" of a hand-crafted, nurtured product. Produced by three generations of the Nelthropp family, this distillery owes its legacy to hundreds of years of Crucian rum culture. Despite the termination of nearly 200+ sugar cane crushing mills on the island, the distillery has increased production capacity to serve a greater global demand for rum and has adapted its technology to remain current without sacrificing quality. Among the largest rum distilleries in the Caribbean, the Cruzan credo is to produce superior rum, as exemplified by its Estate Collection, which has raised the industry standard. Popular Cruzan blends include Cruzan Estate 1-year light, two- year dark, and Single Barrel Estate Rum— the world's only single barrel rum, which has earned the title of "World's Best Rum" and won double gold at the prestigious San Francisco World Spirit Competition in 2010. The oak-aged Cruzan Rum was also voted best in a blind test conducted by The Washingtonian Magazine. For information regarding tours call 692-2280. (Small admission fee.)

While on your tour along the Melvin Evans Highway you will see the huge **Captain Morgan Distillery** previously mentioned in Chapter 1.

Be sure to visit the west side of **Salt River** on the north shore on Rte. 80, just off of Route 75. It is here that Christopher Columbus and his fleet skirmished with Carib Indians on November 14, 1493. The Salt River Park also has the largest remaining mangrove forest left in the territory. The 1,015-acre **Salt River Bay National Historical Park and Ecological Preserve** is jointly managed by the National Park Service and the USVI Government. Within the Salt River Park, ownership is divided such that NPS has 212 acres and the V.I. Government has 653 acres. A Visitor Contact Station is open Tuesdays through Thursdays from November to June. To schedule a free tour call 773-3183.

Guided kayak tours can be accessed through Salt River Marina's office, as can diving the east and west Salt River Canyon Walls with Anchor Dive Shop at Salt River. Guided ecological tours of the **Salt River Mangrove** shore and other breathtaking spots are also provided by Caribbean Adventure Kayaking Tours (778-1522) or Virgin Kayak Tours (718-0071).

Golf buffs will love the world-class Carambola Golf and Tennis Club, located just off Route 69 and east of the Rain Forest. An outstanding course, designed by Robert Trent Jones, Senior, Carambola twists around a beautiful valley. The Buccaneer Hotel (18 holes), and the Reef (9 holes), offer challenging courses for their guests and the general public. For a spectacular view of the island, take Route 58 just outside of Frederiksted, the **Creque Dam Road**, and wind between the mountain tops and through the **Rain Forest**. Because the roads go up hill and down dale, drive them only in the daylight, and with care, in a 4-wheel drive vehicle. The **Mahogany Road**, or Route 76, near Frederiksted, is another beautiful, peaceful drive through the lush Rain Forest.

Staying on the Island...

Since nothing on St. Croix is more than an hour away, stay at a hotel that best suits your fancy or your pocketbook. For top-notch resort vacations, stay at The Buccaneer Hotel, Carambola Beach Resort, or Divi Carina Bay Resort and Casino. Carambola Beach Resort is located on the north side, west of Cane Bay. Divi is at the far east end on   south shore, and the Buccaneer is east of Christiansted. All have beautiful beaches, pools, gift shops, and a range of restaurants from casual to formal dining.

Smaller, but definitely first class beachside hotels, are The Palms, and the Hibiscus Beach Resort, just west of Christiansted, and Chenay Bay Beach Resort (cottages), and Tamarind Reef Hotel, both east of Christiansted. For condo rentals there are many choices: Sugar Beach Resort Condos, Club St. Croix, Colony Cove, west of Christiansted, Schooner Bay at Gallows Bay, The Reef Condos, Caribbean Property Management Inc., and Teague Bay Properties to the east. On the north shore you will find Gentle Winds, Cane Bay Reef Club and Waves at Cane Bay. For the serious golfer, Carambola Golf and Tennis Club has a number of villas avail- able for vacation rental which overlook their spectacular golf course.

St. Croix is known for its charming small inns (bed & breakfast hospitality); to name a few: Carringtons Inn, Arawak Inn, and the remodeled Comanche Hotel. If you should choose to stay in Christiansted, you will find yourself near many of the island's finest restaurants and specialty duty-free shops. Located in town are a number of hotels that reflect the owner's personalities, Caravelle,The Company House Hotel (once the Danish West India and Guinea warehouse), Holger Danske, Hotel on the Cay (a quick 3-minute boat ride), Kings Alley Hotel, and King Christian Hotel (check out their new gift shop), most of which reflect the Danish architects influences. For further information on where to stay call **The St. Croix Hotel &Tourism Association** at 340-773-7117. For rentals try the **V.I. Territorial Assoc. of Realtors (VITAR)** at (877) 253-2448. The **St. Croix Board of Realtors** 344-5618; **St. John Board of Realtors** 1-866-966-9261 and **St Thomas Board of Realtors** 1-866-598-1440 ext. 234.

Dining Out

Experience a little St. Croix history as you are dining in a plantation greathouse, a restored Danish colonial townhouse, or simply sitting by the water enjoying a beautiful sunset. Watch yachts and sailing craft from your harbor-front table, or beachfront table, or enjoy the panoramic view of the Caribbean from a restaurant tucked into an island hillside. There are a full variety of cuisines from West Indian, French, Danish, Continental, Cajun, Latin and American, to fast food and deli specialties.

For upscale dining in downtown Christiansted, enjoy the continental fare at Kendricks. For more casual dining in Christiansted, try: Rum Runners at Hotel Caravelle, Bombay Club, Paradise Cafe , Mexican food at Lunch-eria, and intimate Savant, winner of the 2011 Tripadvisor Certificate of Excellence. In Gallows Bay, The Golden Rail and No Bones offer casual and not too pricey dining. Just outside of Christiansted heading east is Tutto Bene, an Italian favorite. The Buccaneer Hotel, with three restaurants, has elegant dining and entertainment. The Galleon at Green Cay Marina has been an island favorite for a long time. A well-known beachfront restaurant at the east end is Duggan's Reef. The Cultured Pelican, located at Coakley Bay, offers pasta dishes, seafood and continental. Try the homemade pasta at Southshore Cafe (at the old dairy farm site), and the casual popularity of Cheeseburgers in America's Paradise, just before Chenay Bay Beach

Cultural Tidbit

Potato Stuffing
St. John, U.S.V.I.
Yields 8-10 servings

You will find this side dish, thanks to Angela Spencely of St. Thomas, delicious. It's a hit at virtually any West Indian gathering. An inexpensive investment in a potato ricer will make fluffy, not gluey, stuffing that is the perfect accompaniment for roast pork.

Ingredients
• 6 large white potatoes, peeled and diced •1 tbs. olive oil or bacon fat •1 tsp. salt •1 large yellow onion, minced • ¼ cup butter or olive oil •1 large sweet red bell pepper, minced • ¼ cup evaporated milk • ½ small habañero pepper, mince •¼ cup whole milk •1 tsp. dried thyme • 2 tbs. brown sugar •½ tsp. dried marjoram •2 tbs. ketchup •½ cup raisins •1 tbs. tomato juice

Directions
1. Place potatoes in a large, deep kettle or saucepan. Add salt and cover with water. Bring to a boil, reduce heat and simmer until potatoes are soft, about 20 minutes. Drain.
2. Run potatoes through a potato ricer or mash gently. Add ¼ cup olive oil, butter, milks, brown sugar, ketchup and tomato paste. Set aside.
3. Heat olive oil in a large skillet. Sauté onion, bell pepper and habañero pepper until soft, about 3 minutes over medium heat. Stir in thyme, marjoram and raisins. Simmer 2 min.
4. Preheat oven to 350°F. Combine onion with mashed potato mixture and spoon into a greased baking dish. Bake for 20 – 25 minutes until golden.

Resort, where there is also great seaside dining. For authentic local fare try Kim's Restaurant in C'sted, Gertrude's on the Hess Rd or La Reine Chicken Shack in Kingshill.

In Frederiksted, Blue Moon has great food and Friday night Jazz. Just north of Frederiksted there is casual dining at Rainbow Beach and Sunset Grille, both on the beach. Sand Castle Beach Side Cafe (winner of Wine Spectator's 2011 Award of Excellence), Turtles Deli and Mahogany are on the beach south of Frederiksted. Just outside of Frederiksted, off Queen Mary Highway, stop at Villa Morales for the Latin - West Indian flavors of roast pork and fresh seafood.

On the Northshore road try Carambola Resort, Bogey's at Cane Bay Reef Club, Waves at Cane Bay, Cane Bay Beach Bar (EAT), Sprat Net, Off the Wall. Devotees of Wendy's, McDonald's, KFC, Dominos, IHOP, Pizza Hut, and Subway you will find them in several locations on the island. Some favorites for Chinese are China Panda and Fung Kong in Golden Rock. **Some of the above restaurants may close for the summer months, so be sure to call first.**

Shopping Around

St. Croix is a duty-free port with much less hustle and bustle than St. Thomas, and that will make shopping easy. In Christiansted, a collection of galleries, mostly located on properties intersecting Company and Queen Cross Streets, displays the best works of talented local artists. There are art galleries at Henle Studios in Princesse, Danica in the Luncheria Courtyard at Apothecary Hall, No. 6 Company Street, and the Betsy Campen Gallery in Gallows Bay. Several more galleries have opened; just ask around. Don't forget the Caribbean Museum of Art in Frederiksted. One particularly fun way to take in the Crucian art scene is to attend one of Christiansted's Art Thursdays, a November-through-June art walk in which galleries stay open late and provide refreshment and conversation about their work to visitors. For more information, visit www.artthursday.com.

Christiansted also has a lot of fabulous jewelry shops, offering handcrafted original pieces. Visit Sonya's for the authentic 'hook' bracelet; Premier Jewelers and Gifts for custom jewelry and gifts as well as the "hook" bracelet; Crucian Gold for the Crucian Knot bracelet; and the Gold Worker, and IB Designs for custom crafted jewelry. For great sunglasses, jewelry and bric a brac, visit Baci's Duty free. For cigars see Steele's Smokes & Sweets. Unusual glass cut-pieces can be seen at the Mitchell-Larsen Studio on Company Street. Your best bet for duty-free liquor is Kmart. Duty-free means you can take up to $1600 in goods back with you.

Island fashions can be found at the stores at King's Alley Walk, Pan Am Pavilion, and Caravelle Arcade and duty-free perfume at Violette's

Boutique. If you are looking for Native crafts visit Many Hands, or the LEAP in the Rain Forest on route 76. LEAP specializes in locally carved wood artifacts ranging from custom furniture to smaller items made of 18 mahogany, Saman and Tibet. LEAP stands for Life and Environmental Arts Project, which is a special program established to train wood cutters/craftsmen in the utilization of the native woods of the island. There are boutiques, gift and souvenir shops in Frederiksted.

AROUND the ISLANDS....ST. JOHN

St. John is special. Lush mountains drop to white beaches and postcard bays. A getaway for the rich and famous and average Joes, this tiny island

serves as a retreat for Crucians and St. Thomians. The Virgin Islands National Park, consisting of approximately two-thirds of the island, is a major attraction for the more than one million people who visit yearly.

Established in 1956 by the U.S. Congress, the seeds for the Park were sown by philanthropist Laurance Rockefeller who bought and donated 5,000 acres of land on the island. Over the years, the acreage has expanded to 7,200 acres of land with 5,650 acres offshore.

The Park offers gorgeous beaches, camping, prime cruising, snorkeling, and hiking trails.The underwater snorkel trail at Trunk Bay, on the northwestern shore of the island, is world famous. For a glimpse at the island's sugar legacy, visit Annaberg Estate Plantation on the northern shore near Route 20. Lovingly restored by Park artisans, the Estate's stone mill dominates the skyline. The Park often has basket-makers, cooks and other crafts-people on hand to demonstrate and share their skills. On the southern side, the trip through the Reef Bay valley past ancient ruins and stone carvings called petroglyphs dating back to the day when sugar was king, gives hikers a real chance to enjoy the natural beauty of the Virgin Islands.

Visitors can hike on well-maintained trails or through the bush, but keep in mind that some of the land within the Park boundaries is privately owned. The Park strictly enforces the laws that protect the Park's fragile environment. Take only pictures and leave only footprints.

Cruisers will find pristine anchorages and top-notch sailing when they wend their way through the Park. During the winter months, keep a lookout in Pillsbury Sound between St. John and St. Thomas for broaching whales.

To give everyone a chance to enjoy the Park's beautiful waters, sailors are limited to 14 nights per year in the Park. You might want to stop in Cruz Bay and pick up a box lunch before visiting the Park. However, most of the time lunch, restrooms and cool showers are available at Trunk Bay and Cinnamon Bay. Hawksnest Beach has restrooms. Francis Bay, Salt Pond and Lameshur Bay have natural rustic facilities.

If you are in St. Thomas, you can ride a ferry to St. John by going to the Red Hook Visitor's Center, a 15-minute ride. In St. John, see the Cruz Bay Visitors' Center for maps and tour information, and browse through the best collection of books you will find on the different islands. Taxis are available for island tours or you can rent a car. It can take a half day to seethe island if you rush it, but you can relax and make it a full day, or plan to spend more time at one of St. John's inns, condos, or hotels. You can also take a ferry from downtown Charlotte Amalie on St. Thomas versus the taxi ride to Red Hook at east end.

Within the Park boundaries, you will find Cinnamon Bay Campground, Maho Bay Camps, Caneel Bay Resort and a collection of private homes for rent. While the Park is the island's focal point, St. John has much more to offer. The main town of Cruz Bay is now a bustling port. While it doesn'tbegin to rival St. Thomas for traffic, you will see cruise ships' tenders dropping off passengers nearly every day during winter season, sail boats clearing into the territory through the U.S. Customs facility, and barges hauling construction materials. If you want to absorb the local flavor, spend an hour sitting in Cruz Bay Park, just across from the ferry terminal, and watch an entire cross-section of humanity pass by.

Stop at the local museum located on the lower floor of the Elaine Ione Sprauve Library just up from Cruz Bay center off Route 104, called South Shore, which after Fish Bay continues as Giftt Hill up to Centerline Road.

The collection housed in the Enighed plantation great house, includes some pre-Columbian pottery and artifacts from the sugar mill. The museum library hours are 9 a.m. to 5 p.m., Monday through Friday. You can browse its collection of books on the Caribbean. Call the library at 776-6359 for more information.

To see more of the island, rent a car at any of the handful of agencies in Cruz Bay. You can take Centerline Road, which goes straight through the island, or the North Shore Road, which is winding and passes many National Park beaches and scenic lookouts. On Centerline you may encounter truck traffic, so it's slower, with no room to pass. Drive along Centerline Road, Route 10 from Cruz Bay, towards the east end, to the sleepy community of Coral Bay, which is ever expanding. Once out of Cruz Bay, the pace slows. Fill up on gas before you leave, since Cruz Bay has only one station at this time, and Coral Bay has a Domino's gas station. Once you leave the residential area of Cruz Bay, you will find green hills and spectacular views on the 20-minute drive. When you get to Coral Bay, turn right and head down Route 107 and see one breathtaking view after another.Watch for places to stop and take pictures. Also watch out for goats and donkeys that roam the roads. They will put quite a dent in your rental car if you hit one. Also drive slowly and on the left. It is very narrow. If you are truly intrepid, follow the up-hill and down-dale road past **Salt Pond** to **Lameshur Beach** for an afternoon of snorkeling, sunning or dozing in the shade. Explore the ruins of the old Lameshur plantation that hugs the western end of Lameshur Bay beach.

Getting There is Half the Fun

Ferries leave on the hour from Red Hook, St. Thomas for the 20-minute one-way trip to Cruz Bay, St. John, and costs about $6. The ferry from downtown Charlotte Amalie, St. Thomas to Cruz Bay, St. John, costs about $12, takes about 45 minutes and goes less frequently. and costs about $6, though small Children are charged only $1 and seniors, $1.50. You will share the trip with luggage, boxes of groceries, pieces of furniture and dozens of St.John residents returning from work or shopping in St. Thomas. Besides the two passenger companies ferrying between St. John and St.Thomas runs,

TS-Transportation Services (776-6282) and Varlack Ventures (776-6412) and the inter-island boat service to the British Virgin Islands, there are other companies which provide barge service to/from St.Thomas: Boyson and Love City. Car/truck barges run every half-hour or so until about 7 p.m. Car rental companies in St. Thomas do not allow you to take the rental on the ferry to St. John. A car barge is about $30 one way, or $50 roundtrip. A port fee of $3 for cars and $4 for larger vehicles is payable in cash in St. Thomas. Some ferries charge $2.50 per baggage plus a $1.10 fuel surcharge. **(All rates subject to change.)**

Staying on the Island

St. John has a wide variety of accommodations to suit the visitor's taste and budget. From campgrounds to luxury villas, to the gorgeous Westin Resort, with an assortment of budget guest houses in between. Most outdoor types will like the Park's Cinnamon Bay Campground 776-6330, or the privately owned Maho Bay Camps, both on the north side. Harmony Resort, sits just above **Maho Bay** and is an eight-unit eco-resort. Harmony's units are built almost entirely of recycled materials and depend upon solar energy for power. Guests can monitor their power usage with an interactive computer. For those who want luxury, Caneel Bay Resort and the Westin have top amenities. The Inn at

Tamarind Court offers adequate accommodations at a lower price range. Gallows Point Resort and Hillcrest Guest House are within walking distance of Cruz Bay. (Movie stars such as: John Travolta, Kelly Preston, Kevin Bacon and Denzel Washington,have been known to frequent St. John.) If you want a home away from home, there are more than 500 private homes for rent, with pools, hot tubs and spectacular views. Villas and condos are also for rent. Call some realtors on St. John, or phone the **St. John Visitor's Bureau (Dept. of Tourism) at (340) 776-6450.**

Dining Out

From native-style vegetarian to upscale dining, you can find it in St. John. Since the restaurant scene is ever-changing, ask the next person you see in the street for their favorite. For lunch try Ocean Grill at Mongoose Junction. For local flavor, try any one of the local stands selling patés, (a turnover filled with ground beef, chicken or fish), and other Caribbean delights. If you are in Coral Bay, see Shipwreck Landing for fresh fish sandwiches and a cold Carib. Try Skinny Legs Bar and Restaurant adjacent to the dinghy dock, for a reasonably-priced lunch, or the brand new Aqua Bistro. For top-of-the line dining, Caneel Bay Resort, Asolare above Cruz Bay, and The Westin fill the bill. The staff attends to your every wish as you dine on such sumptuous delights as Caribbean lobster and prime rib.

For a more moderately priced dinner in Cruz Bay visit Lime Inn for fish and shrimp, chicken and pasta, or Morgan's Mango. At the Fish Trap, find old favorites. Also see LaTapa in the heart of Cruz Bay. The great scent of Uncle Joe's BBQ at the center of Cruz Bay near the post office, can be smelled all the way to the ferry dock! Many restaurants are closed during the offseason (August and September), so call first.

Shopping Around

From tee shirts to top locally designed jewelry, you are sure to finish your shopping list on St. John. Shopping is centered at Wharfside Village on the beach at Cruz Bay and at the two Mongoose Shopping Centers just past

the Park Office. Don't miss the dozens of boutiques in between. As far as grocery shopping, there are several excellent grocery stores (prices are a little higher than St. Thomas). Try the

Marketplace mall just south of town for one-stop shopping. Look for Starfish Market, the island's largest grocery store; St. John Hardware; Chelsea Drugs; and Kaleidescope Video.

AROUND THE ISLANDS - St. Thomas

Like Rome, all roads or sea lanes lead to Charlotte Amalie on St. Thomas, the seat of government as well as a shopper's Mecca. The downtown district reflects the island's Danish heritage. While many of the streets now have English names; some still bear those given by the Danes, and some carry both names. For example, Main Street is also known as Dronningen's Gade.

A trading port almost since its beginnings in the 1600s, Charlotte Amalie continues its merchant tradition. A duty-free port, you will find prices below stateside. Housed in historic warehouses, the city's brick buildings are filled to the rafters with a mind-boggling array of goods. Wind your way through narrow exotically named alleyways to find jewelry priced from a few dollars to the sky's the limit. Every kind of liquor imaginable, including made-in-St. Croix Cruzan Rum, is there for the tasting. Fine linens, designer leather goods, tropical clothing, electronics, perfume and, of course, yards of tee shirts can be found in the shops of Charlotte Amalie. For a chance to bargain, try the **Vendor's Plaza** at the east end of the shopping district, where you will find an array of tee shirts, African clothing and island-wraps. Over the years, the shopping district has sprawled northward, so don't forget to stroll the side streets to see what the merchants have to offer. For a smaller selection of the same goods, shop at **Havensight Mall** adjacent to the cruise ship docks. **Nearby Yacht Haven Grande** is a great shopping center; and, if you are on the East End, the Red Hook area offers a growing selection of similar items and small boutiques.

If you're interested in the local arts scene, visit **Tillett Gardens**, a cultural cluster of craft stores, visual art, music and theater. Patrons will find raku pottery, jewelry, candles, and a gallery displaying water colors, oils and acrylics by local and Caribbean artists. Tillet Gardens also hosts two music studios featuring lessons in piano, violin and voice. And an outdoor theatre accommodating 300 people is an annual home to four classical concerts and four non classical concerts, all performed by top international talent.

For a look at the art of Virgin Islands politics, stroll eastward along the waterfront until you come to the green **V.I. Legislature Building**. Built in the 19th century as a barracks for the Danish militia and used by the U.S. Navy when it governed the island, it also served, at one point, as the island's only high school. The public is welcome to sit in when the 15 senators meet in full session, or in committee on the second-floor chambers. The receptionist just inside the front door can tell you what is on the calendar for that particular day.

To glimpse the heart of the island's history, walk across the street toward Fort Christian and the museum located on the huge edifice's inland side. Built in 1671 by the Danes, the newly-refurbished museum has a changing series of exhibits on the island's culture and history. Explore the dozen plus cells that served as St. Thomas' only jail until the 1980s. There is also a pay public parking lot adjacent to the Fort that is one of the best places to park your car while you explore old Charlotte Amalie. You will find public bathrooms on the north side of the parking lot.

Continue inland across **Norre Gade** until you find one of several sets of stairs that lead up to **Government House**. Recent renovations to the 19th century building are complete, and escorted tours are usually available. One block over, you will find **Frederick Lutheran Church**, an 18th century building which is open to the public. Venture down the hill to the U.S. Post Office and follow **Garden Street** inland until you hit **Crystal Gade**.

Turn left and walk about three blocks until the brick Synagogue appears on your right. The Synagogue, open from 9 a.m. to 4 p.m. is called the **Congregation of Blessing and Peace and Loving Deeds** and is the second oldest synagogue under continuous use in the western hemisphere. While this building went up in 1833 following a disastrous fire that wiped out much of Charlotte Amalie, the congregation dates back to 1796.

Magen's Bay

A guide will point out the sand floor and the 19th century chandeliers.

Head back into the shopping area for a look at the **Camille Pissaro** building on **Main Street**, once home of the Impressionist painter who went off to Paris to seek fame and fortune. The building now houses several of the stores that give St. Thomas its reputation as a shopping Mecca, as well as an art gallery named in his honor.

25

For visitors who want to put some miles on their shoes and get closer to Mother Nature, **Hassel Island** sits in the middle of **Charlotte Amalie Harbor.** Visit the waterfront taxi services and find out how to get there. Once there, follow the trail up to the old fort on the ocean side of the 135-acre **Virgin Islands National Park**-owned island. There is also a trail to the signal tower used by the Danes to alert residents of approaching ships. It can be super hot at mid-day, so be sure to bring water. While seeing the Charlotte Amalie sights can be fulfilling, there are still miles of island to explore. Most visitors head to **Magen's Bay**, a gorgeous strand of white sand on the island's north side. A full-service beach with bathrooms, changing rooms, snack bar, covered picnic tables, sports equipment rental, and boutique await you. Magen's Bay also has an arboretum recently restored by a local Rotary Club. Walk down the beach to the left and stroll through stands of palms and Norfolk pines included among the 200 varieties of exotic trees. The arboretum was established in 1948 by Philanthropist Arthur Fairchild when he donated Magens Bay to the people of the Virgin Islands.

If you have time to spare, plan a circular tour of the island. Head west along the waterfront from Charlotte Amalie to the left turn at the light by the **Veteran's Drive Post Office**. Or, stop for drinks or lunch at **Frenchtown**, an enclave settled by the French from St. Barths. Home to numerous restaurants and bars, the area seems to attract the island's movers and shakers.

Back on Veterans' Drive, continue past the Cyril E. King Airport and see the beautiful buildings of the University of the Virgin Islands nestled up in the hills to your right. Refresh yourself with a swim at Brewer's Bay or continue uphill. As you continue around the island, one panorama after another will unfold as you follow the narrow, twisting roads. Follow Route 30 through areas that still bear the names of Danish estates; Bonne Esperance, Perseverance, and Fortuna, are just a few.

Retrace your drive to Route 301 or West End Road for a trip along the island's northern side. Take northern Rte. 33 to head east. Make sure you have a good map, because the roads on this side of the island can easily confuse.Everybody stops at Drake's Seat because the view is stupendous.

Drake's Seat is located at the intersection between Routes 40 and 35. For still more awesome views, continue along the north side, Route 42, until the land flattens out and you are on Smith Bay Road. Looking east, note the heart-stopping views of St. John and the British Virgin Islands. Turn left at the signs for **Coral World**, a not-to-be missed attraction that features an under-sea viewing observatory. Watch Caribbean sea-dwellers swim by as divers feed them. You can stop for a swim at nearby Coki Beach. Head through Red Hook at the very east end, along the south side on your return to Charlotte Amalie. The drive takes you past several hotels, groups of condos, local marinas and Havensight Mall before you get back to town.

Staying on the Island

From cozy guest houses to posh hotels, and a coterie of vacation condominiums in between, St. Thomas has the accommodations you seek. For a list, call the Tourism Department at 774-8784, or the U.S.Virgin Islands Hotel Association at 774-6835.

If money's no object, stay at one of the newest hotels on the island; the Ritz Carlton. Located near Red Hook; the 180-room hotel dazzles visitors with elegant ambience. Strung along the south side, visitors will find a chain of similarly-sized hotels, all individually-owned, from Bolongo Bay Beach Resort & Villas, to Bluebeard's Beach. Along the north shore you will find a string of smaller, beachfront hotels. Vacationers and business travelers like the 520-room Frenchman's Reef & Morningstar Marriott Beach Resort, a full-service resort facility convenient to Charlotte Amalie, a few miles south of Havensight Mall. Those willing to forego a beach should try the 170-room Bluebeard's Castle. Adjacent to an historic landmark, the hotel is located just above the city and has recently undergone major renovations.

Visitors who want all the comforts of home might want a condominium vacation. There are condos at the Anchorage, Crystal Cove Villas, and Mahogany Run at the golf course. Red Hook Apartments, Watergate, Sapphire Village and Secret Harbor Beach Resort also have condominium rentals.

In Charlotte Amalie, you will find a handful of guesthouses located in some of the historic buildings. Hotel 1829 has been in business since the island's fledging tourism days. You will also find a handful of less expensive guesthouses scattered in and around Charlotte Amalie.

Dining Out ....

From food carts along the side of the road, to top-of-the line dining, you will find it on St. Thomas. If you are shopping in Charlotte Amalie, numerous restaurants are tucked away in alleys and up the hills. For a to-die-for lunch or dinner at top-notch prices, try Virgilio's on the up-hill side of Raadetts Gade. Moderately-priced lunch can be found at Herve's on Government Hill. Room with a View and Banana Tree Grille are both at Bluebeard's Castle. The island's hotels vie with each other to create the best in fine dining, creating, through competition, a culinary experience bar none. For nouvelle cuisine, dine at the Old Stone Farm House on the north side near Mahogany Run. Head out of town to the many selections of restaurants in Frenchtown, or to Romano's in Smith Bay. Other popular Red Hook eateries are: Pesce, Molly Molone's Irish Pub, Fish Tails, and Duffy's Love Shack.

The best bargain in St.Thomas has to be Texas Pit BBQ where you get half a barbecue chicken, spice or mild sauce, potato salad or coleslaw and a roll on a styrofoam plate and plastic utensils for a steal. The wagons are located in Red Hook,Wheatley Center and the Charlotte Amalie waterfront. They also offer tasty ribs and briskets. Of course there are always McDonalds, Kentucky Fried Chicken, Subway, Wendy's and Pizza Hut at various locations around St. Thomas.

Associations

Now that you have a modest acquaintance with St. Croix, St. John and St. Thomas, their similarities, differences and a little about their personalities, the following information on associations and Clubs has been provided to give you some ideas on how to join the community.

Get involved! That's the best advice for anyone who wants to become a part of their new community. Like everywhere, many volunteer organizations fill in the gap where government stops. Others will help you discover a new hobby. All will help you to meet new friends. Everybody needs help. They will welcome you with open arms. Check the local papers for activities or call one of the numbers listed below.

General and Special Interest Groups (all Area Code 340)

A.A.R.P.	V.I.	866-389-5633
	St. Croix	719-2277
	St. Thomas	776-8236
Alcoholics Anonymous	V.I.	776-5283
	V.I.	690-5283
American Cancer Society	St. Croix	778-2882
	St. Thomas	775-5373
American Hibiscus Society	St. Croix	513-2543
American Red Cross	St. Thomas	774-0375
	St. Croix	778-5104
Animal Care	St. John	774-1625
Animal Welfare Center of	St. Croix	778-1650

Bethlehem House for Homeless	St Croix	777-5001
	St Thomas	777-4463
Catholic Charities Services	St. Croix	773-0132
	St. Thomas	777-8518
Civil Air Patrol	St. Croix	778-1280
C.M. Cancer Institute	St. Thomas	775-5433
Continuum Care	St. Croix	772-2273
	St. Thomas	714-2273
Council on Alcoholism & Drug Dependency	(StT/StJ)	774-4358
Crime Stoppers	VI	1-800-222-TIPS
Diabetes Association of the	VI	693-1399
Disability Rights Center	St. Croix	772-1200
Family Resource Center	St. Thomas	776-3966
Friends of Denmark	St. Croix	718-0104
	St. Thomas	777-2277
Friends of the Library	St. Croix	773-5715
	St. John	776-6359
	St. Thomas	774-0630
Humane Society	St. Thomas	775-0599
Legal Services of the V.I.	St. Croix	718-2626
	St. Thomas	774-6720
Lions Club	St. Croix	772-3206
Lutheran Social Services	St. Croix	772-4099
National Park Service,	St. Croix	773-1460
	St. John	776-6201
Navy League	St. Thomas	776-0421
Orchid Society	St. Croix	514-5349
	St. Thomas	777-1967
	St. Thomas	774-1347
Queen Louise Home (children)	St. Croix	772-0090
Rotary Club	St. Croix	277-1126
Rotary Club West	St. Croix	772-5287
Rotary Club Mid-Isle	St. Croix	690-8246
Rotary Club Harborside	St. Croix	277-4788
Rotary Clubs –	St. Thomas	774-7304
	St. Thomas	626-4690
Found for Community Dev.	St. Croix	773-9898
Environmental Assoc. (SEA)	St. Croix	773-1989
Landmarks Society	St. Coix	772-0598
Salvation Army	St. Thomas	776-0070

St. Croix Bonsai Society	St. Croix	332-8263/778-9087
St. Croix Shrine Club		772-0030
St. George Botanical Garden	St. Croix	692-2874
United Way	St. Croix	718-0582
	StT/StJ	774-3185
U.S.V.I. Girl Scouts Council	St. Croix	772-1850
Men's Coalition	St. Croix	778-2161
Women's Coalition	St. Croix	773-9272
VI Care (HIV/Aids)	St. Croix	692-9111

Art Groups

American Hibiscus Society	St. Thomas	774-3745
Arts Alive	St. Thomas	776-8566
Caribbean Community Theatre	St. Croix	778-1983
Caribbean Dance Company		778-8824
Caribbean Museum Center	St. Croix	772-2622
Island Center	St. Croix	778-5271
Music In Motion Dance	St. Croix	772-5440
Pistarkle Community Theater	St. Thomas	775-7877
Pointe Dance Company	St. Croix	718-0435
Reichhold Center for the Arts	St. Thomas	693-1550
St. John School of the Arts		779-4322
V.I. Council for the Arts	St. Croix	773-3075
	St. Thomas	774-5984

Youth Programs

Boys and Girls Clubs	St. Croix	778-8990
Boy Scouts of America	St. Croix	201-7959
	St. Thomas	774-2752
F'sted Boating & Sailing Schl.	St. Croix	772-2482
Girl Scout Council	VI	774-1054
Civil Air Patrol	St. Croix	778-3371
	St. Croix	778-1280
	St. Thomas	775-0288
4-H Club	St. Croix	692-4087
	St. Thomas	774-0210
Kids and the Sea (KATS)	St. John	514-3718
Swimming Assoc.	St. Croix	778-1398
Swimming Assoc.	St Thomas	779-7872

Labor

| Amer. Federation of Teachers | St. Croix | 778-4414 |
| Economic Dev. Community | St. Croix | 773-6499 |

Job Corps.	St. Thomas	777-9888
Labor Department	St. Croix	773-1440
Lieutenant Governor's Office	St. Croix	773-6449
Small Business Administration	St. Croix	778-5380
Small Business Development	St. Croix	773-2161
United Steel Workers of Amer.	St. Croix	778-5634

Business & Professional Associations

Advertising Club of the VI	St. Thomas	774-8478
Board of Realtors	St. Croix	344-5618
	St. Thomas	866-598-1440 X234
Casino Control Commission	St. Croix	718-3616
C'sted Retail & Rest. Assoc.	St. Croix	778-9433
New Image Foundation	St. Thomas	777-8883
F'sted Economic Dev. Assoc.	St. Croix	772-0069
Our Town Frederiksted	St. Croix	772-3550
Chamber of Commerce	St. Croix	718-1435
Chamber of Commerce	St. Thomas	776-0100
	St. John	776-0100
Hotel Association	VI	774-6835
Hotel & Tourism Assoc.	St. Croix	773-7117
Licensing & Consumer Affairs	St. Croix	718-2226
Taxi Association	St. Croix	778-1088
Taxi Association	St. Thomas	774-0394
Toastmasters	St Croix dgaliber@hotmail.com	
	St. Croix	773-8582
V.I. Bar Association	St. Thomas	778-7497
	St. Croix	778-7497
V.I. Medical Institute, Inc.	St. Croix	778-6470

Sports & Recreation

Cycling Federation/Triathlon	VI	773-4470
Hiking Association	St. Croix	692-9984
Marksmanship Assoc.	St. Croix	773-8555
Olympic Committee	VI	778-2229
	VI	719-VIOC
U.S. Coast Guard Auxiliary	St. Croix	690-3280
	St. Thomas	998-9227
Yacht Club	St. Thomas	775-6320
Yacht Club	St. Croix	773-9531

31

Settler's Handbook Chapter 3

To be a Virgin Islander
Where Shall You Live?

You've finally made up your mind to be a Virgin Islander. You are ready for the sun, sea and sand and determined to make a new start. Where shall you live? Which island? What kind of life or lifestyle are you seeking? Maybe you want a luxury estate, a condominium or a cozy cottage on the beach, an ocean-side cliff, a mountain top or a simple apartment. To help you make the decision, The Settler's Handbook has provided the following descriptions of the life and lifestyles on St. Croix, St. John and St. Thomas.

The real estate markets on all three Virgin Islands has been dramatically influenced in the last few years by the explosive growth of the EDC tax

benefit program, although this has recently tapered off and leveled out. Almost overwhelming demand for luxury homes and condos had created a strong seller's market and in some cases almost doubled prices. However, the US recession and global economic conditions have since created downward pressures to create an exciting buyer's market. While the tax benefit program has subsided, new projects within the next few years are expected to bring new residential and condominium inventory to the market.

St. Croix

In its own inimitable style, St. Croix combines all the best of the Virgin Islands. More laid back than St. Thomas, a few paces faster than St. John, the island called "the quiet Virgin" has amenities and beauty.

While St. Croix has its share of shopping centers, strip malls and local businesses, recent slower development has led to an atmosphere that's more town and country. It always seems to be feel less crowded and more roomy than the other two Virgin Islands. There is still plenty of room for development. The island is large enough to go for an afternoon drive without traveling the same roads twice. It is blessed with abundant picturesque architecture from the sugar plantation days, and much of that architecture is incorporated into the newer buildings. The rural surroundings offer natural settings that can be breathtaking. There is a closeness to nature's treasures that strongly influences the visitor as well as the resident. The island does have cosmopolitan Christiansted, the uniqueness of Frederiksted, Island Center for the Performing Arts for concerts, superb restaurants and charming boutiques. The sparkling blue waters and white clean beaches make sailing, swimming, snorkeling, scuba diving and just enjoying the sunsets a Crucian pastime. St. Croix is an island of sports-minded people and family-oriented outdoor types, evident in the island's three golf courses, numerous tennis courts, rain forest hiking trails and active sports programs for adults and kids. The island also has many professional groups that will make it easy for you to meet others. With four Rotary Clubs, an active Chamber of Commerce,The American Legion, Whim Greathouse Plantation and Museum's Landmark Society, St. George Village Botanical Garden, youth groups, sports associations and more, you will find sufficient volunteer work to help you learn about the people and the island.

In St. Croix, the median residential house was sold at $297,000 for the August 2011 to August 2012 season. The median condo sales price, $125,000, is just slightly lower from previous years though condo closings have dipped significantly. Residential lots range from a low of $25,000 a lot to the ultra luxurious $750,000. Lower valued plots are sold at a median of $28,500, while higher valued plots are sold at a median of $59,200. Despite the current world economy, land prices on St. Croix continue to be the best buy in the Caribbean. Building costs stayed flat but continue to spiral upward with bare bone construction starting at $200-$500 per square foot. Luxury construction continues at $500 per square foot with no ceiling in sight. Monthly rents range from $950 to $4,500 per month. Perhaps more than any real estate market in the three islands, St. Croix is weathering the biggest drops. Due primarily to the Hovensa refinery closure in 2012, one real estate agent reported before the VI senate, land values have decreased by 50 to 60 percent and houses by 35 to 45 percent since their 2008 peak. For the opportunistic settler, the big island is definitely a buyers market!

St. John

With two thirds owned by the Virgin Islands National Park, St. John is the epitome of peace and serenity. Starting in 1950 with 5,650 acres, the park now encom-passes more than 27,000 land and underwater acres.

Though it has a land mass of only 20 square miles, St. John is the purest of the Virgins, possessing steep and lush tropical forests, white sandy beaches unbelievable turquoise seas, and strikingly beautiful vistas. While positively placid by St. Croix and St. Thomas standards, Cruz Bay does buzz, particularly during the winter months, when cruise ships drop off passengers in the early morning hours. Connected to the commercial, educational and medical benefits of St. Thomas, St. John is for the settler who can put up with the short ferry or car barge rides and increasingly high cost of living. Rents, if you can find them, average about $1,000.00 a month for a small apartment. The grocery selection has vastly improved in recent years, but you may not find everything on your list in one of the island's handful of convenience stores, and the prices will be higher. Look for Dolphin Gourmet Market and be sure to visit St. John Marketplace, with Star Fish Market and other stores. A visit will give you a feel get for what it's like to live on an island where everybody knows everybody else and news flies like wildfire on the "coconut telegraph."

Beach gatherings, the Friends of the Virgin Islands National Park, the Audubon Society, the Historical Society, the Lions Club, the St. John Yacht Club, the Business and Professional Women groups and a handful of committees of varying interests keep residents involved. While histo-rically these orga-nizations have mainly attracted flocks of retirees wintering in St. John, the make-up is changing, and youn-ger St. Johnians are participating. Defi-nitely feel free to

attend these meetings. To find out who is meeting, read the Tradewinds Newspaper or the St. John Sun Times, or look for notices on the Cruz Bay bulletin boards. One is located at Connections, where locals get their mail and messages. Another good way to meet islanders is the St. John School of the Arts, which offers various classes aimed at improving artistic ability and physical fitness. As for homes, expect to pay around $300,000 for a handy man special or a cottage in the woods with no ocean view— if they can be found. Average home prices will top $800,000, and there are many multi-million dollar homes. Condos, once a rare commodity, are now plentiful on St. John and can start at $200,000 for a very basic, no-water-view one bedroom, and go as high as $2.5 million for a four bedroom. U.S. and global economic conditions have heavily impacted St. John's real estate market, and prices have recently stabilized to pre-bubble levels.

The growth of St. John is related to construction of condos and villas. Two condo/villa projects have been underway despite some stalled development. The Sirenusa project has 47 planned units, while the Pond Bay Project located by Chocolate Hole is slated for about 44 units and timeshare availability. There is still land left to develop but people are being a little cautious about overcrowding and disturbing the island's natural beauty. Parking and traffic are a problem, although there are now a few parking lots. St. Johns's infrastructure isn't completely keeping up with population growth in its two towns, though in Coral Bay the population growth has spurred development of a few small shopping centers nearby. If you have children, there are two public schools on St. John, one at Coral Bay, the Guy Benjamin grades K-6, and the Julius Sprauve nearer Cruz Bay is K-9 years. The Gifft Hill School is private and is nearer Cruz Bay.

St. Thomas

St. Thomas offers tropical mountain scenery and a coastline scalloped by picturesque bays fringed with inviting beaches. Homes tucked into mountainsides offer the owner views of numerous islands, reefs and coves of the Caribbean. The terraced hills on the north side, perfect for gardening spots, have a magnificent view of St. John and the British Virgins. The resorts and condos are primarily located on the east end. With style and energy, the twenty-eight square mile St. Thomas juggles her dual role as the territorial capital and as the shopping center of the Caribbean. Her magnificent harbor at Charlotte Amalie receives about a thousand cruise ship visits a year; and, after three centuries as a trading center, the people and merchants know how to serve the passengers well. The stone warehouses from colonial days now glitter with an amazing array of products and goods from all over the world.

Many settlers have made St. Thomas home because of the career opportunities and a climate ripe for entrepreneurship. Membership in the island's numerous civic organizations will give you the opportunity to meet other residents. There are several Rotary Clubs, a Chamber of Commerce, the St. Thomas Yacht Club and various associations and organizations devoted to special interests such as the Hibiscus and Orchid societies.

With the airport, supermarkets and entertainment at your fingertips, stateside amenities with a Caribbean ambiance can be found. You can eat out at a different restaurant every day for months or try a different beach every weekend, and not retrace your steps. You will find the island is the perfect jumping off spot for short trips to St. John and points east. Compared to her sisters, St. Thomas is the island of energy and hustle.

Home prices on St. Thomas range from $140,000 for a three bedroom one acre to mansions that go for $20 million. A three bedroom, two-bath family-style home on a half acre will generally begin at about $350,000. Houses are generally situated on a half-acre lot, though quarter-acre lots are common for densely developed locations.

Luxury homes with pools range upwards from $500,000. Condo prices from $75,000 to $150,000 for an efficiency or one bedroom, while three bedroom luxury models can range from $375,000 to $650,000, depending on condition and location. Fractional ownership in luxury condominiums has also become more popular with up to a month's occupancy available. Like anywhere, make an offer.

Water Island

Often called "the last virgin", Water Island is the most recent addition to the USVIs. It consists of 491.5 acres, and offers a unique, informal, private vacation. There is a small full time / part time population of about 200 with private homes, one restaurant, and a great beach. You get there by private boat or water taxi. The taxis or ferries leave from **Crown Bay Marina** by Tickles restaurant and drop you off at **Phillips Landing**. Since it is largely undeveloped and non-commercial it is very peaceful. There are really no cars, so very little traffic other than bikes or golf carts. A restful vacation could consist of: hiking, biking, beaching, line-fishing, or snorkeling. For accommodations your choices are: private villas, cottages or apartments. You can visit the ruins of **Fort Segarra** and **Carolina Point Plantation**. However, Providence Point Plantation has been converted to a home. Fort Segarra was an underground fort from U.S. defense strategies in WWI. For lunch, dinner, or provisioning needs, visit Pirate's Ridge Restaurant Deli & Bar on Honeymoon Beach. For more info visit: www.vinow.com

Your Decision...

Of the three islands, where you finally drop your hat will depend on your own expectations and challenges. There are those who recommend vacationing on each island before taking that leap to make the territory home. Some discover they really don't like living on a "rock" in the middle of the Caribbean, so "rock fever" becomes a reality. Keep in mind that cures come in the form of sail boat charters or airplane rides that can whisk you away for a day, weekend or week.

Aside from that, what these three wonderful islands have— sky blue waters, great beaches, a marvelous climate and people with a real love for their home— might help you to narrow your decision. With these brief descriptions and in the vernacular of the American lifestyle, you can just about determine that St. Croix is the small city, St. John, the small town, and St. Thomas, is where all the big city slickers live. The following information will help you in your preparation for the Virgin Islands, no matter your decision, and no matter which island you should choose.

Shipping and Moving

Now that you have decided on which island you prefer, unless you are one of those individuals who can move through life with nothing more than a toothbrush, you will find moving here a major expense.

If you only have boxes to move, consider the USPS. Boxes shipped this way will not have to go through U.S. Customs and can arrive at your general delivery address if you do not have a post office box. Delivery can take several weeks. Boxes shipped priority mail cannot weigh more than 70 pounds, while the combined length and girth must be less than 108 inches. Since rates vary from where you are shipping, check with the USPS where you live.

The cheapest way to move your entire household is by ship under $5 per cubic foot of household goods, and/or personal effects port-to-port. The items must be delivered by yourself, or a moving company, in crates to shippers located in port cities. Most national moving companies have agents in the U.S. Virgin Islands to facilitate your move. Shipping from Florida to either their St. Thomas or St. Croix office will take one to two weeks. Going door-to-door back to states, about four weeks due to customs. You must hire a trucker to move your goods to your house. St. John residents must hire a trucker to pick up their goods at the shipping company in St. Thomas for the barge trip to St John. Best to call around since prices vary greatly.

Do-it-yourself movers once used the major airlines to airfreight their household goods; however, that has all changed since 9/11. Prior to that, one would ship from a major airport because feeder planes are too small to carry large-sized freight. (Boxes or crates couldn't exceed " height or 126" in width.) Prices also may be high, if it is available at all. It was also on a space available basis. Since the rules and regulations have changed, you need to check with your local airport, and with the airlines to find out who flies here. Since this may not be a possible venue anymore, best to expect to ship by truck by a professional moving company to place on containers for boat shipment. It does pay to shop around and compare, or let the specialists handle it.

Some freight handlers make a specialty of consolidating less than-trailer load shipments into full trailers for a single destination. By sharing a trailer, you save money. A freight forwarder where you live can advise you on how to get your car, trailerable boat, or almost anything else on wheels, into these ships. A freight forwarder's services are required except when using a national moving company or a consolidator.

Hiring one of the big nationwide movers to pack, ship, and unpack your island home is the easiest, but most expensive way to move. You will prepay the entire cost in the States after your shipment has been packed into huge sealed containers and an accurate weight determined. Check with the movers listed in this section as they may represent a nation-wide mover. The whole moving process will take several weeks.

Furniture, or fragile and precious things should be handled by professionals. Other goods that can survive amateur packing will probably be alright if they arrive via USPS. You can also bring some items as excess baggage on the airline in conjunction with your trip. Check with your air carrier on prices and how many pieces are allowed. Compare shipping times, insurance coverage while in transit, handling costs on the ground at both ends, storage if needed and ultimately, the speed of delivery. Also, new items should always have an invoice accompanying them.

However your goods travel, except via the USPS, U.S. Customs will check them when they arrive, for firearms, or any resaleable goods. Used

check them when they arrive, for firearms, or any resaleable goods. Used personal effects enter duty free. For door-to-door help in shipping contact the numbers listed in this section.

Household Movers (all area code 340)

	St. Croix	St. Thomas	
Bob Lynch Moving/Storage	778-1813	Bob Lynch	774-5872
Brandon Transfer V.I. Corp	778-6660	Carib Trans	776-8660
Ferrol Trucking	778-9602	The Viking Corp.	776-1536
Flemings' Transport	778-9160		
O'neale's Transport	778-1111		
The Viking Corporation	773-2105		

Shipping Companies and Agents

Bob Lynch Moving and Storage	778-1813, 774-5872
Brandon Transfer V.I. Corp	778-6660 (St.C)
Merwin Shipping & Trading	778-6199 (St.C)
Tropical Shipping	776-8767 (St.T)
	778-6767 (St. C)
The Viking Corporation	776-1536 (St.T)
V.I. Cargo	778-6331 (St.C)

(These carriers will connect you to their stateside companies.)

Crowley	774-2933 (St. Thomas)
Sea Star	714-1361 (St. Thomas)
Tropical Shipping	776-8767

Bringing Your Car

To import a car from the U.S. mainland, you must arrange to have it shipped on one of the carriers that call in the islands. When it rolls off the ship, collect the bill of lading from the shipper, and, take it to the Internal Revenue Bureau to pay the 16 cents per pound road tax. You must pay in cash, certified check or money order.

Once that is done, go to the Police Department's Motor Vehicle Bureau for a permit to move your car. It's located off Melvin Evans Highway, close to airport. Next, clear U.S. Customs at an office near your shipper. If the car is made totally in the U.S., that means its serial number starts with a one or four, it may come into the Virgin Islands duty free. You will pay a six percent duty on cars made in Canada or Mexico or with foreign-made parts (fees may change since printing). None on U.S. Cars. U.S. Customs takes cash, certified check or money order. Call 778-2257 for clarifications. Next, get insurance through a local agent, then go back to the Motor Vehicle Bureau to get your vehicle inspected and registered. Bring your road tax receipt and the title or bill of sale and a lot of patience to get your new island license plates.

Hook (St. Thomas), but plan on spending all day at this since the various offices are located hither and yon around the islands. Check ahead for their hours of business both at Customs and Motor Vehicle.

Household Goods and Personal Items:

These items do have to be cleared. This should be easier to clear. There might be a "customs duty" but it is not an excise tax. If they are used items, and not of a foreign make, there should be no customs duty. Cars can be moved separate from a trailer of personal items. It is easier for the inspector to find and would clear faster so you have your car and drive it away, while your other items may not be delivered till a moving truck picks them up. It could all be same day.

Bringing in Your Animals

If your pet is moving with you, you must obtain a health certificate from your local veterinarian stating the animal has not been exposed to any communicable diseases and is not sick. The certificate must state that the animal is not coming from an area under quarantine for rabies. Your pet must be vaccinated against rabies. This **must** be done within ten days in advance of arrival. Since most veterinarians are reluctant to give new puppies rabies shots before they are three to six months old, it is not necessary to have your puppy vaccinated. The veterinarian should indicate this on the health certificate. Check with your vet regarding status of your pet's parvo-virus shots. In Chapter 6 of this book you will find more information on helping your pet adjust to living in the tropics. Note the list of vets to call in Chapter 6, if you have specific questions, especially regarding exotic pets. Also, be sure to check with the airlines about any restriction on animal moving, especially May 15 — Sept. 15 because of heat considerations if they must travel in baggage.

By Car

Aaah, life in the left lane! That's us! We even have bumper stickers and signs to keep you on track! The practice is a holdover from Danish days which no one has bothered to change. If you have trouble remembering, put a sign on your dashboard until it becomes second nature. Price of gas varies, so it pays to shop around. Fuel costs and fluctuations are currently being monitored by the Department of Licensing and Consumer Affairs. As of press time, for regular, self-serve unleaded St.Croix's lowest gas price was $3.99 per gallon, St. Thomas' was $4.75, and St. John's was $4.64. To put that into perspective, the national average for regular unleaded during the same period was $3.28 per gallon. Traditionally, St. Croix stations have had cheaper prices for pump-it-yourself gas by virtue of its on-island oil refinery. *How the refinery's closure will affect Crucian gas prices in the long run is yet to be determined.*

prices in the long run is yet to be determined.

Before importing a stateside car or buying one here, it pays to discover what the car is up against: many short trips, very steep hills, narrow twisting roads, and downtown streets that, while picturesque, are often hot and crowded. What about parts? Arrival time for automobile parts can take longer than you like. Many residents rely on backyard mechanics (get referrals) or knowledgeable residents whose skill in scavenging parts from other cars can get you driving again.

You will need a car with a sturdy engine, high-capacity cooling system and an axle ratio designed for mountains, with good brakes, a tough suspension and tight steering. With those constraints in mind, many people opt for four-wheel drive vehicles. Depending on where you live and where you will drive the most, residents can get along with a non-four-wheel drive. If you have dirt roads to travel, particularly in rainy weather, a four-wheel-drive vehicle with a lot of ground clearance is a wise choice. Some locals rely on a "solid" running vehicle rather than a good-looking one, for the roads and salt air can play havoc on "good" vehicles. As far as driving etiquette, those honking horns can either mean "hello" or, "I'm giving you the right of way", or maybe annoyance at waiting for something.

Automobile Insurance

Auto Liability insurance is mandatory in the V.I. Except for certain programs such as USAA, no mainland companies write policies here. The companies based here, the UK or Puerto Rico are fully licensed. As on the U.S. mainland, it pays to shop around.

Driver's License

If you already have a valid driver's license from the U.S. mainland, it is good here for 90 days. If your license comes from somewhere other than the U.S., you must immediately get a temporary V.I. license, which will be good for 90 days (small fee). In both instances you must obtain a valid Virgin Islands license by the end of your 90-day grace period.

To become permanently "licensed", get a physical examination from the Motor Vehicle Bureau and have a brief physical, including a blood and eye test, at your doctor or Health Department clinic (The eye test is the most important). If you know your blood type, the blood test is not required. Return the physical exam form and two, two-inch square, head-and-shoulder photographs of yourself to the Motor Vehicle Bureau. Photos must be taken wearing clothing with sleeves.

Also, to meet requirements of Congress' REAL ID Act of 2005, which creates new authentication measures for homeland security and immigration-related purposes, applicants for a VI driver's license must provide proof of name and physical address. The BMV will accept any two bills, telephone bills, cable tv/satellite tv bills, auto or life insurance policies, filed taxed forms, voter registration cards, credit card statements, property deeds or local rental agreements. The BMV is also no longer accepting Puerto Rico birth certificates issued prior to July 2010 as documentation. This is because earlier forms of the Puerto Rican document were deemed easily forgeable, and the Puerto Rican government has recently issued a more security sensitive alternatives. For other documents that are admissible contact the BMV.

You may call ahead or reserve an appointment online at *http://usvibm v.org* to take the written test. Bring your social security card, birth certificate or passport to prove your age. Be sure to study the loaner manual supplied by the Bureau of Motor Vehicles at Public Safety, located in the Golden Grove area just off Melvin Evans Highway opposite the Industrial Park. On St. Thomas the BMV is near to the shipping center at Subbase in Charlotte Amalie. On St. John it is in the large parking lot by the Cruz Bay fire station.

If you do not have a valid driver's license, you will need to take a road test. Schedule once you pass your written test. If the road test is not necessary, the Motor Vehicle Bureau will snap your photo and issue your photo-laminated license on the spot. The license will cost $35, seniors $17.50 with card, and is good for five years and will expire on your birthday. To renew, simply visit the Motor Vehicle Bureau just before your

Virgin Island Traffic Hints
• Drive on the left
• Carry a valid driver's license
• Watch and obey traffic signs
• Even if a school bus' red flashers do not work, following and on-coming cars must stop for loading and unloading
• Make sure the road ahead is clear before passing traffic
• Put low-beam headlights on a half-hour before sunset and a half-hour before sunrise.
• Use hand signals or blinker signals for turns and stops
• To help others see you in the rain, turn on headlights; and use emergency flashers when your car is disabled.
• Obey speed limits. They are low due to the islands' sharp curves, steep grades, narrow shoulders, and poor visibility. In St. Croix and St. Thomas, it is 20 miles per hour in town and 35 miles per hour outside of town. On St. Croix's Melvin H. Evans Highway, the speed limit is 55 mph. In St. John, the speed limit is 10 mph in Cruz Bay and 20 mph elsewhere.

Cultural Tidbit

One of the hardest adjustments for newcomers to the Virgin Islands to make is learning how to drive on the left side of the road. Indeed, the territory is a curious case because we use vehicles made for stateside, right-hand driving. Why then is it, one may ask, that Virgin Islanders have insisted on this tradition? Crucian cultural aficiando, Dr. George Frankin says he has the answer: "Back in the days donkey was king. We used the donkey for everything especially for transportation. Well sir, when cars came they started right-hand drive but the vehicles kept bumping into the donkeys who were trained to walk on the left. Well, to make things run smoothly, because you know donkey stubborn, the cars had to follow the way of the donkey. And donkey still run things up to this day.

The Democratic party symbol is the donkey. So you know, the donkeys will always win out in the end."

birthday. You must be 18 to be licensed, but those graduating driver's school, may get a license at 16. The driving age for rentals is 25.

If You Get a Ticket

You can pay tickets for parking or minor violations by mail or in person at the Superior Court's cashier where personal checks are accepted. If you wish to contest your ticket, a personal appearance is required. Tickets for more serious violations require a court appearance. All tickets that are paid late will incur a delinquency fee of $75. For more information visit *http://www.visuperiorcourt.org/clerk/Traffic.aspx.*

If You Have an Accident

Remain on the scene and do not move the vehicles. Ask a passerby or, if you have a cell phone, call police and an ambulance, if necessary, or 911. When the police arrive they will fill out the forms on the spot. If an extreme emergency should make you leave the scene before the officers arrive, exchange driver's license plate numbers and names and addresses with the other driver. Report the accident to the police later yourself.

Buying a New or Used Car

There are dealers in the islands for most makes of domestic and foreign cars. While prices may seem high, they do include U.S. Customs duty, and if it's a foreign car, local road tax, and freight charges. The territory has a lemon law, so do not hesitate to complain if the car has problems. Be cautious when buying a used car. Take a test drive and have your mechanic check it out. To find a used car, check the classified sections in the daily newspapers, weekly free shopper guides or online at the increasingly popular VI craigslist: *http://virgin.craigslist.org/cta/.* Ask your friends if they know of anyone leaving the islands, or have referrals. You often can get a good deal from people leaving the islands. Car rental agencies will often sell off their older models.

Car Titles

All automobiles need titles, and the fee is $15.00. If you have moved here from the U.S. mainland, apply for the title at the Bureau of Motor Vehicles with your current title attached to the application.

Vehicle Registration and Inspection

You must get your vehicle inspected and re-registered every year at the Police Department's Bureau of Motor Vehicles (also called Public Safety). See your registration paper for expiration date, you have 30 days grace. This applies to private cars. Business cars and trucks as Virgin Island government vehicles have their inspections done in December. St. Croix 713-4268 and St. Thomas 774-4268.

You must bring your current registration and a valid driver's license to register your automobile, as well as your proof of car insurance certificate. Inspectors will check the low and high beams on your headlights, parking, side and back-up lights, turn signals, windshield wipers, horn, emergency brakes, tinted windows and brakes. They also may check to see if you have a spare tire and a jack. If they find an overly rusty spot on your car or a piece of loose metal, your car may be rejected. If you fail any test, you will have until the end of that month to institute repairs and then have your vehicle re-inspected.

Once the inspection is finished, you will be handed a typed registration and a dated sticker for your windshield and, in certain years, a set of new plates. Cash, credit cards, and certified checks are accepted in payment for vehicle registration. No personal checks are accepted. Annual registration fees range as follows: Cars and trucks up to 2500 pounds are $34.00; cars, jeeps and SUVs 2501-3500 pounds are $43.00; trucks at 3000 pounds are $55.00; Vans from 3001 to 4000 pounds are $77.00; vans 4001 to 5000 pounds are $109.00, and Vans 5001 to 6000 pounds are $141.00. The fee for most motorcycles is around $21.00 and, horse and boat trailers are around $40. Vehicles for Hires: Taxis, limos, safari buses and such. 0-3000 pounds $53; 3001-4000 pounds $74; 4001-5000 pounds $96; 5001-6000 pounds $118; 6001-7000 pounds $140 (all rates subject to change). Before visiting the BMV, visit *http://usvibmv.org* for more information or call.

Vehicle Rentals

It's a good idea to reserve vehicles well in advance. Expect car rentals to be in high demand during holidays and the busy winter months. The national chain rental companies have offices at airports, hotels and other locations on the three islands. Most locally owned independent car rental agencies will deliver to those same locations. Check the local tourist publications for any special discounts. Many car rental agencies will offer discounts on long-term rentals. When checking prices, remember that there are additional taxes & fees. Make sure the price quote you receive includes them. Read the rental conditions carefully to make sure you understand all charges, insurance coverage and liability limits. If you rent a motorscooter, the law mandates that you wear the helmet provided by the company. VI Motorcycle Safety Education Act 2009 mandates the establishment of Standards for rider training courses, improvement of licensure requirements and promotion of motorcycle safety through education and public awareness. Registration for Motorcycles is $15 for up to 250cc, $18 for 250cc-750cc, and $21 for over 750cc.

Car Maintenance

If rust appears, sand the spot down, treat it with a rust-inhibiting primer, and retouch with the original color from your car dealer. Salt crystals in the air make quick work of your car. If you park near the water, do so with your car's radiator away from the sea to protect the aluminum grill from the salt air. Salt also speeds deterioration of electrical parts and rubber, so try to keep battery terminals and distributor caps clean. Treat your battery to frequent additions of rain or distilled water since it will go dry very quickly in the tropical heat. Be generous with lubrication and oil changes. Heat plus dust are constant enemies.

Dial a Ride

Persons with disabilities, elderly residents, and tourists with disabilities, may use Dial-a-Ride services. The service has wheelchair accessible vans. Please call 24 hours prior to schedule pick up. They also have a reference of hotels, restaurants, and attractions that have services for persons with disabilities. In St. Thomas call 776-1277. For assistance on St. Croix, call the St. Thomas number for a referral number. On St. Croix you can also call Wheel Coach at 719-9335 for a 24-hour in advance prearranged pick-up for handicapped. On St. Croix and St. Thomas VITRAN-PLUS, a public service, is available for persons with disabilities. To qualify, go to Public Works to submit an application This application goes through an approval process for acceptability. On St. Croix call 773-1290 ext. 2238, and on St.Thomas, call 774-5678.

St. John

Settler's Handbook Chapter 4

Settling in...

Local Architecture and Your Home

The climate of the Virgin Islands has inspired a style of architecture quite different from that in the states. Most mainland homes, even in Florida, are heavily built, insulated and designated for heating and air conditioning efficiency. Most contemporary Virgin Islands homes are designed to take advantage of the cooling trade winds, offer shade from the brilliant sunlight and protect the interiors from heavy rains. They feature open floor plans to maximize air flow and are often only one room wide for optimum cross ventilation. They may well be designed in long, narrow arrangements or surrounding a large open patio or pool. A wide spreading roof with large overhangs to keep out sun and rain and wide gutters to capture the rain, may float on columns with just enough wall space to give some privacy. Other outside walls are either glass, for enjoying the beautiful views, or louvers, jalousies or concrete grill work for ventilation and semi-privacy.

High, open ceilings are best for coolness while ceiling fans are a must to keep air moving when breezes are light. Roofs are sometimes made of concrete, but more often they are constructed with heavy wooden beams, topped with a waterproofed plywood, or in some cases, galvanized metal to reflect the heat. Floors are cooler and most practical when made of ceramic tile or terrazzo. Area rugs may be used to define special areas, but wall-to-wall carpeting is not appropriate for the tropical climate, since they may harbor dust, mildew or insects. Throw rugs are a nice touch, and easily cleaned.

Lush greenery and area landscaping well placed around the outside and the inside of the dwelling add to the coolness of the home. The brilliant colors and scents of blossoms abound, especially following heavy rainfall, and add to the beauty of your dream home.

Rent First

Try before you buy is good advice. Don't begrudge the time and money you spend under a rented roof, for what you are really after is a period of adjustment. Can you adapt your mainland habits to the realities of living, working and housekeeping on a tropical island? Better to discover how you feel about living in the tropics before you burn your bridges back

47

home. If you own a mainland home, try to find a renter. If you live in an apartment try to sublease it if you can. Be sure to bring a few of your favorite things to make your temporary island house feel like home. The islands have a variety of furnished, semi-furnished and unfurnished rentals in all price ranges. Several years ago it was almost impossible to find housing if you arrived in winter months, but that has changed. The choice is even greater in the summer low season. If you plan to stay only a few months, you will pay more than if you sign a longer term lease. And, don't be afraid to bargain. You may be able to keep the rent down by offering to garden, for example. Some winter residents will occasionally rent out their homes or condominiums for a part of the year. Once you are an established island resident, you may be able to luck into an occasional house-sitting arrangement with an absentee owner.

Persistence pays off. Start with the classified sections of the daily newspapers, check with real estate agents, and ask everyone you meet if they or anyone they know has a rental unit. The best deals often come through unconventional methods.

Buying a House or Condominium

Prices are high by most stateside standards. While you can buy a house or a condominium directly from its owner, your best bet is to start with a real estate agent. They know more about its realistic value and can help you locate financing. Many homes are bought for use as short-term rentals, and to keep for retirement. While federal tax laws are no longer as generous as they once were, it provides an income as well as an island getaway several weeks a year. Homes often include a rental apartment, normally under the main house or in an adjacent cottage. The presence of renters adds to the security of your house and will add income.

Because of moving costs, a lot of homes change hands fully furnished. If you buy a furnished home, the sellers may ask you to pay separately for the furnishings so they can save on the capital gains tax. It also keeps property taxes lower for you.

You may be asked to pay yearly dues to a homeowner's association. Because the government is not responsible for privately-owned subdivision roads, the homeowner's associations frequently control road improvements. Be sure and check with the homeowner's association, for they may have rules prohibiting hanging laundry outside, limiting pets and other constraints.

People who do not live here year-round usually buy a condo. They try to combine the tax advantages of home ownership with the reduced responsibilities of apartment living. However, the monthly fees often run in the $400 to $1200 range, due to the high cost of windstorm insurance,

Monthly Home Rentals for Long Term Rentals			
(Utilities not included)			
Size of Rental	St. Croix	St. John	St. Thomas
Efficiency/Studio	$550-$800	$775-$1200	$775-$1500
Cottage	$1200-$2000	$1000-$1800	$800-$1800
1 bedroom Apt.	$550-$1200	$850-$1800	$800-$1550
2 bedroom Apt.	$800-$1800	$1000-$3000	$1000-$2200
2-3 Bedrm Condo	$1200-$2400	$1400-$4000	$1400-$3500
3-4 Bedrm House	$1000-$4000	$2250-$5000	$1500-$6000

and, like other condo associations, the owners share the responsibility of upkeep for the common areas such as the pool, tennis courts, walkways and also for the management and maintenance costs.

Is Your Dream House Historically Significant?

The ruins of old sugar plantations are strewn across much of St. Croix's landscape. While some of the plantations are restored to serve as the landscaping centerpiece of elegant homes, other plantation ruins may need the loving touch of a creative architect and a sensitive builder to find their former glory. If you decide to undertake such a project, ask your local real estate agent to show you the market. Count on paying double for a lot that may contain such historical ruins.

Christiansted, Frederiksted and Charlotte Amalie are designated historic districts by the local government and the National Register of Historic Places. If you would like to register your 50-yr. old-or-older house, call the Planning and Natural Resources Department for an application. If the house is so designated, you will receive a plaque with the information. If you restore your Historic District house, you will receive a 20 percent tax credit on your income tax.

Houses in Christiansted can date to the 18th century and many of the houses in Frederiksted are Victorian in style and era. Devastating fires over the years have wiped out many of the older homes in Charlotte Amalie. The remaining ones date back to the mid-1800s.

Any changes to houses in those areas are governed by rules set down by the Planning and Natural Resources' Historic Preservation Commission. While you can demolish a building in those districts, you have to explain in great detail to the Historic Preservation Commission why it is necessary.

The Commission works to maintain the historic aspects of those districts. Citizens groups, such as the St. Croix Landmarks Society, The St. Croix Foundation, the St. Thomas Historical Trust, Our Town Frederiksted, encourage local residents to restore their houses with the island's history in mind.

Buying a Homesite

Want to build your own home? Before you buy your dream lot, take the advice of your real estate agent, friends who know or the experts at the

building permit office in the Government's Planning and Natural Resources Department (DPNR).

Are the access roads drained and passable in the rainiest weather? Who is responsible for road maintenance? It is usually left to the sub-divider, association of owners or the homeowner to build and maintain the roads. Most homesites are half-acre lots

Courtyard fountain with tables— Linda Moreland

with quarter-acre lots available in denser areas. However, lots zoned before the 1972 ordinances went into effect could be irregularly-sized or shaped. While the Planning and Natural Resources Department has been working on a comprehensive land and water use plan that will restructure all zoning in the U.S. Virgin Islands, as of now it has not been reported or implemented. There are numerous caveats when buying a lot. If it is on a hillside, check the impact of extra structural requirements and site preparation to make sure your budget can meet these demands. Orientation to the wind, grade, salt spray, road access and availability of utility connections will affect the desirability, cost and the home you will build.

In St. Croix, some building sites will go for as little as $28,000. You can buy attractive one-half acre lots with a view from $125,000 to $200,000 and

waterfront lots ranging from $400,000 to $1,000,000. Depending on their location, half-acre lots in St. John range from

Tropical St. Thomas house— Richard Goldberg

around $100,000 and go up. St. Thomas home-sites may start as low as $60,000 to $175,000 for just a quarter acre, while a half acre rarely starts below $120,000. More expensive lots in high end locations even as small as a quarter acre, typically are not available under $200,000. Waterfront sites bring a premium and are rarely found under $400,000. On St. John, rare waterfront parcels cannot be found under $800,000.

Getting Ready to Build

While you could do it all yourself, settlers should depend on the experts when it comes to building here. Building here is a horse of a different color than building a home on the mainland. Your architect, builder or designer can shepherd your plans and permits through the government red tape process.

While you will be getting involved with much of the same types of building codes and permits as elsewhere, the Virgin Islands Building Code, based on: the Universal Plumbing Code 2009, National Electrical Code 2008 (which changes every 3 years), Fire Codes and the Uniform Building Code, all have special provisions to insure all structures are hurricane and earthquake resistant.

If you are a do-it-yourselfer, do your research and find out if the land you like is zoned correctly for your use. Check the zoning maps at the Planning and Natural Resources Department for their regulations. Copies of zoning ordinances and plot layouts are for sale in the cadastral, or registration section in the Lieutenant Governor's office. (773-6449 StC, 774-2991 StT).

Your plans must be prepared by a licensed architect, engineer or draftsman. You can pick up the requirements for a properly detailed set of plans from the Planning and Natural Resources Department and with that information, if the home will be your own, draw the structure. At this point, meet with the building inspector to insure that you are on the right track. After all, he is the one who will put the final stamp of approval on your house. Next, submit three copies of the working drawings and the site location for an earth-change permit from the Planning and Natural Resources Department's building permits section. After you have secured

your earth-change permit from CZM, then bring the three final sets of working drawings to the Planning and Natural Resources building permits section for building, electrical and plumbing permits. This also puts your job on the building inspector's schedule.

Before you start to build it is best to visit DPNR to learn about, and review, all permits etc. required. For example permits for plumbing, power, central air, demolition, flood. Currently they run $20 for residential application fees for each application, and $40 each for commercial applications. Rates are subject to change. There are review plan fees. Those fees are 35% for residential and 65% for commercial of the cost of the building. Please note these are rated with the International Building Code of 2009. (See V.I. Code Title 29,Chapter 5, Section 296 (b) (1)). The plumbing and electrical permit fees, obtainable only by licensed plumbers and electricians, are also based on the cost of the job. Driveway permits from the Public Works Department will cost you about ten dollars. To start your search on St. Croix call DPNR 773-1082 ext.2295. On St. Thomas call 774-3320. The website for DPNR is steadily improving: *http://www.dpnr.gov.vi.*

To connect to the potable water line, if you are building in an area where it is available, apply at the Virgin Islands Water & Power Authority office. It costs around $120 for a single-family residence. Any construction along the shore or offshore up to the three mile limit, or up to the British Virgin Islands sea boundary, if you are on the north side of St. John, needs a Coastal Zone Management permit from the Planning and Natural Resources Department. You must plead your case before the Coastal Zone Management Commission and the local Legislature. Projects in navigable waters also need a U.S.Army Corps of Engineers permit. This includes dredging, removing piers, seawalls, sand mining, filling and just about every kind of alteration to the fragile and precious coastal zone. It pays to ask before you invest.

In St. John The IBGA (Island Green Builders Association) was established in 2004 by a group of concerned construction industry professionals and island residents to promote responsible and sustainable development there. They suggest thinking about greening up the house you own, are buying, or consider building a green home. Current home owners can start buy making a few enhancements / changes a few at a time. Incorporate some of these thoughts into your building plans. It isn't only a matter of economics but environmental impact too. Homes can be certified with an IBGA logo designation. Green certified homes seem to sell faster. For information on going green and building green go to: www.igba-stjohn.org

The site suggests that attention can be given to reduce erosion pollution and destruction of marine and terrestrial communities. Retain native / natural vegetation; use setbacks as green belt area. A tropical architectural design can take advantage of trade winds and sun paths. Use renewable, recyclable, local, sustainable, non-toxic materials. Build for protection against hurricanes and earthquakes. Develop rain water and gray water collection systems. Design an energy system to maximize the use of renewable energy. Solar panels and wind generators play a key role.

Construction Cost in the VI

The Virgin Islands, and all Caribbean island locations, require a more stringent construction technique. First, the structures need to be built to withstand hurricanes and flooding. Secondly, homes will typically require a water collection system and a cistern to store the collected water for both drinking and sanitation. Thirdly, an on-site septic or waste water treatment plant must be constructed. For remote islands, electricity generation may be the only way to have power. So all of these issues conspire to impact the cost of home construction. The costs are varied and not fixed. Luxury features and extravagant materials tend to raise prices disproportionately and cause average per square foot prices to escalate. Following is a list of average construction cost per island.

As these figures plainly show building in the VI is more expensive. But the positive aspect is that homes built today are far more energy efficient and habitable then in the past.

Most houses have a septic tank with septic pit or drain field rather than

	St. Croix	St. Thomas	St. John
	All prices are dollars per square foot		
Single Family to 1500 sq ft	200-350	250-600	400-800
Multiple Family	175-350	250-600	350-700
Luxury	350-750	450-800	600-2000

a sewer. In your new home, make sure they are not installed in a place where roots could clog the openings. Some houses have graywater systems in order to reuse household water for gardening or landscape areas. Try to design your home to maximize on tropical breezes, and sunlight to save on utility bills.

Houses with **cisterns** for water storage require an intricate system of gutters and drain pipes. This water may be used for drinking and other personal household purposes. Ten gallons of cistern capacity are required for every square foot of roof on a single story residence. This includes roofs over porches and decks. For a two-story residence, it is 15 gallons for every square foot of roof. Commercial buildings must have five gallons per square foot of roof. The cistern may account for almost 10 % of your final building costs. The roof surface that catches the precious water must not degrade in any way. To make your hot water supply efficient, buy a well-insulated hot-water tank and insulate the supply pipes. Using solar collectors mounted on your roof for heating the water, can save you 20-40% of your electric bill. Check with the Virgin Islands Energy office to see if they might be offering one of their periodic rebates for energy saving devices.

Security

As elsewhere, crime is also a problem in the U.S. Virgin Islands. Prevention is the key to keep your house from becoming a statistic on the police blotter. If you are going to be away for more than a day or two, consider finding a reliable house sitter and tell your neighbors when you will be off-island. If you live in a high crime area, install decorative wrought iron grills on your windows and doors and consider a high-tech alarm system. If you are a fulltime resident, there is no better deterrent than a good watchdog.

Since it only takes a minute for burglars to be in and out, do not go out and leave windows or doors open. As in the states, make your house look occupied to deter burglars. Invest in a timer that will turn lights and radio on and off. Forget those wimpy door locks that turn with a flick of the finger. Instead buy solid deadbolts that need a key to open. Invest in a locking device for your sliding doors that pushes a strong pin right through the frame into the sliding panel and cannot be opened if the regular lock is broken.

Again, as in the states, police recommend that you engrave your social security number in bold print in a visible spot on your television set, CD player, home office equipment, cameras and other appliances. This will make it harder for burglars to fence your property and will serve as a deterrent. Record the serial numbers so you can claim them if they are stolen and keep an inventory of those possessions for insurance purposes. Use good judgment when you are out and about. Do not pick up hitchhikers and avoid questionable, unfamiliar areas and keep your car doors locked, especially at night. In case of emergency, call 911 to reach the Police Department, Fire Department or an ambulance. From cells, 340-772-9111.

Financing

Financing in the Virgin Islands is similar to the States except the available programs are somewhat limited. Conventional loans are offered and FHA, VA and Rural Development loans are available for primary residences. Allied Mortgages offers reverse mortgages both purchase and refinance for seniors 62 years of age. The borrower will normally apply and qualify for one of these loans through a local bank or mortgage broker. Since we are located in what is called an ultra high cost area, our loan limits are somewhat higher than Stateside.

Conventional loan limits start at $625,500 for a one unit property and go up from there depending on the number of units. The current VA limit is $625,500 up to four units. FHA limits vary by island and the number of

Conventional loan limits start at $625,500 for a one unit property and go up from there depending on the number of units. The current VA limit is $625,500 up to four units. FHA limits vary by island and the number of units. The FHA single family lending limit for St. Croix is $327,750, St. Thomas $466,200 and St. John $623,300 says Bonnie at Schaffer Mortgage. These limits are influenced and adjusted by the median housing price. The FHA "Rescue Bill" which was passed and signed in the summer of 2008 may have additional impact on lending limits. Check with a local bank or mortgage broker to see which program is best for you. As in the States, normal closing costs apply and excellent real estate attorneys are available.

Property Insurance

Whether you rent, buy or build, you need coverage. Virgin Islands banks require fire, earthquake and windstorm insurance with a mortgage; and, depending on the location, you may need flood. Your agent can help you select the best for your particular needs and location.

Property Taxes

Residential property taxes are .37 percent of the market value of the property. Property owners can qualify for certain discounts, including a homestead tax credit ($400), a veteran's tax credit ($650), a senior tax credit ($500), and a disabled tax credit ($500). The tax year runs from January 1 to December 31. Tax bills for the previous year are mailed June 15 and are delinquent by September 1. The interest charge is 1 per cent each month up to 25% until paid.

Other forms of property incur separate tax rates. Commercial property is taxed at .71 percent of market value; unimproved commercial property is taxed at .49 percent of market value; and time share real property is taxed at 1.4 percent of market value. Tax bills are issued on or before June 30th of each year. Tax bills are mailed to the last known mailing address on file in the Tax Assessor's Office. Property owners are responsible for notifying the Tax Assessor of their correct mailing address.

Property taxes are payable at the Office of the Tax Collector, a division under The Office of the Lieutenant Governor. Taxes become delinquent if not paid within sixty (60) days of issue. If taxes are paid after ninety days, they become delinquent, and an interest rate of one percent (1%) is added per month to the amount of tax that is due. For more information contact the VI Tax Assessors Office at http://ltg.gov.vi/office-of-the-tax-assessor-cadastral.html, or by phone at the following numbers: St. Croix (340-773-4052), St. Thomas (340-774-1270), or St, John (340-693-9916).

Problems and Solutions to Your Décor

How to furnish your house depends on your taste, your environment and you can dunk in the washer instead of carpeting. Wall-to-wall carpeting is an option only for dust, mildew and bugs. Colorful sheets will also brighten up a bedroom and with the warm, tropical climate, bedspreads are often not necessary.

When deciding whether to move, store or sell your furniture, keep in mind that the tropical climate can take its toll. The sun will fade fabrics, while termites and humidity can ravage some wooden furniture. What is cozy in the cool north will feel heavy and hot in the Caribbean. Mahogany and pitch pine resist termites while fruitwood, pine and oak do not. Humidity can cause stuck drawers, splitting veneers and loose joints. There are ways to protect your fine furniture. Coat all unfinished parts, bottoms of legs, inside cabinets, and under drawers, etc., with pentachlorophenol, which will prevent the onslaught of termites, fungus, and wood rot, while minimizing humidity-induced swelling. To protect your baby grand piano against humidity, purchase an electric heater rod. Should you discover a pile of termite droppings under your furniture, (a small, round pile that looks like dark sand) call a professional exterminator who will spray the piece for termites and look for other insect infestations.

Furniture with a minimum amount of upholstery is the coolest and the most practical, hence the great popularity of rattan and cane. However, after several years of living with cushion-only furniture, some folks long for the deep comfort of fully upholstered furniture. In this case, occasional airing and sunning are helpful in dispelling any musty odors that might develop during a damp spell. Choose all cotton or a cotton polyester blend simply because they are washable and cooler.

If you like the look of metal, try aluminum with a baked enamel finish, for rust happens quickly in any tropical climate. For your outdoor furniture, look for aluminum frames with vinyl straps to hold the cushions. If you buy woven mesh cushions made of Tixtaline, you can leave them out in the weather since the rain drains through. Know, however, that the sun will take its toll on the padding as well as the color. New breathable vinyl, which has minute holes or an open mesh, is much cooler than regular vinyl or plastic that sticks to the skin. The new vinyl will also stand up better to spilled food and wet bathing suits. Always use plastic hangers, not metal. Keep bedspreads up off floors, just so floor creatures don't stray!

The best drapery fabrics are verels, polyesters and dacrons. These stand up well in the sun and are washable. Those with high percentage of acetate are not washable and deteriorate rapidly in the sun.

Maintenance

The tropics are tough on the contents of your home. Chances are it will fall prey to salt, dust, bugs and a myriad of other problems that need a watchful eye. If a full-time housekeeper is not in your budget, learn to adjust and accept the fact that cobwebs will grow in the corners, fuzzies will appear under your bed and the clothes in the closet and drawers will grow mysterious small brown spots. As for those mysterious brown spots, they appear to come from insects. There's no cure, but bleach or spot remover will take most of them out of clothes or linens. Try drawer deodorizers in the drawer and closet. If you keep up with the outside maintenance, you won't be in a pinch during our tropical storms or hurricane season. Check all joints for caulking and give your home a frequent freshening with paint or caulking or with paint or preservative stains to protect it. Remember that all finishes should be fungus resistant. The local paint stores will have additives that you can mix with your paint for non-treated finishes. Fungus appears as a dark discoloration on the surface, under the eaves or in other shaded areas. Inspect exterior woodwork periodically to make sure dry-rot hasn't appeared in joints that are slow to dry after rains; a problem that won't exist if you use redwood or pressure treated lumber.

While the briny breezes keep you cool, they also eat away at your house and its contents. Salt destroys because it holds moisture, causing corrosion and mildew in the darndest places. Rust can eat through car bodies, belt and shoe buckles, turning them black, create a soggy smell even in line dried linens and your cranky electronics. It's all the work of salt.

To clean your metal objects, sand and scrape to remove rust then scrub clean with fresh water. Dry quickly, prime with rust inhibitor, and paint. Waxes and oils help keep salt from reaching the surface and prolonging the life of painted or plated metals. Rust spots won't go away so try to treat them before they become a real problem.

Refrigerators are particularly vulnerable to rust due to condensation forming on cold spots on the cabinet. Make sure doors and gaskets fit properly and have a service contractor check the insulation. Those cute magnets cause rust spots that spread. You can wax your appliances with car wax to protect from those attacks of rust.

If you live on a dirt road, a film of sand will cover your window sills and screens on the road side of the house. The best solution? Vacuum regularly. To keep things smelling fresh, install louver doors on your closet so the air can circulate. To prevent mildew, never store anything in a drawer or closest that is not clean or dry and be sure to rotate your linens and clothes as you use them. Avoid rust stains on your clothes by using only plastic hangers. Should you find rust stains on your clothes, Whink, on sale at some of the local stores, will make them disappear in a jiff.

Gardening

Is gardening a labor of love for you or just another phase of home

local stores, will make them
disappear in a jiff.

Gardening

Is gardening a labor of love for
you or just another phase of home
maintenance? If it's the former, the
pleasures in store in the Virgin
Islands will last a lifetime. If the latter, welcome to the majority! You will
never have it easier than in the islands where pests are minimal and hardy
tropical plants are abundant. For most who garden, tropical gardening is
mainly a matter of no muss, no fuss. While you can grow orchids,
strawberries or other exotic species, most gardeners are content to grow
native. Your best bets are flowers and fruits that also grow in the wild. With
a little bit of pampering, these native plants and trees will flourish in your
garden or around your home. To make this appropriate setting for your
home, first begin with an evaluation of the soil, slope, rain, sun and wind
on your own lot. One thing to know, Virgin Islands soils are usually quite
alkaline (high pH) so most plants will need extra nitrogen.

While there's a widespread assumption that anything will grow here, it
just isn't so. Plants, like all living things, tend to do best in the environment
where they first evolved. Drought, sudden downpours, high temperatures
in the air and soil all influence the successful growth patterns of your
favorite stateside plants. Rats or mongoose will make a meal out of your
favorite papayas or other fruit. In some areas, goats, donkeys and horses
regularly have lunch on what you have just invested time and money to
plant. But don't give up, because there are ways around the problem. Do-
it-yourselfers should start with a good how-to book that specializes in
warm-weather gardening. In St. Croix, the St. George Village Botanical
Garden has frequent classes on tropical gardening. The University of the
Virgin Islands extension service on all three islands has a myriad of
pamphlets on the subject, and the local government's Agriculture
Department will not only give advice but also sell low cost plants. You
might consider joining the hibiscus, orchid, or other plant societies, in either
St. Croix or St. Thomas and meet residents who will love to share their
hard-won knowledge with you.

Now comes the fun! As you read through the plant books to develop your
landscape, remember to check how tall the plants will grow and how wide
they will spread. Plant shade trees first, so you can protect plants that need
partial sun. Think two years down the road to prevent your plants from
overrunning each other. Make sure the roots won't invade the plumbing
pipes or its leaves, or overhead power lines. Be sure to talk to your builder

roots of your already established trees.

One of the most important things to remember before you decide to become a landscaper or gardener is to watch out for hazardous plants. Toxic or thorny plants are far more common in the tropics than in the north, so be careful not to plan them near your walkways or doors. Even some of the more common plants, Poinsettias for one, may irritate the skin of those who are sensitive. The sap of Poinsettia and its cousins, Monkey Puzzle and Christmas Candle, are the troublemakers. Wear gloves, but if you should get some on your skin while pruning, scrub well afterward. Another one of those problem plants, Pencil Cactus, can cause blindness if you get the sap in your eye. Oleander, another poisonous variety, is a beautiful large garden shrub bearing clusters of deep pink or white blossoms among long straight branches. While it is one of the few plants not devoured by goats (perhaps they are smarter than what we think), those who would use those handy looking branches as barbecue skewers could, just possibly, get sick or die. Something else to watch for is the Century Plant, or Yucca, which has sharp, sword-like points. Protect your eyes. The Lucky Nut Tree is full of a deadly white latex. Eating the fruit is not a good idea for to do so may cause hearing failure, or death. While few people plant Manchineel in their yards, it is more common near the shore, watch out for this spreading tree with a fruit resembling a crabapple for it is highly poisonous. The sap or rain drippings from this tree or even the smoke from its burning wood can cause a nasty rash. Ackees, commonly eaten as the national dish in Jamaica, grow here but the use of these yellow colored, fleshy arils in red pods are highly toxic should they be picked prior to the pods maturing and opening on their own. It's best to consult with the University or someone local who knows how to prepare them. Trees in the Virgin Islands National Park in St. John and the Buck Island National Monument in St. Croix are often marked with "red skull and crossbones" to indicate their danger to you.

If allergy sensitive members of your family react to some plant pollens and spores, have them be careful around Cassia and Mango trees or Bermuda and Guinea grasses, since these plants are known to cause problems. But, all these problems will be addressed through your reading materials or through conversations with your neighbors or friends. To see what does well in your neighborhood, drive around to observe what your neighbors have planted. Try asking those neighbors for cuttings of plants you like. In the true island spirit, most people will even root them for you, plant several in a pot and, six weeks later, plant the survivors in their own pots. When they look hale and hearty, move them to a ground area you have chosen. Water them regularly until it looks like they are established. While some home gardeners say they never water unless they have new plants, even during droughts, the pros suggest that you drip irrigate. A little bit of water every day is better than a whole lot once a week. Sprinklers waste water due to evaporation in the tropical climate. Instead try using your washing machine or kitchen sink water to moisten your plants. While some plants do not do well with soapy water (check with neighbors or friends here, or a local nursery), others will do just fine. Due to the tropical sun most soil is compact with a hard crust so, for a few days before you plant, soak the soil to soften it. When it comes right down to planting, start with a big hole, put peat moss around the roots and fertilize regularly because of the alkaline soil. Mulch around the plant to keep water in and pests out then use a non-toxic brand pesticide like Sunoil or Dipel to keep down the pest population. Consider using potted plants as part of your landscape. Requiring less water, these plants can be sheltered during storms or put out of sight when they are not blooming. To save back strain use large pots with casters or wheels.

Last, but not least, do not clear more land than you are ready to plant immediately. Without plant cover to hold it, the few inches of topsoil that covers the rocks will vanish with the first wind or rain. If you need to, a mulch of tall Guinea grass cut from the roadside will hold your soil in place. Now that you have done your reading on the botany of the tropics from books and pamphlets, have talked to friends and neighbors and have planted your special choices, enjoy the fruits of your labor for in the tropics the results can be delicious and the colors spectacular.

Insects

Let's face it, insects are a fact of tropical life. Some creep, some crawl and some fly, but unless you are a maniac with the bug spray, they are always with you. Learn to love your lizards or geckos. Besides providing hours of entertainment, they eat mosquitoes, probably the number one pest during the rainy season. To combat mosquitoes, dispose of standing water and close open doors at sundown and sunup. Some types of mosquitoes can carry the dengue virus. It may pay to invest in a mosquito net for your bed. Of course you can always spray or fog, as you can for any pest, but prevention is kinder to you and the environment.

The heavier gauge mosquito nets also keep out the gnats, sand flies, or "no see-ums", as they are known by some. They make themselves known, particularly around your ankles, at sundown. If you are really bothered, try Avon Skin-So-Soft diluted with water as a repellent. It's been proven to work by some. It's been rumored that sheets of "Bounce" placed by you, by the bed and in closets helps with that, as well as keeping the air fresh.

From time to time, every house suffers with ants in sizes that range from minuscule to downright huge. Wipe up crumbs quickly and set traps to prevent them from overrunning your house. To keep out flies, cover your food and take garbage to the dumpsters promptly. Despite your best efforts, big brown cockroaches will make their appearance, usually when your most fastidious aunt makes her annual visit. Sprinkle boric acid tablets in every nook and cranny of your house to keep them under control. You can also call one of the local pest control companies and get a yearly contract for a quick easy monthly maintenance spray. Check occasionally for hives hanging around your eaves or yard trees. They often have hives in the old sugar mill ruins too.

Watch out for Jack Spaniards if you are out hiking. Members of the wasp family, they will sting if you disturb them. Try ammonia, baking soda or a chunk of papaya to stop the stinging. Creatures that look somewhat like a caterpillar with many pairs of legs, are centipedes and their toxic bites can hurt your toddler. Some adults can have a very bad allergic reaction to them. Scorpions are poisonous and their sting hurts. While it is rare to find one lurking about, every once in a while one appears. Termites can eat the wooden parts of your house quicker than your kids can down a pizza. Dozens of tropical varieties live in subterranean nests, building a mud tube up the walls or making big globular nests in trees. Others live entirely within dead lumber like your furniture or rafters with no clue to their presence except an occasional mysterious pile of sawdust or tiny pellets. Prevention is imperative. Use masonry construction over treated soil, pressure treated or naturally resistant lumber. You may be able to knock out an infestation in a single piece of furniture with a drenching of wood preservative, but if they are munching on the building, call the exterminator. In fact, monthly calls by the exterminator does keep down the pests. Many residents would not live without this visit.

If you are bitten by any island creepy crawlies, you may experience some redness, swelling and itching. If it grows, call your doctor. Allergic reactions to insect bites can be serious. Another little crawler found regularly in these parts, as well as worldwide, is the Gongolo, or millipede. They are about 2" long, red, yellow or dark brown and skinny. Normally they dwell outdoors, but often times after heavy rains, tend to meander indoors. If they are kicked, they usually curl into a hard ball. If threatened, they exude a yucky odor and brown substance to deter enemies, which can burn or rash the skin. They enter through door, window, and wall cracks, so be sure to check these spaces. While regular pesticides treatment might kill them, the most common pest control is the swift whip of a broom. Also, if you come across leeches, it has been said that salt dries them out. Do watch out for centipedes. While they hunt roaches and crickets, they have a nasty bite (sting). Take a shoe to them instantly.

Clothing

Boutiques on all three islands carry chic tropical wear for men, women and children for almost every occasion. For those who like bargains, Kmart is available. Savvy shoppers and locals wait for end-of the-season sales to stock up. Since some items are a little harder to find, many residents depend on trips to the mainland or mail-order. Yes, you need a sweater for those cool winter nights and you probably need more bathing suits than you did in the north, but your clothes budget should shrink. For those who must go north, it is common practice to borrow an overcoat from a neighbor.

What you will wear for the day depends on where you work. Government workers and bank employees tend to dress to the nines. Those in more casual offices dress down. It does appear that "anything" goes in the islands and nothing is "in" or "out." Locals dress for their job, dark suits for banks, colorful cottons for regular office jobs, colorful cotton shirts and casual slacks for men, unless you're a lawyer. Women wear long skirts basically for shade. Island wrap skirts can be dressed up or down. As far as shorts and tee shirts, you can't go wrong with cotton. It breathes, is lightweight, and you can throw it in the washer. Look for loose-fitting styles that allow air to circulate. Sandals help to keep your feet cool. Unless you are familiar with your surroundings, never go barefoot, you will leave your feet unprotected against insects, plants, and hot surfaces.

Keep in mind that the law requires you to cover up even if you are on the way to the beach. The U.S. Virgin Islands is neither Miami Beach nor Cape Cod, and islanders frown when they see a tourist on the street wearing only a bathing suit. In fact, they may just tell you to cover up. A long tee shirt does just fine. Men must wear shirts.

At night, some crowds dress up and others down. If you are invited to a special local event, know that Virgin Islanders like to dress up. Only a few hotel dining rooms require jackets for men; you can ask when you make your dinner reservations.

Cooking

Cooking in the islands elevates the art of compromise to new levels. Pueblo, Plaza Extra and Cost-U-Less in St. Croix and St. Thomas are all stocked to the rafters with goodies. But the truth of the matter is, if you have set your heart and your menu on mint jelly with your lamb chops, it could be the week that the Miami or Puerto Rico supplier didn't send any. Should you depend on St. John's small grocery stores to fill your pantry, you may never find all you want. You may want to plan a shopping day to St. Thomas and combine it with other business.

You could spend half a day visiting stores to complete your menu or you can adjust and serve what is available. Sometimes you may want to spend

You could spend half a day visiting stores to complete your menu or you can adjust and serve what is available. Sometimes you may want to spend the time on the hunt and other times you may decide to keep it simple. You will also find roadside fresh fruit and vegetable stands (in season), or specialized seafood markets and delis. When not in season, you can usually find them frozen or canned. Normally there will be varieties of lettuce, peppers, mushrooms, potatoes, and scallions in stock. Stateside fruits like peaches, pears and plums are sometimes mealy and tasteless due to early harvesting for shipping. Citrus fruits, bananas, papayas and pineapples are always a good bet. For a real treat, try grafted mango. While the smaller ones are usually stringy, the larger ones melt in your mouth. You can depend on the fact that you will find just about anything here you see in the mainland stores, although there may fewer brands to choose from and the package size may not be adequate for a desired recipe. The new products you see advertised on cable television will probably take several months to arrive in the islands.

Cultural Tidbit

"White, grey, purple, green, brown, and sable, are all the colors that bundle themselves tightly up in this juicy, pulpy, fruit. Sugar Apple is a staple treat on the island. Entire calypso songs have been sung celebrating this fruit!

The first thing that greets you when you open a sugar apple is the scent. It is such a mild, peppery-clean, and sugary-warm aroma. I would honestly buy anyone's perfume that was made entirely from this fruit. The first taste you get is a very subtle mellowed sweetness. Smooth caramel undertones that suspend the fruit's seeds in a soft, edible, cotton-like sac. Sugar Apple really defies description.

This is one you will simply have to come down to the island and taste for yourself.

Are you packing yet?!"

— Taisha Bailey-Roka, local food blogger and attorney. Visit her blog at http://www.cruciancontessa.com

Retailers blame the price on shipping but costs may run as much as 25 percent higher than expensive Washington, D.C. or nearly 20 percent higher than in nearby San Juan, Puerto Rico. Local food, a little cheaper, does add a new dimension to your menu. For the freshest local and some stateside how to cook it is always free.

Native foods reflect the varied local history. Caribs, Arawaks, transported Africans, Caribbean immigrants and U.S. mainlanders have all left their mark on the cuisine. The Spaniards left a legacy of red beans and rice. Recipes often reflect a European tradition cooked up with what was available here. Those odd-looking roots and tubers you see in the veggie departments date to antiquity. Dasheen, cassava breadfruit, taro and genuine white yam are cooked as side dishes or served as the basis for breads and meat dishes. Banana's not-so-sweet cousin, the plantain, appears as a vegetable baked or fried. Local tangy greens and okra are used mostly for their seasoning qualities rather than served alone.

Chefs are masters at creating tasty stews and entrees from fish, chicken, pork, goat or conch which is harvested locally. The entrees are accompanied by a seasoned rice or a cornmeal dish called fungi. For a taste of native cuisine try kallaloo, a stew of seasoned meat, crab and fish boiled with greens and okra, Roti and conch fritters, as a taste suggestion, are wonderful samples of local fare. The Roti, similar to a floured tortilla, can be stuffed with a combination of potatoes, in a spicy curry sauce with chicken, beef or conch added to it. The conch fritters, similar in appearance to a hush puppy, are often served as appetizers at restaurants and cocktail parties and again, taste will depend upon the individual chef. Gundi, another unusual dish, is a cold, molded salad made from fish or lobster with potatoes, onion or beets.

A Johnny cake, a fried dumpling, is served up wherever West Indians gather whether it be at political rallies, festivals or roadside food carts. Pates, another finger food staple, are spicy fried turnovers filled with fish, chicken or ground beef. To sample West Indian food at its best, be sure to attend the food fairs that are held on all three islands' festive holidays. To learn about local cooking, look for the numerous cookbooks at local bookstores or call the extension service at the University of the Virgin Islands for their "Native Recipes" booklet.

While most local foods won't cause any problems, on rare occasions the **ciguatera toxin** in fish can cause trouble. Despite what you may hear, ciguatera is not fish poisoning. It is caused by a toxin produced by a single-celled animal that lives on algae. Ingested by algae-eating fish, the toxin heads up the fish chain when those fish are eaten by other fish. Since the toxin is cumulative, the bigger the fish, the more likely the problem. Barracuda, some jacks, some snappers, the larger kingfish and groupers may have the problem. Some claim that the toxin only affects fish caught in certain waters, but there is no scientific proof of that. If you eat a fish with ciguatera, you will ache all over. And what is hot will feel cold and vice versa. You may also suffer nausea and diarrhea. If you suffer these symptoms, head for the hospital where a drug called Mannitol is available. While there is no known cure, the Federal Drug Administration is working on a test kit to help doctors determine if what you have is really ciguatera.

If a stomach upset is your only symptom, you probably have eaten a fish with scrombrid toxin which is found in larger fish with red meat. Those fish should be iced immediately after catching to prevent development of the toxin.

Drinks

Hot sun plus warm temperatures equals a big thirst in the tropics. It is always wise to carry some bottled water with you on long planned errands around the island. While water is the best thirst quencher, there is also a big variety of fruit juices from which to choose. In addition to the mango, tamarind, guava, soursop and coconut nectars on the local supermarket shelves, you will also find the usual orange, cranberry and apple juices.

Look for Vita Malt, a non-alcoholic drink produced throughout the Caribbean. Try coconut water right from the coconut at roadside stands. You will also find locally-brewed maubi, ginger beer, sorrel and sea moss, an alleged aphrodisiac, at native restaurants. Also try the Schnapps (i.e. Akvavit), the Danish drink served right from the freezer. It is often chased with beer. Most stateside beers can be found here, but of course the most popular island drinks are anything made with rum. That special Cruzan Rum is distilled right on the island of St. Croix. Local bars all have their favorite special rum cocktails.

Weather in the Tropics

Most of the weather patterns come from the East, out of the Atlantic Ocean and, in some cases, all the way from the shores of Africa. The haze seen at times during the year is the "Sahara dust" floating across the Atlantic Ocean from the African continent. Some of the most beautiful sunsets seen in the Virgins are created by these "imported" dust particles.

On the U.S. mainland, high and low-pressure systems bring well-defined weather changes to a region before moving eastward. While these air masses rarely penetrate as far southeast as the Virgin Islands, when they do, the warm seas warm their passage. Occurring in the winter months, the result could be strong northerly winds, rough seas, rain, a temperature drop and what the locals call the cooling, refreshing "Christmas winds," which usually start in December. Seasonal changes are subtle but they are there with temperatures 10 degrees cooler in winter than summer— around 70 low / 80 high winter and 80 low / 90 high in summer months. Trade winds help to cool. For those who are

Cultural Tidbit

*T*hough the seasons in the Virign Island's are not as visually dramatic as in the northern U.S. mainland, when summer time comes you will feel the change. It will show in the form of damp, sticky shirts and often oppressive humidity. To help ease the transition to summer, here is a cooling elixir created by the Crucian Contessa, Tanisha Bailey-Roka

Ingredients: • About 50 Ounces of Water •1 1/4 Cups (Organic Evaporated Cane Juice) •Sugar •1/4 Cup of Local Honey •2-3 drops of Banana essence (to taste) •6 Bags of Orange Pekoe Black Tea (Lipton) •2-3 Limes •2 Cups Passion Fruit Pulp

Directions: • In a large heat-resistant pitcher, pour gently boiled water over six tea bags and allow to steep for no more than 4-5 minutes. If you let the tea steep longer it will turn bitter. While the water is still warm, add the passion fruit pulp, the sugar and the honey. Stir until the sugar and honey dissolves. • Add the juice of the limes and the banana essence. Be careful with the banana essence. • It is very powerful and can add a bitter-ish taste to your drink if too much is used. • Let the drink cool to room temperature, and then refrigerate.

Suggestions: You can leave it overnight to ensure that all the flavors properly marry. You can also strain prior to serving. However, I prefer to let the passion fruit seeds show themselves off, as a great visual contrast. I also add ice to the cups instead of to the pitcher, since it tends to dilute the flavors. It is to your own taste and preference. It literally looks and tastes like SUNSHINE in a cup! Enjoy!!— *Tanisha Bailey-Roka. Check out her food blog at http://www.crucian-contessa.com.*

accli-matized, it can feel cooler in winter months, especially at night.

The trade-winds, drifting across the Atlantic and into the Caribbean with their accompanying ocean waves, always move west. While these are not as well defined as the Lows and Highs of the northern air masses, they can cause cloudiness, rain and a predictable wind-shift pattern and therefore changes in the weather.

When an easterly wave forms just north of the equator in the Atlantic, as often happens during the late spring and late summer, a tropical wave may appear. Should this wave intensify, the weather system grows in magnitude, with wind speed rising over 34 miles per hour, it will become a tropical storm. Once the wind speed reaches higher than 74 mph, the tropical storm is then designated as a full-fledged hurricane. During the years from 1928 to 1989, there were no major storms in the Virgin Islands. In September 1989, Hurricane Hugo roared through the Caribbean and stalled over St. Croix for almost 18 hours on September 17 and 18. The island suffered massive destruction. St. John and St. Thomas were hard hit by Hugo, but one comment about the island of St. Croix "of the trees still standing there wasn't a leaf left." When Hurricane Hugo hit the islands in 1989 some areas clocked the wind speed at over 200 miles per hour and one anemometer on St. Croix broke at 217 mph. Heavy rainfall in West Africa may create major storms in these areas but, research has uncovered the coincidence that when Africa is dry, as has been the case up until 1995, the threat of hurricanes appear to diminish. Tropical weather systems are also affected by conditions referred to as La Nina (more favorable to development), and El Nino, some-what opposite.

In early September 1995, Hurricane Luis, while devastating St. Maarten and Antigua and the other islands in the Eastern Caribbean, was kinder to the U.S. Virgin Islands. Mainly causing waterfront destruction by its high tides and wave surges, Luis did not affect the infrastructure of the Virgin Islands. However, Hurricane Marilyn, ten days later, was a different story. St. Croix suffered moderate damage to its structures, utilities and landscape. St. Thomas and St. John received the brunt of Marilyn with 90% of its homes, hotels and utilities severely damaged. An extensive reconstruction program was conducted. Building codes have been revised since, resulting in more stringent codes and more reinforcement to all structures being built.

St. Croix's new pier in Frederiksted was not damaged by Hurricane Marilyn, and cruise ship lines re-routed some of their ships from St.Maarten and St.Thomas to St. Croix. After a few years of visiting the same port, and because of repeat customers, cruise ship operators often change ports for a few years. St. Croix saw an increase in cruise ship visits in 2009 with more in ensuing years. St. Thomas has always been a port of call because of its natural deep water port, and now two docks, one at Havensight and one at Crown Bay.

While residents have always observed Hurricane Supplication Day around the end of July, and Hurricane Thanksgiving Day in the month of October, the observance of Thanksgiving Day took on a deeper meaning following Hurricane Hugo in September of 1989, Hurricane Marilyn in September of 1995 and Lenny in November of 1999. With adequate warning and few lives lost, residents flocked to their churches giving thanks. The Virgin Islanders have pulled together, and by most accounts, have recovered and regrouped from the force of two major hurricanes. With the result of these two Hurricanes, buildings have been rebuilt with better hurricane specification codes.

Tropical Storms

Since Hurricane Hugo 1989, the U.S. Virgin Islands government tuned up its hurricane response system and was prepared for Hurricanes Luis and Marilyn. Communication systems have been improved, shelters identified and fortified and emergency personnel trained. Thanks to up-to-the-minute weather forecasting, residents get fair warning when a hurricane threatens. And since then, the Hurricane Hunters have made their summer forward home base in St. Croix and are here from June till October yearly. They fly the storm and send data back to the Hurricane Center in Miami. Don't wait until a storm threatens, instead, be prepared. Long before there is any storm on the horizon, make sure you have enough plywood to protect windows and doors. In the last few years, companies here have specialized in supplying secure hurricane shutters. Keep a supply of large plastic bags to store your small appliances, books and other valuables. A battery-operated radio is a necessity. Radios and newspapers give plenty of warning a few days prior to help you prepare.

Tarps are handy to have if your roof blows off. Invest in a generator to insure you have enough power to run your refrigerator. Of course, you will need to keep an adequate supply of gasoline in a proper container on hand. If you live in an all-electric house, buy a camp stove that runs on sterno or white gas to make sure you can warm up a can of soup, make coffee or tea. Buy several battery-operated flashlights and lanterns and enough batteries to last until the power comes on again. Since you could be without electricity for days, don't depend on the rechargeable kind. Battery operated lanterns work best, since wind can blow out kerosene oil lamps or candles, possibly increasing the danger of fire.

At the start of hurricane season in June, stock up on non-perishables. Keep bottled water, an assortment of basic canned goods, and a manual can opener on hand. Store dry goods such as powdered milk, cereals, pasta products, sugar and crackers in plastic bags to keep them moisture free. Don't forget food for your pets, too. Make sure you have enough toilet paper, bleach to purify contaminated water, your basic tools, a fully-stocked first aid kit, and adequate supplies of any drug prescriptions you feel are necessary. Also, store your important documents in plastic bags.

Settler's Handbook Chapter 5

The Infrastructure..Services..Utilities...Airlines..Medical

The infrastructure within the Virgin Islands has vastly improved in the last decade. Electrical power failures, which used to be a way of life, are now the exception. The city water, through desalination, is safe to drink. All major streets, though they still have the proverbial pothole here and there, are paved and considered some of the best in the Caribbean. The telecommunications system is better than in some areas in the United States. But, like all structural systems, problems do exist and it is considered part and parcel of living in the islands and the tropics.

Communications

Innovative Companies provides a broad range of telecommunications and cable TV services. Innovative's family of services for both the business and residential markets include local telephone, long-distance, internet, cable TV, wireless and business phone systems.

The Innovative family of companies consists of Innovative Telephone, Innovative Wireless, Innovative Cable TV St. Croix, Innovative Cable TV St. Thomas-St. John, Innovative PowerNet, Innovative Business Systems and CBS-TV2(collectively, "Innovative"). Innovative is the only telecommunications provider in the U.S. Virgin Islands with the ability to bundle all voice, wireline, data and video services. Innovative has one-stop customer care locations at Estate Diamond on St. Croix; Tutu Park Mall on St. Thomas and Starfish Marketplace on St. John. Additionally, Innovative has Wireless Retail Stores at Estate Diamond and Plaza Extra West (Kiosk) on St Croix; Tutu Park Mall and Nisky Center in St. Thomas and Starfish Marketplace in St. John.

Innovative has embarked on an aggressive plan to upgrade its network. It's modernization project is a two-year plan to address the need for new modern services and to improve the reliability of voice, video and high-speed data offerings throughout the U.S. Virgin Islands. This new suite of services, called EVO by Innovative, is a telecommunications platform that delivers service via a state-of-the-art hybrid fiber and coax cable (HFC) network. Innovative anticipates that at the end of the project up to 100MBps speeds will be available.

Some specific benefits Innovative customers receive are: bundled multi-service discounts through their Innovative Advantage program, custom solutions for many of their business and government clients, one-stop, convenient customer service through their integrated billing and customer service centers, and the dedication & commitment of their employees to serving Innovative's customers. The following is a brief description of each of the services Innovative offers.

Innovative Telephone

The US Virgin Islands has a state-of-the-art communication system provided and operated by Innovative Telephone (previously known as The Virgin Islands Telephone Corporation (VITELCO)). The company was the first in the Caribbean and one of the first in the continental United States to have a fully digital switching network. All central offices are connected by fiber-optic cable, allowing for significantly higher transfer speeds as compared to copper. Digital radios and undersea fiber-optic cables connect the islands of St Thomas, St. Croix and St. John. Innovative telephone offers a number of custom calling and CLASS features including: speed dialing, call waiting, three-way calling, call forwarding, conference calling, caller ID, call return, call screening, and voicemail.

The entire territory consists of one calling area, meaning that Virgin Islands customers call anywhere in the VI for a flat fee and there is no limit on intra-island calls. Tolls are charged only when calling outside the territory.

The area code for the U.S. Virgin Islands is (340). Telephone service is linked to the world through three long-distance carriers, Innovative Long Distance, Sprint and AT&T. To make a long distance call to the continental US or Canada, customers must dial l, the area code and the phone number. Toll-free 8XX numbers are available for either incoming or outgoing calls.

Innovative Cable TV St. Thomas – St. John

Innovative Cable TV St. Thomas-St. John, the Caribbean's oldest cable television network, offers services to St. Thomas and St. John such as basic cable, a variety of upgraded packages and premium channels, Pay-Per-View, adult programming, local programming, and High Definition (HD) TV and Digital Video Recording (DVR).

Innovative Cable TV St. Croix: Offers services to St. Croix such as basic cable, a variety of upgraded packages and premium channels, Pay-Per-View, adult programming, local programming, and High Definition (HD) TV and Digital Video Recording (DVR). Both systems offer over 200 digital video and audio channels.

Innovative Wireless: Offers the premier wireless service catering specifically to Virgin Islanders. Choose from plans that include local-only calling, calling to the U.S. and Puerto Rico, special rates for calling other Caribbean countries, unlimited data plans, and a variety of texting and messaging options. Innovative Wireless offers the newest technology (3G and 4G) in mobile devices from top providers like, Samsung Galaxy phones and tabs, I Phones, BlackBerrys and accessories available in the Caribbean.

Innovative PowerNet: Offers high-speed internet over the Virgin Island's only fiber optic network. Available in a variety of symmetric speeds, with additional services like data back-up, email service, and online storage, Innovative offers reliability like no other provider in the USVI.

IBS Business Systems: Allows Innovative's services to work for businesses of all sizes. From small offices to corporations and governmental agencies, Innovative has a package to support all professional needs. Innovative offers dedicated T1 lines, multi-line calling systems, as well as other internet, television, and wireless phone service packages.

CBS-TV2 is a U.S. Virgin Island's local source for news, sports, and weather, via the local news channel, News 2. TV2 is the USVI's CBS affiliate and also produces the Island Tour Network, a guide to living and traveling in the USVI. With studios on St. Croix and St. Thomas, TV2 also has a complete production team to produce all forms of media including TV, radio and print.

Information about the Innovative Companies, EVO by Innovative and current rates and promotions is available at www.innovativevi.net and customers may also call 340-779-9999 to speak to a Customer Care Representative.

Television and Radio Stations

The territory has several local channels, and also Spanish-language stations from Puerto Rico. Residents on all three islands can stay in touch with the rest of the world through cable television. From CNN to the Disney Channel with stops at HBO, ESPN, and a religious channel among the many in between, cable television brings them all 24 hours a day. It also hooks you up to Digital Music and cable radio for a variety of top-notch audio entertainment.

New settlers should make a point to watch WSVI, the local ABC affiliate in St. Croix and Public TV station WTJX in St. Thomas, and St. Croix, Channel 12, to get in touch with events and locally-based programming.

Also, TV-2 (Cable Ch.2) has local news and produces local commercials and production for industry and non-TV use. UPN-39 (Ch.39) features network programming and CNN news.

In St. Croix, 97.5 AM, 95 FM and 99.5 FM are the major news radio stations. In St. Thomas, listen to WVWI at 1000 AM and WSTA at 1340 AM for news. 99.5 also reaches St. Thomas and St. John. Numerous other AM and FM stations air many types of music (for different demographics), headline news, sports and community programming.

Radio Stations

WVVI-FM Caribbean Country 93.5 FM, Box 25868, Christiansted VI 00824, 773-5935 (news, country music, talk shows M-F)

WJKC/Isle 95, 95 FM, Box 25680, Christiansted,VI 00824, 773-0995 (urban/reggae)

WMNG, Mongoose 104.9 FM, Box 25680 Christiansted VI 00824 (adult contemporary, some news, local, regional, national)

WVIQ Sunny 99.5 FM, Box 25680, Christiansted, VI 00824, 773-0995 (some news, adult contemporary)

Latino 98.3 (Spanish) Christiansted, St. Croix VI 00824, 773-5935

WVWI-AM 1000, St. Thomas, 776-1000

WVJZ-FM 105.3 JAMZ, St. Thomas, 776-5260

WWKS-FM 101.3 KISS, St. Thomas, 776-1013

WSTA Lucky 1340 AM, St. Thomas, 777-4500

WSTX Ft. Louise Augusta, St. Croix, 773-0390

Broadcast Television Stations

Channel 8 (ABC Affiliate) **WSVI**, Box 8 ABC, Christiansted, 00823, 778-5008

Channel 12 (PBS) WTJX, Box 7879, St. Thomas, 00801, 774-6255 St. Croix, 773-3337, recently acquired four digital channels.

Innovative Cable TV-St. Croix, Box 5968, Sunny Isle, 00823, 779-9999

Innovative Cable TV-St. Thomas/St. John Cable TV, 693-8685, Tutu Park Mall, St. Thomas, 00802, 776-2150

UPN 39, P.O. Box 24027, St. Croix, 00824 (wcvi.tv), 713-9927

TV-2 7 Estate Diamond, St. Croix, 00820, 773-2200 / 779-9999 Tutu Park Mall, St. Thomas, 00802, 774-2200

WVXF (CBS). St. Thomas, 00802, 774-2013

Internet Service Providers (From Dial-up to Wireless)
Broadband VI Wireless 340-719-2943 - St. Croix 340-774-0024
St. Thomas, www.BroadbandVI.com
Choice Communications 340-778-8864 - St. Croix 340-774-0024 - St.
Thomas, www.choicevi.com
SmartNet 340-715-4818 St. Thomas/St. Croix
VIPowernet/Innovative 340-714-3700, www.vipowernet.net

Cellular Phone Company Providers
AT&T Mobility 690-1000 St. Croix / 777-7777 St. Thomas
Innovative 712-5029 St. Croix / 712-5029 St. Thomas
Sprint PCS 713-0055 St. Croix / 755-3232 St. Thomas

Sending a Telegram
Need to send a telegram? Call 1–800-325-6000 to find the locations of the Western Union offices nearest you on whichever island you are on. Both St. Croix and St. Thomas have locations. You can call from a pay phone, pay with your credit card and Western Union will transfer money to the mainland or overseas.

Mail and Parcel Service
Since this is the good old U.S.of A, the USPS first class rates from the U.S. Virgin Islands are the same as in the states.Those rates are subject to increase at any time. Parcel post and priority mail rates depend on where the package goes. Keep in mind that anything that does not go by air must go by ship. This means you have to allow four to six weeks extra when you are shipping your Christmas packages. Most islanders send items by parcel post and priority.

All mail is flown in and out several times a day from the New York and Miami areas with the mail going directly to either St. Croix or St. Thomas. From the rest of the mainland, it goes through Puerto Rico. First class mail up to 11 ounces, and priority mail over 11 ounces will automatically go by air. Priority mail, with a top weight limit of 70 pounds, cannot exceed 108 inches of combined length and girth. Fourth class mail, used primarily for books and parcels will go by ship. Express Mail is available to all areas on the U.S. mainland with service to major cities usually about one day, two days elsewhere.

St. Croix has post offices or branches at Richmond, downtown Christiansted, Gallows Bay, Sunny Isle, Kingshill and Frederiksted. Post offices box availability changes as people move off-island and new people move in. Home delivery is available across the island and if you live in a hard-to-reach location, you can have a mail box on the nearest main road.

Zip Codes and phone numbers for USPS (area code 340)
Postmaster of the Virgin Islands

Sugar Estate Post Office, St. Thomas	00801	774-1950

St. Croix

All Christiansted street delivery	00820	
Mail P.O. Boxes, Estate Richmond	00821	773-1505
Company St. (Downtown) Post Office boxes	00822	773-3586
Gallows Bay Post Office boxes	00824	773-4538
Sunny Isle Post Offices boxes	00823	778-6805
Kingshill Post Office boxes	00851	778-0199
All Kingshill street delivery	00850	778-0199
Frederiksted street delivery	00840	772-0040
Frederiksted Post Office boxes	00841	772-0040
Express Mail		1-800-222-1811

St. John

All street delivery	00830	
Cruz Bay Post Office boxes	00831	779-4227

St. Thomas

All St. Thomas street delivery	00802	774-1950
Sugar Estate Post Office boxes	00801	774-1950
5046 Norre Gade	00804	774-3750
Veterans' Dr. P.O. Boxes, Frenchtown	00803	774-6980
Tutu Park Mall	00805	775-7354
Havensight Mall	00801	776-9897

Courier Companies

Several courier companies offer service to and from St. Thomas and St. Croix. Some companies have drop-off, pick-up and delivery service on all three islands. Prices vary.

American Airlines Cyril E. King Airport Cargo Hangar, StT 774-6550
DHLWorldwide Express Nisky Center, St. Thomas   774-4066
       St. Croix   778-8553
       DHL Toll Free   1-800-225-5345
Federal Express Peter's Rest, St. Croix   1-800-GOFEDEX
       (pick-ups in St. Croix call by 3:30 p.m.)   1-877-838-7834
       Cyril E. King Airport cargo hangar   776-8887
       St. Thomas   1-800-463-3339
       Drop-off box: business accounts, First Bank, waterfront, St.T
UPS Airport, St. Croix   778-7100
       Raphune Hill, St. Thomas   776-1700

St. John has a newly-renovated post office that opened November 1992. You may have to wait for a post office box. If you do, you can pick up your mail at General Delivery until then. The windows are open as posted. Carriers will deliver twice a day to boxes placed along a route on Centerline Road from Cruz Bay to Coral Bay.

St. Thomas has post offices in downtown Charlotte Amalie, Sugar Estate, Veterans' Drive near Frenchtown, Havensight Mall, and at Tutu Park Mall. While you wait for a box at a post office more convenient to your house, again you can receive your mail through general delivery. Hours are as posted.

Private mailbox services are scattered throughout the islands if you can't secure a USPS post office box. Some of the mail services will also offer secretarial, notary and fax services.

In St. Thomas see Red Hook Mail Services at 779-1890 and Messages, Mail & More at 776-4324.

By Boat

Important envelopes or packages, with prices starting around $5.00 can be sent to and from St. John, Red Hook and Charlotte Amalie, St. Thomas via the St. John ferry. You can give your parcel to the ticket seller or to the captain. You must, however, have someone meet the envelope or package when it arrives. You can send packages to other Caribbean islands via an inter-island freighter. Call the Virgin Islands Port Authority marine manager to find out if any such vessels are tied up in St. Croix at Gallows Bay, at the Creek in St. John or along the waterfront in St.Thomas. Also, the inter-island ferry service or the Seaplane will carry small packages for a fee.

Banking and Credit

When relocating to the Virgin Islands there are a few things that may be helpful to know about banking and credit before you arrive. There are four banks in the U.S. Virgin Islands with different locations on each island. Banking hours are usually from 9 a.m. to 2:30-3 p.m. Monday through Thursday, Fridays 9 a.m. to 4:30-5 p.m., with some having Saturday hours of 9 a.m. to noon. Usually deposits made after 3 p.m. on Friday's won't be credited to your account until the next regular banking day. Banks are closed for all Federal and some local holidays including Carnival and Three King's Day. Most of these banks offer online services or telephone banking where you can bank anytime.

Your ATM Card is the best way to insure you have cash on hand when you arrive. You can use any stateside bankcard that carries the NYCE or Plus logo at any of the local banks free of charge. The figure for maximum withdrawals may vary so you need to check before making any major purchases. Traveler's checks are an expensive way to move your money.

Do not however, count on cashiers or bank drafts as some banks will treat them as personal checks and may not allow you to draw against them right away.

Most banks may cash off-island checks, but due to slow transit time to clearing houses often force the banks to be very careful. Allow a minimum of one week for a check drawn on a U.S. mainland to clear, five days for one drawn on a Puerto Rico bank or on a different island in the Virgin Islands and three days for a bank on the same island. Cashiers checks will not be any quicker unless drawn on a mainland branch of an island bank or one of its affiliates.

When here to scout, it may be a good idea to open a savings or checking account, for which you will need 2 types of identification, at least one being a picture ID with your physical address or proof of residence (like a phone bill, electricity bill, etc). As the moving day nears, have your mainland bank transfer funds you want available upon your arrival.

Utilities

The Virgin Islands Water and Power Authority (WAPA) is an autonomous government body that produces and distributes electricity and potable water to approximately 55,000 electric customers and 13,000 potable water customers in the territory. WAPA also installs and maintains street lights. Considered a not-for profit public corporation, WAPA contributes directly to the territory's budget by an annual payment in lieu of taxes (PILOT) to the Virgin Islands Treasury.

The Virgin Islands Legislature created the Authority in 1964, and it is governed by a nine member board of public and private sector members. The governor of the Virgin Islands selects the three public sector members from his cabinet and nominates six private sector board members, who the legislature confirms for three-year terms. Private sector members come from each district.

Electrical service conforms to U.S. standards: 110/220 volts single phase or three phase, 60 cycle AC, making converters commonly required in Europe unnecessary. The Authority's power plants are located at Estate Richmond, St. Croix and at Krum Bay, St. Thomas. Customers on St. Croix and St. Thomas are served by both overhead and underground lines. Customers on St. John are provided power through underwater cables from St. Thomas.

Currently, WAPA relies exclusively on fuel oil to power its electric generating units. Because of its reliance on fuel oil with its volatile prices worldwide, and its dual operations of producing water and power, WAPA's customer rates are generally higher than rates charged by electric utilities in most regions of the United States. Monthly bills will

vary according to customer usage and the prevailing fuel factor which is based on the cost of fuel oil purchased on the world market. The fuel surcharge which appears on the bill is a customer charge that allows WAPA to address increases or decreases in fuel prices. Customer rates, and adjustments to the fuel factor, are subject to approval by the Virgin Islands Public Services Commission.

To reduce rates, the Authority is moving aggressively to diversify its generation portfolio and will integrate 18MW of solar energy into its grid in 2013. Wind studies are underway and the utility is pursuing a move to liquefied natural gas (LNG) as an alternative to fuel oil. To help its customers cope with fluctuating energy costs, WAPA has embarked on an

St. Croix Banks (all are area code 340)

Bank of St. Croix (has ATMs)

Anchor Way, Gallows Bay	773-8500
Peter's Rest	713-8500

Banco Popular de Puerto Rico (has ATMs) www.bancopopular.com

All branches	693-2777
Orange Grove	693-2902
Sunny Isle Shopping Center	693-2935

First Bank (has ATMs) www.firstbankvi.com   866-695-2511

FirstLine Telebanking	775-8899
Orange Grove Branch	775-7777
Sunny Isle Branch	719-8686
Strand St., Frederiksted	712-1020
King St., Christiansted	773-0440

Scotiabank
usvi.scotiabank.com
(safe, secure 24/7 ATMs)

King St., Christiansted	773-1013
Strand St., Frederiksted	772-0880
Estate Diamond (near Sunny Isle)	778-5350

St. John Banks

First Bank (has ATMs)   www.firstbankvi.com   866-695-2511

FirstLine Telebanking	775-8899
Cruz Bay	776-6881

Merchants Commercial Bank

Chocolate Hole	779-2696

Scotiabank   (safe, secure 24/7 ATMs)

The Marketplace www.scotiabank.com	776-6552

St. Thomas Banks

Banco Popular de Puerto Rico

Veteran's Drive 693-2777	Hibiscus Alley 693-2823
Altona 693-2704	Lockhart Shopping Center 693-2880
Fort Mylner 693-2860	Red Hook 693-2873

First Bank (has ATMs) www.firstbankvi.com   866-695-2511

FirstLine Telebanking	775-8899
First Bank Plaza	777-1222
Crown Bay Branch	775-7777
Charlotte Amalie Business Center	775-7777
Waterfront Branch	775-7777
East End Plaza Branch	775-5650
Port of Sale Branch	774-4800
Estate Thomas Branch	775-7777
Yacht Haven Branch	775-1414

Merchants Commercial Bank Tutu Park Mall   779-2265

Scotiabank   www.scotiabank.com

Loan and Mortgage Center, Nisky Center	776-HOME
Shopping Mall Bldg #6, Havensight Mall	776-5880
214C Altona & Welgunst, Altona	774-0037
East End Plaza, Red Hook	777-EAST

aggressive customer education and conservation campaign to curb wasteful consumption and encourage investment in high efficiency appliances including solar water heaters. The utility often distributes Energy Star rated light bulbs at community events, as efficient lighting is one of the easiest ways to save energy.

The Authority also supports netmetering, which allows consumers who install renewable energy systems, such as solar and wind, to reduce their bills by using less electricity from the grid. It also provides the customer with the potential to receive credit for electricity exported to the grid. A "smart grid" system to assist customers in monitoring and regulating their usage as a tool to ensure energy efficiency in their homes and businesses is scheduled to be operational within the next two years. Additionally, a 2012 grant award from the U.S. Department of the Interior has established an energy services business unit which will provide energy audits, technology validation for best in class equipment and supplies, and a financing opportunity for utility customers to acquire energy efficient appliances and equipment.

Recognized as an Energy Star Partner of the Year in 2008, the Authority is an active member of the prestigious program created by the

U.S. Environmental Protection Agency and the U.S. Department of Energy and partners with the Virgin Islands Energy Office (VIEO) to provide information and customer-focused services. In 2009, WAPA was designated an EDIN (Energy Development in Island Nations) partner. EDIN-USVI is a collaborative effort among many public and private sector representatives from the U.S. Departments of Energy and the Interior, the National Renewable Energy Laboratory, the V.I. Energy Office, the University of the Virgin Islands and local businesses. This partnership supports the territory's efforts to reduce fossil fuel usage in the electricity and transportation sectors 60% by 2025.

In recent years, WAPA has invested millions of dollars in upgrading its generating and distribution systems to improve reliability. But because WAPA is not connected to a national grid, as is the case with electric utilities in the mainland United States, periodic power outages may occur. Additionally, the threat of tropical storms and hurricanes from June through November leads many Virgin Islands residents to purchase back-up generators for their homes and businesses.

More information about WAPA's projects and plans is available at www.viwapa.vi and www. edinenergy.org/usvi Customers are also invited to visit WAPA's customer service offices or its website (www.viwapa.vi) for information on no-cost, low-cost energy saving tips. These include:

• Use ceiling fans to cool or be sure to use Energy Star-rated air conditioning units.

• Wash clothes in cold water and only use full loads.

• Hang wet towels, swimsuits and other items outside to dry in the sun rather than using an electric dryer.

• Let dishes air dry in the dishwasher rather than use the automatic dryer mode.

• Consider investing in a solar water heater.

• Change out incandescent light bulbs with high efficiency, long-life compact florescent bulbs (CFL) or LED (Light Emitting Diode) bulbs for the maximum savings

• Turn off all lights, appliances and electronics when not in use.

Water

Recognizing that potable water is one of the most precious resources in the U.S. Virgin Islands, WAPA has taken a lead role in educating customers about water and energy conservation. The U.S. Virgin Islands have no freshwater bodies, so WAPA desalinates seawater for distribution to the most densely populated commercial and residential centers on St. Thomas, St. Croix and St. John. The majority of water is currently produced by reverse osmosis plants at the Richmond and Krum Bay plants. Residents also collect rain water in cisterns attached to their homes or businesses. With an average of only 45 inches of rainfall a year, water conservation has, by necessity, been developed into a fine art. Virgin Islanders talk about water or its shortage the way mainlanders talk about the weather, crab grass or heating bills. Most residents, using cisterns to collect rainwater, will rush to launder slipcovers, draperies or rugs if a storm should cause an overflow.

Helpful water usage hints can be found at www.viwapa.vi, but consider the following:

• Cisterns must be kept clean and free of leaks and obstructions. All openings must be screened to keep out dirt, bugs, leaves and light. In the rare event more rain falls than a cistern can hold, an overflow will keep the water from backing up into your house.

• During power outages, the electric water pump will not work, but residents can often bucket water out of their cisterns or swimming pools for immediate needs. Knowledge of the workings of your water pump, water level and its flow and the quality of cistern water is a necessity. To access the cistern, which is more than likely located under your house, open the cover found in the floor of the home. If your cistern is free-standing, the opening should be fairly obvious.

• The flow at your faucet is produced by an air tank pressurized by an electrical pump. If the pump requires lubrication, stick to a schedule. Learn the sounds your pump makes. If it varies, investigate at once to avoid burning out the pump. If it seems to cycle too often, it may need bleeding or you may have a leak in the system. Call a plumber or ask a handy neighbor for help.

• Don't let the water run while you brush your teeth, shampoo, shave, shower or wash dishes. Wet everything down first, then TURN OFF THE WATER while you scrub. Rinse quickly. Since every flush uses five gallons of water, flush only when necessary and install water reduction devices such as dual flush toilets. Take a shower rather than a bath and install low flow showerheads. Remember to alert your guests that "in this land of sun and fun, we rarely flush for number one."

• Fix every dripping faucet immediately and equip garden hoses with automatic shut-offs. Don't run clothes or dishwashers until you have a full load. In-sink garbage disposals use extra water and increase the build-up of solids in your septic tank which will hasten the day when it must be pumped out. Build a gray water cistern to catch runoff from patios, bathtubs and kitchen waters for garden or lawn use.

• Should your thirst outrun your capacity, private truckers will deliver water. Prices vary widely depending on where you live and how much water the truck carries. Water delivery companies can be located in the Virgin Islands telephone book or in online services directories.

For information on how and where to apply for power or water services, and for rates, call the Virgin Islands Water and Power Authority's customer service departments at 340- 773-2250 St. Croix, 340-774-3552 St. Thomas, and 340-776-6446 St. John or visit www.viwapa.vi .

Waste Management

The Virgin Islands Waste Management Authority (VIWMA) is responsible for the collection, treatment and disposal of wastewater and solid waste in the territory. This includes the operations and maintenance of the sewer collection system, wastewater treatment facilities and pump stations, landfills, and transfer stations.

On St. Croix, the Authority provides residents several types of solid waste services. Some locals receive house-to-house collection twice per week at their homes. For such folks, the pick-up days can be obtained from the Authority's Division of Solid Waste at 712-4962 or by visiting the VIWMA website at www.viwma.org.

Those who do not receive this service are provided with waste disposal bin sites located throughout the island. There are three such sites on St. Croix: Cotton Valley, Mon Bijou and Concordia. A newly opened manned convenience center is located in Peter's Rest. This facility accepts household waste, household hazardous waste materials, and some recyclables.

St. Thomas residents receive limited house-to-house collection and there are 26 public disposal sites located island-wide. St. John does not receive any house-to-house service, as the terrain makes such service challenging, and there are 28 bins located island-wide for residential use.

Virgin Islands law requires commercial and industrial businesses to employ licensed haulers, who are permitted public disposal site acess, to dispose waste. Many small business owners and residents also use private haulers for their solid waste disposal. These haulers are permitted by the VI Waste Management Authority to dispose of waste at the landfill and transfer station, and must display a VIWMA sticker in their windshield to be allowed access to solid waste facilities, which include the Anguilla Transfer Station and Landfill on St. Croix, the Bovoni Landfill on St. Thomas and the Susannaberg Transfer Station on St. John, or wastewater treatment plants (WWTP), such as the Anguilla WWTP on St. Croix, Mangrove Lagoon or Red Point WWTPs on St. Thomas or the Cruz Bay WWTP on St. John. The Anguilla Landfill is closed for the acceptance of waste and currently only accepts construction and demolition debris and scrap metal.

A list of permitted haulers can be obtained from the Authority's Division of Compliance Management and Environmental Enforcement.

Each type of disposal practice requires adherence to various guidelines. House-to-house collection requires that resident's place their waste in a closed bag within a large receptacle with a secure cover at the curbside on the day(s) of their neighborhood collection. Disposal at the bin sites also requires that the waste is placed inside of the bin and not on the ground adjacent to the bin. There are certain items that cannot be disposed of by either house-to-house collection or at the bin sites. The following items must be taken directly to the landfill for disposal: yard waste; scrap metal; appliances; junked cars; bulk waste, like furniture, bedding, and other bulky household goods; gas cylinders; and, construction & demolition (C&D) waste. You can contact the landfills directly for a complete listing of acceptable items for disposal at the bin sites or landfill or visit the VI Waste Management Authority's website, www.viwma.org.

Littering is a criminal offense and individuals or businesses can be cited for violations at a minimum charge of $1,000 per violation and/or up to 180 days in jail. The VIWMA's Environmental Enforcement Officers monitor the waste disposal practices of residents and businesses and will issues littering citations.

Keeping the V.I. Clean

The Virgin Islands continues to make strides in beautification efforts, and has supported various recycling projects to do so.

• There are two local companies, one for the St. Thomas/St. John District and one for the St. Croix District, which purchase aluminum cans and scrap metal for cash. The VIWMA also holds annual aluminum can collection contest in the local public and private elementary schools to educate and encourage students on the benefit of recycling.

• Cell phones are accepted for recycling at local libraries as a fundraising opportunity.

• Scrap metal is currently being crushed and removed at the Territory's landfills.

• Lead-Acid Batteries are not accepted at the local landfills but are recyclable. To ensure they are recycled, return them to the place of purchase.

• Used tires are also not accepted at bin sites or local landfills. Tire dealers accept scrap or used tires, although many charge a small disposal fee.

• Used oil, if disposed of improperly, can contaminate soil, ground water, and surface water. Residents who change their own motor oil can dispose of no more than five gallons per person per month at the VIWMA's Do-It-Yourself (DIY) Used Oil Collection Sites which are located at:

St. Croix – Department of Public Works in Anna's Hope

St. Thomas – Department of Public Works, Motor Pool in Subbase, and Bovoni Landfill

St. John – Susannaberg Transfer Station

VIWMA has developed a campaign, "Preserving Paradise," that educates students, communities and businesses on ways they can help keep the islands clean. As part of the Preserving Paradise Kids' Campaign, VIWMA teaches students about the importance of preservation and encourages them to take what they learn and share it with their parents. Preserving Paradise Communities invites residents to enter into a partnership with the VIWMA to beautify their neighborhoods and common areas.

New business owners on the island can become Preserving Paradise Business Partners. PPBP members work together to sponsor programs, projects and events that educate and inform the public about VIWMA's initiatives. Business Partners can make in-kind, monetary or other contributions to VIWMA's programs that introduce environmental educational information to students, community or civic organizations. Each business that participates in a VIWMA program or becomes a VIWMA vendor or contractor becomes a Business Partner. Contact VIWMA at 712-4962. To report a problem dial 713-1962, or visit VIWMA at www.viwma.org

Streets and Roads

Finding your way around can be a major hassle. Residents often give directions that begin with "turn right at the big tree" or "left just after that paved road". Most areas use plot numbers that date to old Danish surveys and, since many have been subdivided, the result can be quite confusing. It's best to get complete directions before you set out. Keep a map in the glove compartment of your car, and if you get lost, don't be shy about asking directions. It's a great way to meet new folks.

In St. Croix all major roads are named and numbered and both are used. Some of the subdivisions will have street names with signs, some names but no numbers and some may have neither. While the houses all have plot numbers, you may find 5 next to 5-1 or even 7. In Christiansted and Frederiksted, the numbers start upward on one side of the street, cross over at the end, and begin downward on the other side. Don't be surprised to see 4 across from 42. Christiansted's numbering begins at the waterfront, runs inland to the old city limits and then returns on the other side of the street. Frederiksted's numbers begin at the north town limits or at the waterfront on the west. The main streets, and those that parallel them have long blocks. The cross streets have short ones. Corner plots usually take their number from the main streets, though the building's entrance may be around the corner.

Recently, the government has taken on the project of reorganizing street addresses to be compatible with GPS systems. The project, officially known as the Street Addressing Initiative (SAI), creates new street names and assigns new addresses to residences. The format for this address system will use logical number sequences, which increase in standard increments of two, four, or 10, putting odd numbers to one side and even numbers to the other. When complete, SAI should help improve: tax collection, assign voters to correct districts, designate what schools children should attend, improve postal delivery, and facilitate better response time for police, fire and EMS. Once up and running, a Virgin Islands Master Address Repository will be included in GPS devices such as Garmin, as well as on digital maps on the internet. Preliminary planning has been completed for SAI, and, as of press time, pilot programs were slated to commence in Williams Delight on St. Croix, Cruz Bay on St. John, and part of Charlotte Amalie, St. Thomas. Once the pilot programs are complete, the entire territory will be re-addressed in one fell swoop.

SAI will mean a significant change for St. John, where major road names route numbers are things only map-in-hand tourists use. Streets in recently developed areas on the island have been named and have signs. Sometimes the residents use the names; sometimes they do not. In Cruz Bay, the streets have names and signs, but few remember what they are. Houses are numbered by plot, which is no help in finding your way since number 2 probably isn't next to number 3.

St. Thomas is just as bad. Though major roads all have names and numbers, most residents don't know the numbers. Some roads have been renamed and are referred to by both old and new names. Skyline Drive is a good case in point. Some years ago, the town fathers decided to name it after one of their own, Valdemar Hill Sr., but few people ever call the scenic road anything but Skyline Drive. In Charlotte Amalie, buildings have numbers, but they have no relationship to the number on the building next door. Remember to ask for a good map.

Transportation to the Islands

With tourism such a critical source of revenue, transportation plays a major role. The influx of almost two million tourists and a professional or personal need to travel by islanders, has developed a network of the major airlines and local commuters that blanket the Caribbean and all points north, east, south and west.

The islands can be reached from anywhere in the continental U.S., the Caribbean, Europe or South American in one day and, in some cases, a couple of hours. St. John has no airport, but both St. Thomas (Cyril E. King Airport) and St. Croix (Henry E. Rohlsen Airport) have airports capable of handling jets. The Henry E. Rohlsen Airport was recently renovated and expanded to attract new airlines and accommodate more passengers. The airport's new terminal was doubled in size and the runway was extended from 7,600 feet to 10,000. Long-range flights were limited to St. Croix before the runway expansion due to fuel restrictions of smaller aircraft. The control tower is operated under the auspices of the FAA which contracts for private air traffic controllers.

The availability of flights to both islands are subject to seasonal and economic changes. Rumors have been circulating that due to its restructuring process, American Airlines plans to discontinue its American Eagle flights between St. Croix and San Juan.

St. John, the smallest of the three islands, does not have an airport, but has a busy little seaport at its dock at Cruz Bay. Tourists can take one of the many inter-island ferries from Charlotte Amalie or Red Hook on St. Thomas.

Major Airlines - St. Croix

American Airlines – MIA/STX Boeing 737-800 (148 seats) 5 weekly 1-800-474-4884 www.AA.com (adjusted seasonally; be sure to call)
Delta Airlines – ATL/STX – MD88/CR9/E70 (143 seats) (4 weekly flights- Saturday, Sunday, Monday, Thursday) 1-800-221-1212 (adjusted seasonally; be sure to call)
Jet Blue - 1 800 – JETBLUE (538-2583) www.jetblue.com
US Airways – Charlotte/STX Airbus A319 www.usairways.com twice weekly (seasonal) 1-800-622-1015 (adjusted seasonally; be sure to call)

Regional / Commuter Airlines - St. Croix

American Eagle – from San Juan, Turbo Prop ATR 72 - 3 daily (216 seats) 1-800-474-4884
Cape Air – SJU/STX – Cessna 402, twin-engine, single pilot aircraft (9 seater) – up to 8 daily flights in season, also serving St. Thomas and Tortola. Departures are timed to meet jet departures to mainland U.S. 1-800-352-0714   www.flycapeair.com
CoastAir Transport – Scheduled and chartered flights to Anguilla, Nevis, Dominica, St. Barths, and St. Eustatius. Call   (340) 773-6862.
Jet Blue: Flights to San Juan. Call -800-JETBLUE (538-2583).
LIAT – uses Dash 8s – operates from the down-islands to USVI. From St. Croix, passengers can fly to other Caribbean islands after connecting

in Antigua or St. Maarten. St. Croix –778-9930, St. Thomas – 774-2313.
Seaborne Airlines – uses DHC-6-300 and Saab 340B (beginning January 2013). Seaborne offers daily nonstops to and between St. Croix, St. Thomas, San Juan, Vieques and the BVI. This airline also partners directly with Road Town Fast Ferry to offer connecting service from St. Croix to downtown Road Town, Tortola via St. Thomas. For full information about traveling with Seaborne, and to book online, visit www.seaborneairlines.com. You can also call them at (340) 773-6442 or toll free at 888-FLY-USVI. Charters available.
Vieques Air Link – Service from St. Croix to Vieques, Fajardo and Isla Grande Airport, Puerto Rico 778-9858

Major Airlines - St. Thomas

American Airlines: 1-800-474-4884 (adjusted seasonally, be sure to call) MIA/STT – B757-200 (seasonal November to May two daily flights, then back to one) Boston/ STT – B757-200 – scheduled service Jan – Apr on Tues & Sat JKF / STT B757-200 – one daily flight
Delta Airlines: ATL/STT 1-800-221-1212 (adjusted seasonally, be sure to call) Two daily round trips (check with the airline) (additionally, there will be 4 weekly overnight flights – check with the airlines) 4 weekly round-trip same-day flights Copenhagen to ATL to StT: T/F/S/S JFK / STT: seasonal weekly on Saturdays (check with airline). Additional service during season Fridays and Sundays
Jet Blue - 1 800 – JETBLUE (538-2583) www.jetblue.com
US Airways – 1-800-622-1015 (adjusted seasonally, be sure to call) Charlotte/STT – B757-200 daily non-stop service Philadelphia/STT B757-200 daily non-stop service. During the off-season, trips to Philadelphia are limited to two times per week.
Spirit Airlines: Ft. Lauderdale / STT – MD-80 – daily non-stop 1-800-772-7117 www.spiritairlines.com.
Continental Airlines: Newark, NJ/STT – B737-700LR 1-800-231-0856 Four weekly flights (Saturday/Sunday/Wednesday/Friday)
United Airlines: 1-800-241-6522 www.unitedairlines.com Chicago / STT – 3 times per week, Sunday, Wed, Saturday Washington, DC/STT – one weekly service on Saturdays (adjusted seasonally, be sure to call)

Regional Commuter Airlines - St. Thomas

Air Sunshine: Direct flights to San Juan, Vieques, Virgin Gorda, Nevis, St. Maarten and Tortola. Call (888) 879-8900.
American Eagle: San Juan / St. Thomas flights daily
Cape Air - about 8 daily flights, in season (call 1-800-352-0714)
LIAT: Anguilla, Antigua, St. Kitts and St. Maarten. Call 1-888-844-LIAT (5428).

Seaborne Airshuttle – Daily nonstops to St. Croix, San Juan and Vieques and the BVI. Call toll-free at (340) 772-6442 or 888-FLY-USVI www.seaborneairlines.com. Charters available.

Downtown to Downtown

Seaborne Seaplane – The seaplane departs and arrives from the downtown Charlotte Amalie seaport and the downtown Christiansted seaport. Their aircraft fly under the same strict regulations as major US Carriers, with all-day availability on convenient morning, midday and evening flights. If you plan to travel between the islands frequently, or with your family, Seaborne SmartPaks are also available. For full information about traveling with Seaborne, and to book online, visit their website or call toll- free. For reservations and schedules, please call (340) 773-6442 or 888-FLY-USVI, or visit them online at www.seaborne airlines.com

Air Charters		
Air Sunshine	St. Croix	(888) 879-8900
Bohlke International Airways	St. Croix	778-9177
Caribbean Buzz	St. Thomas	775-7335
Coastal Air Transport	St. Croix	773-6862
Island Airlines	St. Croix	344-3900
Seaborne Airlines	Both	(866) 359-8784
Sea Flight	Both	714-3000
Vieques Air Link		(888) 901-9247

By Sea

There are plans in the works for a high speed ferry service between St. Thomas and St. Croix. The trip would take about 75 minutes one way. For more information on schedules and fees call 776-5494 or e-mail caribbean. fastferry@gmail.com.

St. John and St. Thomas are linked with a comprehensive ferry transportation system. The ferry departs and returns from downtown Charlotte Amalie, St. Thomas, for Cruz Bay, St. John from about 9 a.m. to 5:30 p.m. This 45-

minute ride gives you a scenic view of the south shore of St. Thomas and costs about $12 each way. For more frequent. less expensive and quicker departures to St. John, use the ferry from Red Hook, St. Thomas, to Cruz Bay. Boats run from 6 a.m. from Cruz Bay until the last ferry leaves Cruz Bay at 11:15 p.m. From Red Hook the ferries run at 6:30 a.m., 7:30 a.m. and then hourly until midnight. That 20-minute trip costs about $6 one way. Local senior citizens pay $1.50 and children pay $1. Buy your tickets at the booth adjacent to the parking lot in St. Thomas or at the booth on the dock in St. John. For more information on trips between St. John and St. Thomas. call either Varlack Ventures, 776-6412 or Transportation Services, 776-6282.

From the Charlotte Amalie waterfront to Frenchman's Reef Hotel, take the Shopping. The 25-minute trip costs about $7 each way, and it runs from 8:30 a.m. to 5:00 p.m.— on the half hour from the hotel and on the hour from the waterfront. There are no Saturday trips. Call 776-8500 and ask for the ferry station.

If you miss the last ferry or want to travel to almost anywhere between St. Thomas, St. John, or the British Virgin Islands, call Dohm's Water Taxi at 775-6501. They will pick you up in a high-speed boat for a quick trip to anywhere they can dock. Service after midnight can be negotiated. For pricing, visit http://www.watertaxi-vi.com.

Native Son and Smith's Ferry share the route between the Charlotte Amalie waterfront and either West End or Roadtown, Tortola in the British Virgin Islands. Service starts at 7:10 a.m. with departures scheduled for morning, mid-day and evening rush-hour. Times vary depending on the day of the week. The one-hour trip costs about $50 round-trip. Connections to other British Virgin Islands are possible. For information on the ferry trips to the British Virgin Islands, call Transportation Services at 776-6282, Native Son at 774-8685 or Smith's Ferry at 775-7292. For vehicle transportation St. Thomas/St. John call Love City Car Ferries 779-4000.

From St. John, ferries leave the Cruz Bay dock for West End, Tortola, Jost Van Dyke and Virgin Gorda. Times vary by day. While you can go to West End, Tortola every day for about $32 for the 45-minute trip, the boat to Virgin Gorda leaves only on Thursdays and Sundays. The boat to Jost Van Dyke goes only on Saturdays and Sundays. Call to see if any of this has changed and also ask if you need a passport to get from the U.S. to the British Virgin Islands. You may NOT need one getting into the BVI but you may need one getting back!   ALL rates subject to change.

Public Bus Transportation

The government-owned Vitran bus lines operates all three islands. Look for these familiar cream and maroon buses. Stops located frequently across the islands have signs that carry the Vitran logo. Service usually runs from 5:30 a.m. till 8:30 p.m. Senior citizens and students get a discount if they present their identification. In St. Croix, Vitran operates bus routes between Christiansted and Frederiksted with a transfer station at La Reine and Golden Rock. All trips are about $1. Call them at 778-0898 for routes and schedules. In St. Thomas, Vitran buses run between Red Hook in the East and Bordeaux in the west. All buses go through Charlotte Amalie.Trips within the city limits cost about 75 cents. The more distant locations run about $1 with no transfers. Call Vitran at 774-5678 for schedule and routes.

By Private Bus or Van

In St. Croix, private taxi vans pick up passengers with unscheduled and unregulated service between Christiansted and Frederiksted. They stop only along the main road between those towns. Rates vary. Wait for them at shopping centers and bus pull-offs. If you are unsure whether they are a private taxi van or a regular regulated taxi, ask first.

In St. John you can make use of bus transportation service, but residents sometimes stand by the Boulon Center corner exiting Cruz Bay to wait for a kindhearted soul, or someone they know, to deliver them to points east. This personal service works well and gets many St. Johnians to and from school and work.

While you will soon get used to the sight of the familiar open-air safari buses packed with tourists on tour, they also serve as the main means of transportation between Red Hook and Charlotte Amalie. Drivers meet the ferry from Cruz Bay, St. John for the half-hour trip to Charlotte Amalie. Those Safari buses leave at about 20 minutes after the hour from 8:20 a.m. till 3:20 p.m. Trips are about $3. The safari buses leave by the stop light at Market Square in Charlotte Amalie for Red Hook and points in between 15 minutes past the hour from 8:15 a.m. to 3:15 p.m.

By Taxi

Taxis are unmetered, and fares are determined by destination. Fares are fixed by law, but it is best to agree on a fare before you go. If you want to travel solo or leave immediately, you will pay more— particularly at the airports and ferry docks since drivers wait till they have all the passengers they can fit. Because gypsy cabs do try to pick up passengers, especially at supermarkets, look for "P" as the second letter of the license plate to ensure you are taking a regulated taxi.

All major hotels are serviced

by taxi associations. At smaller hotels, the reception desk will call one for you. If you are in town, look for a taxi at the marked taxi zones. In St. Croix and St. Thomas, call one of the taxi associations listed in the phone book for service. If the taxi association does not operate in your area, they will advise you who to call. You cannot call for service in St. John. Tours that cover any or all of the island start at about $12 each for three or more passengers. A solo tour could be about $30. Fares include one suitcase or box and a small piece of hand luggage. Additional pieces cost 50 cents each. Pets must be caged. If you need to make several stops, negotiate with the driver in advance. After 10 minutes of wait time there will be an additional charge.

Should you have a problem, write down the driver number located above the windshield inside the vehicle or the license plate and call the government's Taxi Commission at 776-5354 for help. When leaving the airports the taxi dispatcher will know the rates to where you are going. There are posted rates in some of the tourist publications too.

St. Thomas taxi - Danilo Monqiello

Call for a Taxi

St. Croix

Antilles Taxi	773-5020
CruzanTaxi & Tours	773-6388
Will & Berns Taxi	772-4775
St. Croix Taxi	778-1088

St. Thomas

Dore Edmund Taxi	473-9323
East End Taxi	775-6974
Islander Taxi	774-4077
VI Taxi Assoc.	776-9850

St. John

St. John Taxi Service	693-7530
C&C Taxi	693-8164

st. croix

Point Udall
Eastern Most Point of U.S.

91

Settler's Handbook Chapter 6

Your Basic Needs ...

Health Facilities

The hospitals on both St. Croix and St. Thomas are semi-autonomous agencies and each hospital has a local board to oversee operations. Medical assistance is available on St. Croix, St. Thomas and St. John for low-income patients at a variety of health facilities.

On St. Croix, the **Governor Juan F. Luis Hospital and Medical Center** (JFLHMC), centrally located in Estate Diamond Ruby, is a one hundred eighty-eight (188) bed facility. As the only full-service hospital, it offers acute emergency and ambulatory care, in a wide range of services, including general and specialty medicine, surgery, pediatrics, obstetrics, gynecology, psychiatry, physical medicine, hemodialysis and others. The facility is accredited by the Joint Commission on Accreditation of Healthcare Organizations (JCAHO); certified by Health Care Financing Administration for Medicare reimbursement; is a member with good standing of the National Association of Public Hospitals and the American Hospital Association. The Hospital Pharmacy and Blood Bank are licensed by the Drug Enforcement Agency and the Pathology & Clinical laboratory are also certified by the Joint Commission on Accreditation of Healthcare Organizations (JCAHO). All health professionals are licensed under Federal Regulatory Agencies and meet OSHA standards.

The Juan Luis Hospital provides full health care services for a population of 50,600 residents and to all visitors. The Emergency Room is open 24/7 and can/will refer patients as needed. It has become more efficient by the implementation of Fast Track. Fast Track is open every day from Noon to 8 p.m. to treat all minor cases that come to the Emergency Room to include sutures, fractures, severe flu and the like.

The Virgin Islands Cardiac Center (VICC) has been constructed to become the premier Cardiac Care facility in the Caribbean. The VICC has been outfitted with state of the art equipment to provide world-class Cardiovascular Treatment. The Juan F. Luis Hospital & Medical Center has been performing various cardiovascular procedures in their Cardiac Catheterization Laboratory including pacemaker implants, monitor pacemakers and Angioplasty.

Additionally, the Cardiac Unit does treadmill tests, stress echo testing, Electrocardiograms and arrhythmia detection, 24-hour Holter monitoring and management of congestive heart failure. Diagnostic Radiology includes state of the art CT Scan, open MRI and nuclear medicine capabilities. Their Board Certified OB/GYN physicians and Pediatricians are equipped to handle almost any contingency of high-risk pregnancies; diabetes and hypertension. Targeted ultra sound and amniocentesis are also available. The Hemodialysis facility is in use six days a week and visitors or residents can be accommodated as needed. Services include adult and pediatric evaluation of acute chronic kidney disorders; renal hypertension; diabetes collagen vascular disorders; kidney stone disease; infectious etiologies; renal transplant evaluation and referrals. A Board Certified Specialist in renal nutrition works with both adults and children suffering from acute or chronic renal failure to insure a proper diet is adhered to. For additional information on available services call 778-6311.

In St. Thomas and St. John, three medical facilities operate under the umbrella entity of the Schneider Regional Medical Center: the Roy Lester Schneider Hospital (St. Thomas), the Myrah Keating Smith Community Health Center (St. John), and the Charlotte Kimelman Cancer Institute (St. Thomas).

St. Thomas residents are served by the **Roy L. Schneider Hospital**, a 169-bed acute-care facility located across the street from the Lockhart Gardens Shopping Center. Provision of quality outpatient services is provided, including laboratory, radiology, rehabilitation and physiological testing. These services are in accordance with regulatory standards. The Schneider Hospital is a member of the National Association of Public Hospitals, and has full accreditation by the Joint Commission on Accreditation of Healthcare Organizations.

The Schneider Regional Medical Center employs 600 employees and approximately 80 physicians, with specialties ranging from emergency room, intensive care, hemodialysis, radiology, laboratory, physical therapy, pharmacy, cardiology, catheterization, nephrology, general and laparoscopic surgery, gastroenterology, neonatology, neurology, obstetrics and gynecology, nursery, pediatrics, orthopedics, and nuclear medicine. They also offer oncology, cancer chemotherapy, bone marrow aspiration, needle biopsy, evaluation and treatment of blood diseases, mammograms, skin tumors, lymph node, dissection, melanoma, and other cancer surgeries. The hospital is the only one in the Eastern Caribbean that has a hyperbaric chamber to treat decompression sickness and wound treatment. There is a Community Wide Scheduling Center for outpatient services. By calling a central phone number patients may make appointments and pre-register for a list of outpatient services. The system is designed to reduce the number of trips to the medical center, speed up the pre-admission process and to increase the level of customer satisfaction. (www. srmedicalcenter.org)

The Myrah Keating Smith Community Health Center: in St. John, 24-hour emergency services, family practice, pediatrics, internal medicine, radiology and general laboratory services, high-risk OB/GYN services and women's health services can be found at the Myrah Keating Smith Community Health Center in Susannaberg (693-8900). Appointments are made Monday-Friday from 8 a.m. to 8 p.m. Patients needing hospital care go on the ambulance boat to the Red Hook ferry dock in St. Thomas, where the ambulance picks them up to go to the Schneider Hospital. The MKS helipad in St. John now provides direct acute emergency medical transportation between MKS and the Schneider Hospital in St. Thomas.

Since October 2009 a new service has been available here. Telemedicine makes possible virtual office visits attended by medical personnel on St. John and medical specialists at Cleveland Clinic, Florida. With this collaboration, patients on St John are avoiding much of the cost and inconvenience of off-island travel for services that include: Pulmonology, Rheumatology, Dermatology, and pre/post evaluations for cardiac surgery. The Telemedicine link was funded by St. John Rotary.

Dental and mental health services in St. John are at the **Morris F. deCastro** Clinic in Cruz Bay.

The Charlotte Kimelman Cancer Institute: The $18 million, 24,000 square-foot Charlotte Kimelman Cancer Institute is now open and is the only comprehensive cancer care facility in the Eastern Caribbean. The cancer institute offers a full range of cancer services under one roof: radiation therapy, oncology, chemotherapy, early detection, prevention and wellness programs, surgical consultations, and clinical support services, 775-5433. They now have a board certified Hematologist. The Lynne Cohen Positive Appearance Boutique in the Cancer Center has a Certified Mastectomy Fitter available to see cancer patients by appointment to assist with individualized enhancements to appearance, including top-of-the-line skin care products, swimwear, clothing and apparel. When visiting Schneider, all patients should bring their insurance card, proof of mailing address (utility or phone bill), and picture ID. Call 776-8311, or 911.

On St. Croix, the Health Department's out-patient clinic at **Charles Harwood Clinic**, 773-1311, in Christiansted, provides services which include: primary care, obstetrics and gynecology, dental, mental health care, cardiac, allergy, dermatology, ear, nose and throat, eye care, food, handlers' exams, orthopedics, home care, immunization, Lamaze classes, neurology, opthalmology, oncology, pediatric, sexually transmitted diseases, including HIV and AIDS, and urology.

On St. Thomas, **The East End Family Health Center** provides many of the same services for residents of the eastern portion of the island. Call 775-3700. Family Planning and Maternal, Child Health and Crippled Children services are available in Nisky. Call 774-5256 for Family Planning, and 777-8804 for Maternal, Child Health and Crippled Children services. Mental Health Services are provided at Barbel Plaza South, 774-9000. Call 774-4912, the department's long-term mental health care facility, The Eldra Shulterbrandt Residential Facility.

The Frederiksted Health Care, Inc. (all insurances accepted) is a private non-profit organization, whose principal offices are located in Frederiksted, with a School Based Health Center satellite clinic located at the St. Croix Educational Complex. The services of FHC, Inc., offered on an appointment basis, include: Comprehensive Medical Services of Family Medicine, Internal Medicine, Optometry, Prenatal/High-Risk Prenatal and Gynecological Services, Pediatric and Newborn Pediatric Clinic, Podiatry, Adolescent Health Services, Dietician Services, Lab Services and Immunization by appointment. HIV, Diabetic and Eye Screening Clinics. Walk-in services are offered at the Urgent Care Center to patients of various ages and levels of illnesses from minor to urgent with evaluation, treatment,

St. Croix (area code 340)		
Governor Juan F. Luis Hospital		778-6311
Home Hospice Care		
Hospice & Home Care	*St. Croix*	*718-LOVE*
Continuum Care Inc.	*St. Croix*	*772-CARE*
	St. Thomas	*714-2273*
La Paz Hospice Care	*4B Sion Farm*	*719-3113*
Seaview Health Care (home-nurse assistance)		775-1660
	St. Croix	*719-7921*
	St. Thomas	*775-1660*
VI Kidney Center	*St. Croix*	*773-3227*
St. Thomas (area code 340)		
Roy Lester Schneider Hospital		776- 8311
St. John (area code 340)		
Morris De Castro Clinic		776-6400
Myrah Keating Smith Clinic		693-8900

discharge and/or transfer to the Governor Juan F. Luis Hospital and Medical Center via Emergency Medical Services. The also provide laboratory and dietician services. FHC INC also offers on-site in-kind services which include: Community Health (STD/HIV/TB), Mental Health and Substance Abuse, Women, Infant and Children's Program (WIC), and Family Planning Services. Contact 340-772-0260 (switchboard), 340-772-1992 (administrative offices), 340-772-5895 (general fax).

Air Ambulance

If an unexpected injury or illness occurs that cannot be treated in the USVI, an air ambulance could be needed. These medically equipped jets can cost upwards of $9000 for services to Puerto Rico and about $20,000 to Miami. The planes are chartered from either Puerto Rico or Miami. While local primary health insurance coverage, or whatever you might bring from the states for primary insurance, say they include air ambulance, you may have to pay upfront and get reimbursed later. You may also have to meet a deductible. Also primary insurance companies may not be open 7/24/365 to handle those wee hours of the morning, or weekend calls. These air ambulances want their money upfront first. Primary insurance companies may not pay your return trip home commercially.

One local company that offers Air Ambulance membership plans is SkyMed USVI, which has offices in St. Croix and St. Thomas. SkyMed has 25 years experience (their head office is in Scottsdale, AZ) and 12 years in the USVI. Their phones are answered 7/24/365. SkyMed offers three distinct plans. Their rates are $120 a year single, $240 a year family with the Basic plan to Puerto Rico. Add $96 to each Basic plan for the transport to Florida plan. Add $300 to the basic single, and $420 to the basic family plan for the City of Choice plan. SkyMed members do not pay any co-pay or deductible. Some of their benefits include return trips home for recuperation, and medical escort. They cover you worldwide at no extra cost. You do not have to notify them prior to your international trip. Members can pay annual, or convenient monthly payments can be set up.SkyMed can be contacted in St. Thomas at 1-866-349-1394 or in St Croix at 1-866-349-2398   (visit them at www.skymedusvi.com)

Staying Healthy

The best advice in the tropics? Drink plenty of fluids. Other hints until you have had a chance to acclimate: Why squint? Invest in a good pair of sunglasses, prescription, or not, to protect your eyes from sun damage. While many residents depend on photograys, optometrists say they do not provide sufficient protection for those who spend hours in the sun. Aside from wrinkles, the sun causes cancer and numerous other growths. Wear a hat and use heavy duty sunblock when out. The sun is strongest from 10 a.m. to 2 p.m., so avoid the beach during those hours. Since the rain water collected in your cistern lacks minerals found in ground water, a vitamin and mineral supplement every day is a good idea. Also, never ignore scratches and scrapes. Infection sets in quickly in the tropics. Wash with soap and water before covering loosely with a sterile bandage. If it's slow to heal, or the surrounding area becomes red, see your doctor immediately.

Life and Health Insurance

Like everywhere, health insurance rates have skyrocketed. Private policies and group plans are available through local agents. Contact local insurance companies for more information. Several companies such as: Bupa Insurance Group, Atlantic Southern, Cigna Health Care, Blue Cross Blue Shield, MAPFRE, Mutual of Omaha and United Health Care write policies in the territory. Life, disability, and annuities are available through agents who sell health insurance. Ask local agents what is available here and where these policies are accepted.

Finding a Doctor/Dentist

Start your search by asking your new neighbors, or a business contact, or, look in the local telephone directory (www.viphonebook.com). Call first to be sure which island they are on. Each island has specialists, including: cardiologists, chiropractors, dermatologists, ear-nose-throat specialists, radiologists, rehab centers, urologists, dentists, and many more. Some of them are associated with the local hospitals or clinics and/or may have their own practice. You might want to drive around to check for location of business signs and offices while you are familiarizing yourself with your new home.

Taking Care of Your Pets

Animals are subject to all the creepy crawlies your garden or yard can muster and, like little kids, their curiosity will push their noses a little deeper into the bush or shrub. They will depend upon you for guidance and protection because the tropical climate will spawn a collection of interesting and unhealthy critters. Your pets are subject to the same diseases as those in similar warm climates where ticks, intestinal parasites and heart worm infestations are prevalent. It is important to control ticks with dipping preparations because ticks transmit blood diseases, can seriously threaten the health of your pet, and may set up residency in your home.

Intestinal parasites like hookworm are a constant threat because the warm weather conditions allow the larvae to persist in the soil. Heartworm is transmitted by certain mosquito species and may be treated successfully in most cases. Small monthly doses of medicine, prescribed by your vet, will prevent both heartworm and hookworm. Jack Spaniard stings can cause swelling and centipede bites can really hurt dogs. In both cases, get the animal to the vet. Medical attention is immediately needed if your dog gets entangled with an eight-to-ten inch toad called a "crappo." This toad exudes a substance from glands in the skin which may cause profuse salivation, nervousness with high fever, uncontrollable motions, and even death. In most cases, this toad is entirely nocturnal and can only be found in the daytime under some type of dark, damp cover. Cats are especially vulnerable to wild dogs and feral cats. If your pet has not been spayed, do so before you leave home to prevent encounters with these wild animals. In the islands there is an abundance of animals needing homes, so if your pet has babies, finding homes for them will be extremely difficult.

Two final thoughts on the care of your pets concerning the everyday life on the islands. For their sake, remember the tropics are too hot to leave animals shut in a car or in the back of a truck. And, if your pet becomes an ocean swimmer, wash off the saltwater from the pet's body afterward. You rinse off after swimming in salt water, so do the same for them. Worthy of mention is the unwritten leash law. Dogs, where necessary, should be kept on leashes, and especially off beaches where turtles are nesting. Parrots, parakeets and fighting cocks must come from an area that is not under quarantine for psittacosis or Newcastle's Disease. For information on importing these birds contact any of the local animal shelters.The law mandates pets be registered every year, and new pets or pets brought into the territory must be registered with an identification tag within 30 days.

In **St. Croix**, pets are licensed through the St. Croix Animal Welfare Center currently located in Clifton Hill. Call 778-1650 for more information. The AWC runs an on-line pet tag registry, for which fees are $5 plus $1 for shipping for a basic black tag. Personalized ones are available at an extra cost. Licenses are also $5.00 and can also be purchased at any local veterinarian office(see www.stcroixawc.org/pet-licenses for more information). The AWC shelter is open from 8:30 a.m. to 5 p.m. Monday-Saturday, but closed on Sundays and federal holidays. Owner phone numbers and names are kept at the AWC to help match lost pets. In addition to providing animal control services and operating a humane education program, the shelter works to reduce the huge number of stray and unwanted animals on St. Croix by requiring mandatory spay/neuter of all adopted pets, while offering a Low-Cost Spay/Neuter program to local residents. The adoption fee of $100 for dogs or cats includes heart worm or feline leukemia testing, vaccinations, spaying/neutering fees, and a microchip to aid in lost pets. The shelter is a non-profit organization that depends upon private fundraising, volunteers, and proceeds from their thrift store to keep doors open. This thrift store, called The Flea Market, is located in Richmond and open from 10 a.m. to 2 p.m. Tuesday through Saturday.

Turn after Olympic Car and the Richmond Post Office to their alley. Call 692-5355 for more information.

In **St. John**, The Animal Care Center of St. John issues identification tags. Call 774-1625. Licenses on St. John are $85 for spayed animals and $124 for non-spayed to include spay/neuter. Dog licenses are not issued on St. Thomas. However, the Humane Society of St. Thomas issues an identification tag at $5 per tag. Their mailing address is 7041 Estate Nadir No. 26, St. Thomas, 00802 and their phone is 775-0599. They are open 7 days a week, 8 a.m. to 4 p.m.

The Humane Society of **St. Thomas** serves as the island's main animal shelter and adoption service. Potential adopters are welcome to come to the Humans Society's new Animal Campus, located on Weymouth Rhymer Highway across from Cost-U-Less. The adoption process is pretty straightforward. After filling out a questionnaire, staff will help you decide if the animal you want suits your lifestyle and will direct you to pets that may be appropriate. The shelter encourages prospective pet owners to allow everyone who will live with the animal (pets or housemates) to meet it before adoption. The Humane Society will require proof that you are allowed to have pets if you live in rental housing or in a condominium with animal restrictions in the bylaws. It is expected that adopters come prepared with landlord letters or lease copies that will verify that the animal does not violate rental or condo requirements. Adoption fees for cats are $75, which includes first vaccinations, de-worming, spay/neuter and flea treatment. Adoption fees for dogs/puppies is $105, which includes first vaccinations, de-worming, spay/neuter, flea treatment, license, a microchip and lifetime registration.

Below is information for veterinarian services on all three islands:

St. Croix

Deller Duke L DVM	772-4781
Island Animal Clinic	718-3106
Progressive Veterinary Hospital	718-1256 / 719-7387
Sugar Mill Veterinary Center	718-0002

St. John

Cruz Bay Canines, Cats & Critters	693-7780

All St. Thomas veterinarians make regular visits to St. John.

St. Thomas

Moore Veterinarian Clinic	775-6623
Tutu Veterinarian Services	777-7788
Animal Hospital	775-3240

For more information on bringing your pet from the mainland double check "Bringing in your Pet", Chapter 3 in this *Handbook*.

Education

Public and private education is available for all Virgin Islanders from pre-school through college. The government operates Head Start centers on all three islands and there are numerous private pre-schools. It is best to ask around to find one that fits your needs. Students attend either private non-sectarian, religious or public elementary and high schools. Private and religious schools charge tuition. Government-run schools are free. Most settlers send their children to private or religious-affiliated schools. The government provides bus service for private and public school students in grades kindergarten through six who live over a mile away. It also has classes for handicapped students. While most private school students wear street clothes, those attending religious or public schools wear uniforms.

St. Croix Private Schools

AZ Academy, 35 Estate Orange Grove, Pre-K to grade 10, 773-7909
Country Day School, nursery through grade 12,R.R.#1, Box 6199 Kingshill, 00850, 778-1974, (fax) 779-3331
Good Hope School, pre-K through 12th, Estate Good Hope, 772-0022
Good Hope School, pre-K and K, Estate All for the Better, 778-7136
Manor School, kindergarten through 12 th, La Grande Princesse, Christiansted, 00820, 718-1448 (fax) 718-3651
St. Croix Montessori, 13 Orange Grove (ages 2 1/2 to 9) 692-2859, (fax) 773-6036, www.stxmontessori.org.
Star Apple Montessori Preschool, 24 Strand St. Christiansted 773-8071
Stone House Pre School, 30 Estate St. John, Christiansted 718-5606

St. Croix Religious Schools

Church of God Holiness, Peter's Rest, Christiansted, 719-1220.
Free Will Baptist School, Baptist, pre-school through 12 Box 6265, Sunny Isle 00823, elementary, 773-3179, high school, 778-8030.
Randolph Lockhart Christian School, 21 Orange Grove, Christiansted, 719-2000.
St. Croix Christian Academy, 26 Golden Rock, Christiansted, 718-4947.
St. Joseph's High School, Roman Catholic, grades 9 through 12, No. 3 Mt. Pleasant, Route. 2, Frederiksted, 00840, 692-2455.
St. Patrick's School, Roman Catholic, Grades one through 12, 406 Custom House Street, Frederiksted, 772-5052
St. Mary's Catholic School, P.O. Box 224620, Christiansted, V.I. 00822, 2184 Queen St., Christiansted VI 00820 Grades Pre-K through 8, 773-0117
School of the Good Shepherd, pre-K through grade 8, 772-2280
Seventh Day Adventists, Holgers Hope, K to 12, 773-6350 The Public

Elementary Schools are located in Fredensborg, Richmond, La Grande Princesse, Kingshill, Concordia, St. Peters, Frederiksted, Sion Farm, Mount Pleasant, Strawberry and Grove Place. St. Croix has two public high schools, **Central High School**, with Grades 9 through 12 at Kingshill. In August of 1995, a new combined high school and vocational school was opened on the Queen Mary Highway opposite the University of the Virgin Islands campus called **The St. Croix Educational Complex**. The island has three junior high schools grades seven and eight. They are Elena Christian Junior High located in La Grande Princesse, Arthur Richards Junior High in Stoney Ground, and John H. Woodson Junior High in Fredensborg.

<h3 style="text-align:center">St. John Public and Private Schools</h3>

In St. John, private elementary school students attend **Gifft Hill School** on Gifft Hill Road. It runs from pre-school through sixth grade. Many elementary and high school students take the ferry to St. Thomas to private or religious-affiliated schools. Recently Pine Peace, 776-6595, combined with Coral Bay High School (7 to 12), 776-1730, to be called Gifft Hill School. There is also the **St. John Montessori** 775-8071, and **St. John Christian Academy** – 693-7722

Public school students attend Julius E. Sprauve School in Cruz Bay, which goes through grade nine, or the Guy Benjamin School in Coral Bay which is kindergarten through grade six. St. John high school students take the ferry to Ivanna Eudora Kean High School at Red Hook. A special ferry runs at 7 a.m. to Red Hook to transport the students to their classes. They return home, at their convenience, using government-issued passes on any of the regularly-scheduled ferries.

<h3 style="text-align:center">St. Thomas Private Schools</h3>

Antilles School, pre-school through grade 12, P.O. Box 7280, Charlotte Amalie, V.I. 00801, 776-1600
VI Montessori School, accredited, ages 3 through 12, 6936 Vessup Bay Road, St. Thomas, V.I. 00802-1001, 775-6360

<h3 style="text-align:center">St. Thomas Religious Schools</h3>

All Saints Cathedral School, Episcopal, pre-kindergarten through 12, P.O. Box 308, Charlotte Amalie, 00804, 774-0231
Bethel Baptist Day School, kindergarten through 3, P.O. Box 4465, Charlotte Amalie, 00803, 774-1378
Church of God Academy, kindergarten through 12, P.O. Box 502187, Tutu Park Mall Post Office, 00805, 775-1252.
Memorial Moravian School, kindergarten through 8, P.O. Box 117, Charlotte Amalie, 00804, 774-7579 and 774-2670
Saints Peter & Paul School, Catholic, pre-kindergarten through 12, P.O.

Box 1706, Charlotte Amalie, 00803, elementary school, 774-5662, high school, 774-2199

Seventh Day Adventist School, kindergarten through 12, P.O. Box 7909, Charlotte Amalie, 00803, 775-3525.

Wesleyan Academy, pre-school through 12, P.O. Box 302779, Charlotte Amalie, 00803, 774-5438

Public School elementary students in St. Thomas attend schools in Sub Base, Tutu, Hospital Line, Frenchman's Bay, Nazareth Bay, Bournefield, Sugar Estate, Donoe, Mandahl, Mafolie, Savan and several in Charlotte Amalie.

St. Thomas has two high schools. One, Charlotte Amalie High School is located just outside of the island's main town and serves grades nine through 12. The other, Ivanna Eudora Kean High School, located at Red Hook, serves grades 9 through 12. Addelita Cancryn Junior High School serves grades seven and eight from its Frenchtown campus. Bertha C. Boshulte Junior High has grades seven and eight at its Bovoni campus.

Vocational students in St. Croix learn skills at the St. Croix Educational Complex & High School. Programs may include carpentry, computers, culinary arts, plumbing, hospitality, boat building, office skills, or practical nursing. In St. Thomas, vocational students take similar classes at the Rafael O. Wheatley Skills Center in Charlotte Amalie. All the junior and senior high schools offer vocational programs for their students.

University of the Virgin Islands

The University of the Virgin Islands (UVI) is a liberal arts, land-grant institution established by public statute to meet the higher education needs of people from the territory and throughout the Caribbean. The university is accredited by the Commission on Higher Education of the Middle States Association of Colleges and Schools, which is an institutional accrediting agency recognized by the U.S. Secretary of Education and the Commission on Recognition of Post Secondary Accreditation.

UVI has campuses on St. Thomas and St. Croix — with an Academic Center and Environmental Resources Station on St. John. The St. Croix campus is located at Golden Grove, midway between the towns of Christiansted and Frederiksted. Via the Queen Mary Highway, the entrance to St. Croix's Albert A. Sheen Campus is lined with royal palm trees leading to the residence halls, Student Center and the Melvin H. Evans Center for Learning. Other main buildings include the Great House, the Northwest Wing, the Nursing Complex, Agricultural Experiment Station and the Research and Extension Center, which contains administrative offices and the U.S.V.I. Cooperative Extension Service.

The 388-acre St. Thomas campus is located three miles west of Charlotte

Amalie overlooking Brewer's Bay. In addition to academic facilities, administrative and student service buildings, residence halls, the UVI Sports and Fitness Center and the 1,196-seat Reichhold Center for the Arts, the St. Thomas campus includes the Herman E. Moore Golf Course, Brewer's Bay beach and tennis courts.

Students who come to UVI choose from a broad array of associate and bachelor's degree programs in more than 20 curriculum areas. The university maintains five colleges and schools: the College of Liberal Arts and Social Sciences, College of Science and Mathematics, School of Business, School of Education and School of Nursing, and offers master's degree programs in public administration, business administration, mathematics for secondary education, marine science, and education. A new post-master's degree program in school psychology is also being offered. UVI is one of few HBCUs to offer undergraduate and graduate degrees in marine science.

The faculty is comprised of 250 highly qualified, full-time and part-time members. Faculty members represent diverse ethnic and cultural backgrounds, from the mainland U.S., the Virgin Islands and abroad. Cooperative agreements between the University of the Virgin Islands and many other leading universities exist to allow UVI students to receive degrees not offered on the UVI campuses.

The Boston University School of Medicine cooperative agreement allows UVI students, who meet certain qualifications, provisional acceptance into the medical school at the end of their sophomore year. The College of Science and Mathematics has developed an articulation program in engineering with Columbia University in New York and Washington University in St. Louis. These articulation agreements allow students to begin their studies at UVI and then complete requirements for graduation at one of these schools.

UVI's 2,500 full-time, part-time and graduate students come from: the U.S.V.I., 34 U.S. states and about 14 other countries, primarily in the Eastern Caribbean. Undergraduate tuition for Virgin Islands residents is $4,190 per year. Non-resident tuition is $12,570 per year. Per-credit undergraduate tuition is $140 for residents and $420 for non-residents. Total room and board charges per semester average $2,477 double and $3,220 for a single room, depending on meal plan choice.

In addition to academics, UVI is home to the Virgin Islands' **Research & Technology Park (RTPark)**, an economic development initiative that leverages visions of the business community, UVI and the public sector. RTPark is a world-class, near-shore provider of technology solutions for knowledge-based, information technology and e-commerce companies.

Part of its mission is to attract businesses from these sectors to the USVI, stimulate creation of new jobs and career opportunities for residents, and strengthen UVI's academic and financial capabilities. RTPark can directly extend compelling benefits and incentives to qualifying knowledge-based businesses, including significant reductions – up to 90% – in income taxes for USVI-sourced income. Alternatively, in certain cases, knowledge-based businesses can obtain similar benefits from the USVI Economic Development Authority (EDA) if those businesses are first referred by RTPark. Other key strategic and competitive benefits include access to world-class broadband connectivity that leverages the USVI's unique concentration of switching facilities for undersea fiber networks, and legal protections for intellectual property, investments and contracts under federal law.

For more on the RTPark, including application requirements, browse to http://www.uvirtpark.com/ or call (340) 692-4200. For information on UVI, refer to the website: http://www.uvi.edu/ or contact the university's Public Relations Office at (340) 693-1057. Current and incoming students are advised to contact UVI's Financial Aid Office at 340-693-1090 to determine opportunities that exist with federal grant programs, other scholarship opportunities and loans.

UVI Directory (Area Code 340) (Voice / Fax)
St. Croix Campus

Admissions	692-4158/4115
Agricultural Experiment Station	692-4020/4035
Alumni Affairs & Development	692-4023/4025
Campus/Executive Administrator	692-4000/4005
Cooperative Extension Service	692-4080
Financial Aid	692-4193/4145
Housing/Residence Life	692-4194/4184
Human Resources	692-4160/4165

St. Thomas Campus

Admissions	693-1150/1155
Alumni Affairs	693-1047/1045
Campus/Executive Administrator	693-1147/1175
Development	693-1040/1045
Financial Aid	693-1090/1095
Housing/Residence Life	693-1110/1104
Human Resources	693-1410/1405
President's Office	693-1000/1005

Libraries

There are public libraries on St. Croix, St. Thomas and St. John. Library cards are free to residents and valid at each facility, which offer services for children, young adults and adults. There are also services to patrons remotely located via the bookmobile; in a major shopping center (the Sunny Isle Public Library); and from the Regional Library for the Blind and Physically Handicapped. In St. John visit the Sprauve Library.

The libraries are fully automated on the VIALS (the Virgin Islands Automated Library System) to include the Public Library Learning Center and access to the book/materials collections of all the public libraries and three of the four public high school libraries and two curriculum centers in the Territory. Internet access is free to the public.

Special collections on V.I. and Caribbean history, culture and related topics are housed in the Florence Williams Public Library Caribbean Collection and the Enid Baa Public Library and Archives Von Scholten Collection. Researchers are asked to make appointments

Religions

V.I. multiculturalism has led to diversity of spiritual culture here. Western religious tradition in these islands can be traced to the Moravians, who arrived in the 1700s with the blessing of the Danish governor. The Moravian missionaries were English speakers and tought their language to local slaves. Spanish services were also common, particularly on St. Croix.

Today there are more than 150 congregations and world religions in the territory, including hundreds of Christian denominations, Bahai, Islam, Hindu, Judaism and many more

The Congregation of Blessing and Peace and Loving Deeds on St. Thomas is the second oldest continuous-use synagogue in the U.S.

Settler's Handbook Chapter 7

Community Life: Island Style...

Folklore and Culture

Seven flags have flown over St. Croix and three over St. Thomas, a remarkable number for Caribbean islands since all were fought over for their agricultural advantages and strategic outposts on the trade routes to the New World. During the unending series of European wars and shifting alliances that lasted from the mid-1500s until the Napoleonic Wars in the early 1800s, settlers and Christian missionaries from about a dozen nations were merged to create the island culture. However, the dominant contributor was Africa, origin of the enslaved peoples who tilled the plantations in the Caribbean.

The definitive Virgin Islands form of music is quelbe, which is performed by scratch bands and makes use of gourds and washboards. Close to Christmas on St.Croix don't be surprised if one morning before dawn you find yourself jigging down the streets behind a truck of musicians. No, you are not in Hamlin – it's just St. Croix's Pied Pipers, Stanley and the Ten Sleepless Knights playing their infectious scratch music during their Annual 'fore Dawn Serenade, the local equivalent of mainland caroling. 'Jamesie and the Allstars are known as The Kings of Scratch music throughout the Caribbean'.

Another cultural music tradition is cariso, a slave-pioneered, lilting music with words that tell a story. Not allowed other communication as they toiled in the fields, the slaves sang as a way to pass on the news of family, friends and events to the other slaves. Cariso

Cultural Tidbit

Dr. George Franklin, principal of the School of the Good Shephard on St. Croix and cultural humorist, has volunteered the following instruction for newcomers to our islands.

Plural Nouns

What is the plural for mongoose. No not mongeese, or mongooses, but mongoose dem.

In fact, the plural for anything is the proper word followed by the suffix dem.

Virgin Islands GPS

If you are a visitor and you are trying to find your way around our island using a map and the road signs you better forget it because none of us native have a clue about route this and route that. If you want to get from point A to point B you have to ask for landmarks (mango tree, a big white house with a lady sitting on the gallery, there's a red car in the yard, down by cousin so and so house).

developed like the well-known calypso that now satirizes political figures and local issues and describes the folk medicine of the healers or "weed women" of long ago. One of the ingredients described for a particular problem was the aloe plant which now is included in many skin creams. Various teas and tisanes, or herbal concoctions, which will cure, sedate or stimulate are put to song. Story tellers today create their own theatre as they tell the folk tales from their African-West Indian culture. The island youngsters know all about Mickey Mouse but they also know of the "Bru Nancy" spider tales as well, which are the Caribbean equivalent to the Br'er Rabbit stories of Uncle Remus.

Virgin Islands traditional folk arts are still practiced but by very few. While fishermen continue to construct practical fish pots, it's only a few of the older generation, and even less of the territory's youths who continue to weave beautiful baskets, create original needle work or build mahogany furniture and fine caned chairs, though a tri-island woodworking group is growing. The social melting pot of the islands and the hardships endured during and after slavery have made Virgin Islanders a gracious and somewhat conservative people. They cherish privacy and are rather undemonstrative, at least by stateside standards, until you smile and say "good morning". To a native islander, good fortune is nice but fragile, which is why the automatic question "how are you" often receives the reply "not as good as you".

Mocko Jumbies

These masked stilt walkers walk and dance the streets during parades or festive occasions and entertain with colorful, meaningful costumes. But the mocko jumbies have their serious side. Depending on whom you talk to, jumbies are supernatural beings for either good or evil. Never to be seen by nonbelievers, they reflect the islands' African heritage and are thought to be either one's ancestors or one's connection with the spiritual or superstitious world. That superstitious force, called the Obeah, which creates those good and bad occurrences, is African rooted and similar in some ways to the more familiar Voodoo. While belief in Obeah has never been prominent in the U.S. Virgin Islands, it has been part of the territory's ambiance for years. You won't find many people who actually claim to believe in Obeah themselves, although the natives will tell you stories of something that supposedly happened to someone else. Some of the characters you see during Carnival or parades are mere interpretations of the spirits and superstitions of long ago.

Carnival

Author Herman Wouk wrote the truth when he said "rain don't stop de

Cultural Tidbit

Richard Allsopp in his text Dictionary of Caribbean English Usage, says the term mucko jumbie hails from African terms nsambi, 'God', and nsumbi, 'Devil', "the linking of good and evil with the same cosmic powers."

My definition of a Jumbie is a chance encounter of the living with a deceased relative, family or friend, in a guise recognizable to the seer.

Their intent for the most part is not to scare but to assist the living, or protect them from harm, bring them good news or luck, alert them of impending death of a family member, or to warn them of dangers. In this sense they are generally not haunts, although there are some "bad" Jumbies that are haunted and thereby are intent on doing harm. However, this is by far a rare occurrence.

Then there are those who use Jumbies as a way to scare children into behaving. "Imaginary bogey man called on the frighten children." — from *Wah a Jumbie Beh*, by **Dr. George Franklin**

Carnival. Indeed, all other activities cease when the Carnival comes through town. The event occurs on St. Croix, St. John and St. Thomas at different times, and each is unique. These celebrations begin slowly, as locals spend months building floats, sewing costumes, training horses, and selecting queens, princes and princesses. But on carnival days the action intensifies as groups gather for the hours-long parade through the streets with participants dressed in glitter and glitz. Look for floats, bands and twirlers, floupes, troupes and mocko jumbies. In the interim look for calypso contests, horse races, dances and night after night of fun, music and food at Carnival Village. Then there's J'Ouvert, a West Indian invention, which usually starts around 4 a.m. when thousands of people tramp through the streets behind their favorite bands. Boat races, baby contests and other events change from year to year depending on who's in charge and what the residents want. The entire event usually wraps up with a fireworks display. The newspapers and the local grapevine will let you know when and where the action starts.

If you are not up to the crowds, be sure to catch the parades on television. The St. Croix version of Carnival, called the **Crucian Christmas Festival**, begins before Christmas and runs through Three Kings' Day or Epiphany on the religious calendar. Three Kings' Day is a major holiday for the numerous residents of Puerto Rican descent who live on St. Croix. Crucians first celebrated the festival during the final years of the Danish government. Although the holiday was abandoned over the years, residents revived it again in the 1950s. In some years, Carnival villages are erected near Frederiksted or near Christiansted. The parades (children's and/or adults) used to alternate yearly between the towns of Christiansted and Frederiksted, but are now all in Frederiksted.

Not to be outdone, St. John residents celebrate their **July 4th Festival** in a special style. Although smaller than Carnival celebrations on the other islands, residents enjoy it just as much. In fact it is growing yearly. Boatloads of sister-island folk crowd St. John. Just before the July 3rd parade, the ferries from St. Thomas run all day. Look for the Food Fair in Cruz Bay Park on the celebration's first Sunday.

© Joyce Hickock

St. Thomas has a lollapalooza of a Carnival. Usually held a few weeks after Easter, **St. Thomas Carnival** is second only to Trinidad's in scope and size. The tradition began in 1912 but subsequently lapsed. Revived in 1952 by Ron de Lugo, who later served as the territory's representative in Washington, D.C., the extravaganza consumes the minds and hearts of the islanders for weeks. Don't miss the parade through the streets of Charlotte Amalie. The costumes are known to rival those seen at the Mardi Gras in New Orleans.

Entertainment and the Arts

Though not Broadway, there is plenty of entertainment in St. Croix and St. Thomas during the winter season. The pickings are slimmer on St. John, but late-running ferries allow residents to sample the St. Thomas night life. From major hotels to the corner bar, you will find a wide variety of musical

entertainment during dinner and afterwards.

Since 1967, **Island Center for the Performing Arts** on St. Croix has headed the entertainment bill. A premier spot for artistic performances, Island Center has hosted such noted groups as Island Center has hosted such noted groups as the Boston Pops Traveling ensemble, Ebony Fashion Fair, Alvin Ailey, The St. Petersburg

Ballet and the London Ballet. Such notable artistes as Eartha Kitt, Cab Calloway, pianist Awadagin Pratt, the Naumberg award winner Tomohiro Okumura, the Preservation Hall Jazz Band, Jose Feliciano, Third World and Victor Borge have headlined during the winter season. Island Center also dance programs, theatre presentations, and youth activities, while serving as a community resource for special events, including performing arts workshops and public interest meetings. More than half of its 1100 seats are under cover. *Call 778-5271 for program information.*

Also on St. Croix, the **Caribbean Community Theatre** holds performances at #18 Orange Grove, behind Golden Rock Shopping Center. This non-profit performs Broadway-style musicals, comedies and local plays from October to July. Contact: 778-1983, www.cct.vi.

On St. Thomas, **Reichhold Center for the Arts** is celebrating 34 Years of in the arts. The center was the dreamchild of Philanthropist and businessman Henry H. Reichhold, CEO of Reichhold Chemicals, Inc. Reichhold endowed and oversaw

India Arie- Courtesy Reichhold Center

development of a state-of-the-art amphitheater just west of the University of the Virgin Islands' St. Thomas campus. It has since grown a top regional performing arts center. Reichhold Center has hosted some of the world's top performers, including: Itzhak Perlman, Ray Charles, Sarah Vaughn, Puerto Rico Symphony Orchestra, Alvin Ailey Dance Company, Beres Hammond, George Benson, Chris Botti, and McCoy Tyner, just to name a few.

Artists and audience members alike are enthralled by the theater's natural setting, nestled within the lap of a natural valley whose mouth opens to the crystal blue waters of John Brewer's Bay. Performances take place under the stars and moon, adding a unique ambience to each performance in this nearly 1,200-seat theater. The Center's season runs from October to June each year. For a current performance schedule and ticket information, call 693-1559 or visit www.reichholdcenter.com. In addition to the Reichold Center, St. Thomas has a community theatre called **"The Pistarkle Theatre Group,"** which performs at **Tillett Garden**s.

The government-supported **Virgin Islands Council on the Arts** provides matching yearly grants, funded through the National Endowment for the Arts, to artists and organizations. The Council on the Arts participates in and sends exhibits and musical groups throughout the the world. For further info call 774-5984, St. Thomas and 773-1095 or 719-2246. Anytime you are in the islands look and listen for calypso, steel bands, quadrille dancing, marching bands and baton twirlers as well as ballet and modern dance performances. Check local newspapers for the latest entertainment updates.

Holidays

If it seems like there is a holiday every time you turn around, you are probably right. Many of the local holidays are celebrated on Monday to give workers a three-day weekend. Local government offices are closed for those listed below. Banks and Federal offices close only for those marked with an asterisk (*). The Governor usually gives government workers a day or half-day off for Carnival activities. In election years, those days are also declared holidays.

Usual Annual Holidays

*This is 2013, dates in subsequent years will be similar. *Banks may be closed most of these days.*

Jan. 1	New Year's Day
Jan. 4	Crucian Festival Children's
Jan. 5	Crucian Festival Adult's Parade
Jan. 7	Three King's Day observed*
Jan. 21	Martin Luther King's Day*
Feb.18	President's Day*
March 31	Easter Sunday/Transfer Day, V.I.
March 28	Holy Thursday
March 29	Good Friday*
March 31	Easter Sunday
April 1	EasterMonday
April 26	St.T Carnival/ J'Ouvert
April 26	St.T Carnival Children's Parade
April 27	St.T Carnival Adult's Parade
May 27	Memorial Day*
July 3	Emancipation Day V.I. *
July 4	Independence Day*
Sept. 2	Labor Day*
Oct. 14	Columbus Day / USVI-Puerto Rico Friendship Day*
Nov. 1	D. Hamilton Jackson Day
Nov. 11	Veteran's Day*
Nov. 28	Thanksgiving Day*
Dec. 25	Christmas Day*
Dec. 26	Boxing Day

Newspapers & Magazines

To quickly get an understanding of the islands and know what's going on, read the two local newspapers, the *St. Croix Avis*, and the *V.I. Daily News*. Both newspapers carry wire services reports on breaking stateside and world news. For more in-depth world coverage, read the *New York Times,* the *Miami Herald, Washington Post*, the *Wall Street Journal* or the *San Juan Star.* They are available at outlets in the islands at prices quite a bit higher than stateside. The Sunday New York Times will arrive a day later because the plane comes in the next day. A good selection of national magazines is available at many convenience stores, supermarkets, Kmart and at news outlets. The prices run about a dollar more per issue.

Annual Events

January: *St. Croix* - Crucian Christmas Festival (includes Three Kings DayParade on or close to Epiphany); Candlelight Concerts at WHIM sponsored by St.Croix Landmarks Society (run November – April); Sunset Jazz, Frederiksted 3rd Friday every month; Orchid Society Show
February: Miss UVI Pageant; *St. Croix* – Agricultural Fair; House Tours by St. Croix Landmarks Society thru March; Agricultural Fair; Jump-Up Christiansted Block Party (streets closed and stores stay open late 4 per year); *St. John*- St. John Race, Eight Tuff Miles (last Saturday); *St. Thomas* - Valentine's Ball (Fur Ball) to benefit Humane Society
March: *St. Croix*-St.Patrick's Day Parade; University of the Virgin Islands Golf Tournament; Orchid Society Show: *St John* – St. John Blues Festival; *St. Thomas* - Arts Alive Festival Tillett Gardens; Hibiscus Society Show
April: *St. Croix* - LPGA Pro-Am Tournament, Carambola Golf Club; Golden Hook Fishing Tournament; Taste of St. Croix (fantastic wine/food sampling!) *St. Thomas* - St. Thomas Carnival; Rolex Cup Regatta ; Easter Bonnet Contest, Blackbeard's Castle Hotel
May: *St. Croix* - Ironman 70.3 Triathlon; Memorial Day Race, St. Croix Yacht Club; Amer. Cancer Society Walkathon: *St. John*- Beach to Beach Swim by Friends of the Park
St. Thomas: Spring Charter Yacht Show – (alternates each year between USVI and BVI –call 774-3944 for info)
June: *St. Croix* -Annual Women's Race for Women's Coalition
July: *St. Croix*- Mango Melee, SGVBotanical Garden; Summer World Music Series July/Aug/Sept at WHIM plantation, St. Croix Landmarks Society; *St.John* -July 4th Carnival Celebration; *St. Thomas*- Open Sport fishing Tournament ; French Heritage Week ; Bastille Day King-fish Tournament; St. Thomas Billfish Tournament, American Yacht Harbor
August: *St. Thomas*- Arts Alive Festival, Tillett Gardens; Texas Chili Cookoff; Atlantic Blue Marlin Tournament
September: *St. Thomas* - Women's Laser Regatta,
October: *St. Croix* – Fall Heritage Day; Virgin Islands/Puerto Rico Friend ship Day; MOTTEP Family Walk
November: *St. Croix* – International Sailing Regatta, Yacht Club; Starving Artists Fair, Whim Museum; *St. John* – Annual Thanksgiving Weekend Regatta; St. Thomas -Arts Alive Festival, Tillett Gardens; AgriculturalFair; Paradise Jam Basketball Tournament ; Fall Charter Yacht Show
December: *St. Croix* - Crucian Christmas Festival kicks off; Boat Parade of Lights *St. Thomas* - Hibiscus Show

Newspapers

The *St. Croix Avis*, a St. Croix daily, except Mondays and major holidays, Box 750, Christiansted, VI 00821 718-2300, (fax) 718-5511. (call for subscription). (In St. Thomas it is sent there as The Avis.)

Virgin Islands Daily News, St. Thomas and St. Croix daily, except Sundays and Christmas Day, 9155 Estate Thomas, St. Thomas, VI 00802. 774- 8772. St. Croix Bureau, 773-4125.

News On-Line

•www.visource.com   •www.virginislandsdailynews.com

Tourist and Island Information Websites

•www.gotostthomas.com   •www.gotostcroix.com
•www.gotostjohn.com   •www.stcroixhotelandtourism.com
•www.virgin-islands-hotels   •www.visitstcroix.com
•www.visitthevi.com   •www.vinow.com

Local Periodicals

Island Trader, free weekly, call for classified rates, (contact Daily News). *St. John Tradewinds*, bi-weekly news of St. John, P.O. Box 1550, Cruz Bay, St. John VI 00831, 776-6496.*St. Croix Crucian Trader*, weekly,published by Daily News,773-4145

Tourist Publications

Discover St. Thomas - St. John - St. Croix -Published by HCP/Aboard Publications and found in hotel rooms, 1-800-829-9405.

Marine Guide (Media Marketing Inc.), 774-0920, all three islands, British Virgin Islands and Puerto Rico. www.vimarineguide.com

Places to Explore (Media Marketing, Inc.) 774-0920, all three islands.

Places to Eat Map, St. Thomas and St. John (Media Marketing, Inc.) 774-0920. www.viplacestoexplore.com

St. Croix Explorer, an annual tourist guidebook with information on shopping, dining, accommodations, activities, and watersports, with map, P.O. Box 2797, Kingshill, St. Croix VI 00851 718-5128. www.stcroixexplorer.com

SSt. Croix This Week, 774-2500 published monthly: events, shopping, maps, tourist information, Box 224477, Christiansted, St. Croix, VI 00822-4477, http://www.stcroixthisweek.com.

St. Thomas This Week, 774-2500 free every Saturday: shopping, maps, dining, and tourist information, updated weekly. P.O. Box 11199, St. Thomas, VI 0080, http://www.stthomasthisweek.com.

Books

Many wonderful books have been written about the Caribbean and in particular about the U.S. Virgin Islands. Some of the older ones could be out of print although you may find them at a local library. Below is listed but a mere selection of good books written about the U.S. Virgin Islands. You can also go on-line with Amazon.com, or Barnes & Noble. When you arrive at your chosen island, visit some of their local book stores: in St. Thomas: Dockside Bookshop, Island Periodicals (airport); and in St. Croix: Undercover Books, WHIM Museum gift shop, Design Works, National Parks Visitors Center, (also the one on St. John), Island Periodicals (airport); St. John at Connections in Cruz Bay and Papaya Cafe (Bookstore) at Marketplace. Also try the University Bookstores at: 692-4162 St. Croix, and 693-1561 St. Thomas.

Architecture / Living Here
Architectural Heritage of the Caribbean – Andrew Gravette
Caribbean Elegance (exotic furniture from the sugar islands)
Caribbean Houses, both – Michael Connors
Gardening in the Caribbean – Bannochie and Light
Historic Buildings of St. Thomas and St. John – F.C. Gjessing,
    F.C. & W.P. MacLean
Life in the Left Lane – Emy Thomas

Children's
A Caribbean Journey from A-Y – Mario Picayo
Caribbean Capers – J&M Santomenna
Caribbean Colors of Rainbow – Skylon & Woodruff
Daniel and the Christmas Festival– Denise Bennerson
Lenny the Lobster – Katherine Orr
My Island and I - The Nature of the Caribbean – A. Silva Lee
Pabi, Beega & The Mongoose Monster – Patricia Gill
The Illustrated Animal Folk Tales (Anansi Stories) – P. Sh

Cookbooks
A Taste of the Virgin Islands– Angela and Richard Spencely
Crucian Confusion Cooking – St. Croix Landmarks Society
Just Add Rum – Angela Spenceley (other similar ones by her)
My Little Virgin Islands Cookbook– Kathleen Querrard
Native Recipes – UVI Cooperative Extension Service
Virgin Islands Cooking – Carol Bareuther

Culture / History
A Brief History of   Caribbean – Rogozinski
A History of the   . of the U.S. – Isaac Dookhan
Alexander Hamilton: American – Richard Brookhiser
Annals of the Big Island, both – Robert Hoffman
From Columbus to Castro – Eric Williams
Fruits and Vegetables of the Caribbean – Seddon

I am Not a Slave – Eugene LaCorbiniere
Kallalo – Richard A. Schrader, Sr. *(plus others by Schrader)*
Me and My Beloved Virgin – Guy H. Benjamin
Negotiating Enslavement – Arnold Highfield, George F. Tyson
Peter Von Scholten– Hermann Lawaetz
Pirates of the Virgin Islands – Fritz Seyfarth
Romantic History of St. Croix – Florence Lewisohn
St. Croix Historic Photos – Elizabeth Rezende, Anne Walborn
Saint Croix 1770-1776 – Robert Johnson
Say It In Crucian – Robin Sterns
The Night of Silent Drums – John L. Anderson
This Little Island Mine – Richard A. Schrader, Sr.
Time Longa Dan Twine – Arnold Highfield

Fiction

A Bunch of Real Jumbie Stories, Meh Son – George Franklin
A West Indian Fish Tale – A. Anduze
Andy Browne's Departure – S. B. Jones-Hendrickson
Buddhoe and Cape of the Arrows – Patricia Gill
Caribbean – James Michener
Don't Stop the Carnival – Herman Wouk
Lagoonieville Series – Bert Emrick
The Caribbean Writer - Volume 1-22 – Erika J.Waters
The Mangoes Series – R. D. Dowling
Transfer Day– Sophie Schiler

Nature/Wildlife

200 Tropical Plants of the Caribbean – John Kingsbury
A Guide to the Birds of P.R. and the V.I. – Herbert Raffaele
Caribbean Wild Plants & Their Uses – P. Honychurch
Diving Pioneers and Innovators – Bret Gilliam
Guide to Corals & Fishes – Idaz Greenberg
Island Peak to Coral Reef – Toni Thomas & Barry Devine
Traditional Medicinal Plants – Toni Thomas
Tropical Trees of Florida and the V.I. – T. Kent Kirk
U.S. Virgin Islands – National Park Handbook

Poems

Sugar Is All – Annette Walwyn Michael
Under the Taino Moon – Arnold R. Highfield /Richard Schrader

Settler's Handbook Chapter 8

THE GREAT OUTDOORS ...

With an endless array of sunny days, a climate unsurpassed, and the blue Caribbean at your feet, playing in the outdoors is a natural way of life. It's just how do you decide what to do! You can bask on the beach, float in the gentle surf, hike, ride horseback through a rain forest or on the beach, play a championship golf course, dabble in tennis, sail, snorkel, SCUBA dive, cast a line in the turquoise waters, or play softball or basketball with a local league. The more sedate or curious person might want to do some bird watching in bushes, or watch the sugar birds right from a porch. A lazy afternoon could be spent collecting shells along the beach. The choices are endless.

Swimming

Virgin Islands' law states that the beach area is measured 50 feet from the low water mark, which means that all beaches in the Virgin Islands are open to sunbathing or swimming for locals or visitors. This law ensures that the beaches will never be closed. The hotels on the islands do not own the beach on their property, but it pays to use discretion and common sense when using any of those beaches. Since they have an investment in the property, they usually try to keep it clean for their guests. But if you have to cross private property to get to that beach, permission is necessary. Everyone has a right to use the beaches, but please help keep it clean for others too.

New residents to the islands will likely frequent the beaches as much as possible, but believe it or not, this novelty will wear off, as you either enjoy different recreation, or your back-yard pool. The longer you live here, the

more you will find that even you will think the water temperature is colder in the winter months. The water is in fact about 10 degrees cooler in the winter months. For local divers that means using a shorty wetsuit! Snorkelers feel comfortable in a lycra suit or, even a t-shirt to prevent some sunburn and to keep a little warmer. The sun is still at its strongest between

10 a.m. and 2 p.m. That's because we are closer to the Equator here. Just like vacations, don't overdo it, always wear good sunblock, and a hat. Take a break and sit in the shade. Sun reflection from ocean and sand can give you a faster burn that you may not realize until later. Ouch! You'd probably rather not want to look for the Aloe!

Everyone always asks locals where their favorite beaches are. You will get mixed reviews, because every island has its share of great beaches. On St. Croix check out beaches at: Tamarind Reef Hotel, Chenay Bay Beach Resort, Cramer Park, Divi Resort (east end southshore), Hotel on The Cay, Club St. Croix, Hibiscus Beach Hotel, The Palms (formerly Cormorant Beach Hotel) (north side), Cane Bay Beach, Carambola Beach Resort, and all the sandy beaches along the shore at the west end. On St. John, National Geographic says Trunk Bay is one of the most beautiful beaches in the world. Residents frequent: Hawksnest, Cinnamon Bay or Francis Bay. St. Thomas' Magens Bay is the most favored by locals and tourists, while east enders prefer Secret Harbor, Coki Point or Sapphire. Local swimming associations offer lessons for infants through adults. On St. Croix call the Swimming Association at 719-7946. They sponsor the local Dolphins swim team. On St. Thomas call 779-7872. For St. John call the V.I. National Parks 776-6201.

Shell Collecting

While shell collecting has been a favorite pastime of many over the years, one may soon come to realize that it can dwindle the resources, and those pretty shells you might want to take home in a suitcase, or to your residence here, will soon smell if not cleaned properly. While some like to collect souvenirs and some scientists like to collect "live specimens", legal clarification on what can or can't be taken should be queried with the Department of Planning and Natural Resources. Beachcombers should be conservative. An old saying holds true, "take nothing but pictures, leave nothing but footprints."

Snorkeling

The United States Virgin Islands of St. Croix, St. John and St. Thomas were listed in the SCUBA Diving Magazine's Readers Choice Awards as "one of the finest spots in the world for snorkeling" (and SCUBA diving too!) There is great beauty and fascination under the waves here. If you didn't bring your own snorkel gear, check out the many local dive shops to buy your own personal gear, or rent it. They would be the best place to start either for quick lessons or for advice on the best places just to snorkel. There are techniques for beach diving, like either putting your fins on near the water's edge and walking backwards, or walking in waist deep and slipping your fins on there. As for the mask, one must either use a defog rinse, or spit into the mask and rinse it around. You want a clear mask to see everything. You can float along the surface and just breathe out of your snorkel, but if your snorkel goes below the surface you should leave enough air in your lungs to blow out the water in your snorkel when you surface.

Dive shops will tell you what not to touch underwater. They also stress not removing any souvenirs. Leave something for the next person to see and try not to disturb the eco-system. The best thing is to float, not stand, on any of the coral heads since they are pretty delicate and can be crushed. It is always recommended to swim with a buddy. If you can't, stay close to the shore and avoid any place with a current. Try not to touch anything because it can leave a substance on your fingers which may result in itchiness or even being poisonous. Don't step on those spiny sea urchins, and be careful of yellow hard coral with white trim. That's fire coral and it can burn the skin.

If you should cut yourself on coral, wash with soap and water as soon as possible. Infections develop more easily in a warmer climate so apply antiseptic cream as soon as possible. For stings, neutralize the cut with ammonia, baking soda or a piece of papaya.

If you have an open cut, stay out of the water. Do not drag around your "catch of the day". Curious barracuda are attracted by smell, as well as shiny objects like jewelry. Also, when the water is warmer, jellyfish may drift through the waters. If you have an allergic reaction from any of these type of stings, see a doctor immediately.

Diving

Crystal clear waters with visibility up to 100-feet invites the new diver to learn about exploring its depth, and the experienced to add to their diving log. With thousands of coral reefs, rocky pinnacles, drop offs and ledges, the Caribbean Sea especially around these three islands, are home to an abundance of marine life and shipwrecks. For a lot of vacationers it is the number one reason to visit. *Diving Magazines* rate the clear, azure waters of the Virgin Islands as the *"most beautiful in the world for diving"*. Take lessons from some of the finest instructors in the Caribbean. If you can swim, you can dive. If you like the water, you can learn how to dive. Each of the three Virgin Islands offers its own unique spots for diving and they all have great dive shops who know their areas well. For a fascinating experience in this undersea world, take an introductory SCUBA diving course from any of the local dive shops. They teach to national and world standards and will walk you through the basics step by step from the pool to the beach, to a boat dive. You will soon discover the sea gardens that boast a myriad of flora and fauna, sea fans, feather dusters, colorful fish, reefs, slopes, walls, crevices, canyons and shipwrecks. After a resort course, advanced certification courses can be obtained. All instructors here promote safety for yourself and the environment. They enforce "take pictures and leave nothing but bubbles". For safety's sake there is much to learn before you go off on your own. (Of course, never dive alone, but always with a buddy.) You should especially learn about which sea life can sting. If you are certified, the local shops will rent you gear. Please use them as dive guides because they know the areas. They fly the red with white diagonal diver down flag, or the blue/white alpha flag to warn boaters that divers are in the area. You should fly one if you are diving from a float. Each of these Virgin Islands has its own great diving spots. St. Croix has wall, wreck and reef diving. St. Thomas is more flat, with great reefs and shipwrecks. St. John has great reef diving, and the St. Thomas/St. John dive shops will take you on certain days to great diving in the British Virgin Islands, especially to the wreck of the Rhone.

For **St. Croix** wall diving visit Cane Bay Dive Shop 718-9913, (1-800-338-3843) www.canebayscuba.com on the north shore right at the wall. They have other locations too: Cane Bay West, Strand Street, Frederiksted; Cane Bay East, the Pan Am Mall, Christiansted; Cane Bay Dive Shop, Divi Carina Bay Resort.

Many of the most exciting wall diving is off the north shore at Cane Bay, Annaly Bay, Davis Bay, North Star, and Salt River East and West Wall. See Anchor Dive 778-1522 at Salt River to get to that site quicker. The Frederiksted Pier is known for its abundance of sea life, for you are apt to find: seahorses, Christmas tree worms, sponges, puffer fish, trumpet fish and needle nose fish. You can't dive when cruise ships are in. This pier is also very popular for night diving. To the south of the Pier, Kings Reef reveals a gentle slope full of corals, fans and sponges. To give you an idea of the depth of the slope, several hundred feet off the western shore near Frederiksted, the U.S. Navy used to conduct submarine and airplane night detection training. There are several dive shops in Frederiksted, at the west end, to assist with rentals, and boat diving, or a snorkel guide tour. Check out: N2Blue 772-DIVE or at www.N2blue.com.

Most of them have boats to take you to wrecks at Ham's Bluff. West end shore diving usually has calmer water then the rest of the island's shores. The Christiansted dive shops are: Dive Experience, 773-3307, 1111 Strand St., or at www.divexp.com, and SCUBA 773-5994 or at www.stcroixscuba.com. The dive shops in St. Croix, in conjunction with a group called the Island Conservation Effort, established mooring areas around and near the dive sites. Those mooring sites, Scotch Banks, Eagle Ray, Cormorant Reef, Luv Shack, and win Anchors (to name a few), were set up to prevent damage to the reefs by not anchoring just anywhere. There are over 60 moorings to dive, both on the west end and north shore. The The **Buck Island National Monument** offers extra crystal clear water and is marked by signs on an underwater trail to identify local flora, fauna and fish. Contact Caribbean Sea Adventures at 773-2628 to visit this site, and also Big Beard's Adventure Tours at 773-4482.

St. John's shallow water diving is excellent at **Watermelon Cay** and **Stevens Cay.** The underwater trail at **Trunk Bay** offers an abundance of coral formations and marine life. There is a small reef in the middle of **Salt Pond**, with an array of marine life, sure to be a snorkelers delight. The rocky ledges at **Carvel Rock** are decorated with gorgonians, seawhips and sponges. Some of the dive shops to contact there are: Low Key Water-sports 693-8999 and Cruz Bay Watersports 776-6234.

St. Thomas boasts the best wreck diving at: the **Grain Wreck, General Rogers**, and several others. On the north side, popular dive sites include **Outer Brass, Hans Lollick, Thatch Cay** and **Coki Beach**. Off the south side, you will find good diving at **Fortuna Beach, Sail Rock, Cow** and **Calf, French Cap Cay and Caverns, Capella Island**, the **Ledges at Little St. James,** and the **Stragglers at Great St. James.** Contact some of the dive shops on St. Thomas for more information: St. Thomas Dive Club 776-2381 at Bolongo Beach Resort; Hi-Tec Watersports 774-5650; Dive In at Sapphire Beach Resort 777-5255 and Aqua Action 775-6285 at Secret Harbor.

Boating

Whether you are an old salt or a novice, under power or sail, boating in the U.S. Virgin Islands offers spectacular sparkling waters, cozy anchorages, tradewinds and plenty of little islands to visit. Sheltered bays dotted with palm trees, and white sandy beaches invite you to drop anchor. This part of the Caribbean is a favorite cruising ground. St. Croix, the biggest island, offers good anchorages in both Christiansted and Frederiksted harbors. Buck Island Reef National Monument, just a few miles north of St. Croix, has an underwater national park with fabulous snorkeling, swimming and anchor sites. Getting into Christiansted harbor especially at night can be very tricky. While there are channel markers and buoys, there are many shallow reefs surrounding this area. From St Thomas, head up the Pillsbury Sound, going east, into the sheltered Windward Passage between St. John and Jost Van Dyke to the stellar anchorages in the British Virgin Islands.

If you are a novice boater, take a boating safety course from the U.S. Power Squadron or U.S. Coast Guard Auxiliary. While these waters and islands are all too inviting, let the sailor beware that dangerous squalls can come up fast.

On the average, swells run from one to five feet; waves are one to three feet and the wind up to 20 knots. In the winter, the winds blow from east to northeast with northerly swells. While in the summer, the wind shifts south to east to southeast with swells from the south.

As with any large investment, try before you buy. Sail with friends, charter, or visit boat yards to see what's available. Check the classifieds, and also *Triton, All at Sea* and *Island Trader.* If you find a "favorite boat" back home, arrangements can be made with them, or locals, to set up a delivery crew. Learn to sail at Jones Maritime, St. Croix, 773-4709.

Call the U.S. Coast Guard Auxiliary at 714-2861 in St. Thomas for a free safety check of your boat. They will advise you as to what needs to be fixed up. Other useful numbers are the Resident Inspection Office on St. Croix 772-5557, and St. Thomas, 776-3497.

Since there were not any pump-out stations anywhere in the territory, The Department of Planning and Natural Resources worked with marinas to ensure their installation. At the present time, there are pump-out stations at several marinas on both islands, or boats can go beyond the three-mile limit to empty their holding tanks.

If you sail into the U.S. Virgin Islands on a vessel registered on the mainland or in a foreign country, you can cruise for 60 days without registering here. You can anchor for 14 days in any one bay. If you want to stay longer, you must apply for an anchoring permit at the DPNR. Anchoring permits run $2 a foot per month. If you want a mooring, you must apply to the DPNR. Mooring fees are $5.00 per foot per year. They will pro-rate your registration fee since all boats must register in June. Noncommercial boats pay $25 under 16 feet, $50 for boats 16 to 25 feet, $100 for boats 26 to 39 feet, $150 for boats 40 to 65 feet, and $200 for boats over 65 feet. Commercial vessels pay $37.50 under 16 feet, $75 for boats 16 to 25 feet, $150 for boats 26 to 39 feet, $225 for boats 40 to 65 feet, and $300 for boats over 65 feet. Call DPNR at 773-5774 in St. Croix, or 774-3320 in St. Thomas for more information.

Charts

Charts from the U.S. Coast and Geodetic Survey will help you find your way around these islands. All marine stores sell selected charts, but Brad Glidden Charts and Books at Caribbean Inflatable Service has the most complete selection in St.

Photo by Sam Halvorson, Dive Experience

Thomas, and in St. Croix see St. Croix Marine. Christiansted Harbor - No. 25645, Frederiksted Roadsted - No. 25644, Pillsbury Sound (St Thomas/St. John) - No. 25647, St. Thomas Harbor - No. 25649, Virgin Islands - No. 25649, Virgin Passage, Culebra, Vieques - No. 25650, Culebra - No. 25653, Puerto Rico - U.S. Virgin Islands - No. 25640, British Virgin Islands and Anegada - No. 25609, Roadtown Harbor, British Virgin Islands - No. 25611, Virgin Gorda, British Virgin Islands - No. 25610

Marinas

On St. Croix, boats can be docked at St.Croix Marine,Green Cay Marina or the Salt River Marina. Permanent moorings are allowed in Christiansted and Frederiksted harbors, Chenay Bay, Cotton Garden Bay, Salt River and Teague Bay. St. Croix Marina, a full service marina has a marine railway and a 60-ton travel lift, and is the only place to haul your boat. You will find launching ramps at Altona Lagoon in Christiansted, and at the foot of Fisher Street in Frederiksted; also at Cane Bay and the Great Salt pond, and several coves along the southshore.

There is no boat docking in St. John. Permanent moorings are permitted only in Cruz Bay, Great Cruz Bay, Chocolate Hole, Coral Bay or Johnson Bay. The Friends of the National Park organization have set up more than 200 moorings in National Park waters around St. John to protect coral reefs and sea habitats from anchor damage.There is a small marine store near

the Coral Bay dinghy dock St. John Hardware near the Enighed Pond should have a small selection of marine parts. All Coral Bay is a launching ramp. Currently the Virgin Islands National Park will not allow boaters to use the Park's launching ramp in Cruz Bay. (Check if that has changed.)

On St. Thomas, Crown Bay Marina in Subbase, Saga Haven Independent Boat Yard, Compass Point Marina, American Yacht Harbor Yacht Haven Grande Marina, Pirates Cove Marina, Frenchtown Marina CYOA and Sapphire Marina have dock space. Permanent mooring is permitted at Elephant Bay, Honeymoon Bay, Flamingo Bay Frenchtown/Villa Olga, Careening Cove, Long Bay, Hull Bay, Bolonge Bay, Jersey Bay, Benner Bay, Compass Point, Secret Harbour, Vessup Bay and Red Hook in St. Thomas.

To haul your boat call Haulover Marine in Subbase or Independent Boat yard at the Benner Bay Lagoon. Gas and water is available at Crown Bay Saga Haven and American Yacht Harbor. The new Yacht Haven Grande

Marina is another place to get fuel and water. Trailer boaters can launch their craft from shore at Red Hook, Magens Bay, Hull Bay or Crown Bay. The Virgin Islands Port Authority will allow small boats to tie up for a few hours without charge, space permitting, at its harbor facilities on all three islands, but check with them first. You should leave a dinghy ashore since there is no launch service.

Visit www.vimarineguide.com for information on marine industry and services. Some useful numbers for boaters are: St. Croix Power Squadron, 778-5247 / 719-9686, St. Thomas Power Squadron, 774-3320, Coast Guard Auxiliary, 998-9227.

Yacht Clubs

St. Croix Yacht Club at Teague Bay offers club privileges and guest memberships to visiting boaters. Racers gather at the Yacht Club for the prestigious St. Croix International Regatta over President's Day, and the winner takes home their weight in Cruzan Rum! The course is laid out between the Yacht Club, Buck Island and, at times, through Christiansted Harbor, permitting a great view of the race for spectators situated in town and along the north shore of the island.

They encourage members to participate in inter-island racing and also teach Junior sailing. These young sailors often participate in Opti, Laser and Sunfish Regattas on other islands, the mainland, or even internationally. For further info call the St. Croix Yacht Club at 773-9531.

While there are no yacht club facilities in St. John, the **St. John Yacht Club** and the **Coral Bay Yacht Club** do have meetings. Call Skinny Legs Bar and Restaurant at 779-4982, for Coral Bay Club info or Connections at 779-4994 for St. John Club info. The clubs sponsor the annual Thanksgiving Weekend Regatta which draws casual and serious racers.

The **St. Thomas Yacht Club** at Vessup Bay provides reciprocity to visiting yacht club members. On Easter weekends, or close to that timeframe, the club hosts the acclaimed Rolex Cup Regatta, which draws competitors from the States and all over the Caribbean. St. Thomas has top-notch sailor Peter Holmberg who has participated in many world-wide races such as the America's Cup. For further info call them at 775-6320.

Chartering

To experience boating first hand, charter a boat, with captain and crew, or bareboat, by yourself and friends. That of course means you do the navigating, swab the decks and cook. For a little more dollars, you can let someone else do all the work while you relax on deck or jump in for a snorkel .You can sign up for a day or for a week. There are many charter companies and different size boats available for small or large groups. Check with tourist publications, or your travel agent, or for a spur of the moment trip, walk along the dock and see who is in port. For further information call the Virgin Islands Charter Yacht League in St. Thomas at 774-3944, at Yacht Haven Grande www.vicl.org, or any of the three marinas on St. Croix: St. Croix Marine, 773-0289; Green Cay Marina 718-1453; Salt River Marina 778-9650. The Spring Charter Yacht show is May in St. Thomas with a much larger show in November to kick off the season.

Fishing

The fishing waters in the U.S. Virgin Islands are considered some of the finest in the world for tuna, marlin, sailfish, kingfish and wahoo. You will find lots of challenges whether you fish from the family yacht, a chartered fishing boat or a rented runabout. Major fishing tournaments, in the Johnny Harms' Tournament Series, are held annually on St. Thomas July through October. The tournaments in the Johnny Harms' Series include three Billfish events in St. Thomas, one in the British Virgin Islands, one in Puerto Rico and, The Golden Hook Challenge in St. Croix. For information on the tournaments in St. Thomas call American Yacht Harbor at 775-6454, or the V.I. Fishing Game Club at 775-9144.

The Golden Hook Challenge, held in late February, is one of four annual St. Croix tourneys. The three other Crucian tournaments include: the Dolphin Tournament, mid-April; the Guy/Gal Reel Challenge, early October; and the Wahoo tournament, ocurring in late November. Call 778-0487 for information on Crucian sport fishing.

In St. Croix, championship marlin, yellow fin tuna or wahoo can usually be found several hundred feet off the north shore, along the northeast corner to the southeast corner of Lang Bank (extending nearly 15 miles). The drop off near Sandy Point just south of Frederiksted is also a popular spot. Local fishing professionals will tell you to go out about a half mile and drop your line.

About ten miles north of St. Thomas and St. John, head for the famous North Drop to look for blue and white marlin, wahoo, sailfish, dolphin and yellow fin tuna. About 20 miles north of St. John and St. Thomas is the Puerto Rico trench, at 25,000 feet the second deepest trench in the Atlantic ocean. Ten miles south of St. John and St. Thomas, is the south drop, another popular spot. Reefs closer to shore are where you can find smaller fish like bonito, rainbow runner, jack, grouper, snapper and mackerel. Check tourist publications or the hotel bulletin boards to see who is going out.

You won't need a license from DPNR to fish with hook and line or your bare hands. You do need one to use a net or trap. Spearfishing is prohibited in any of the Virgin Islands National park waters. Commercial fishermen will need a license.

You can fish for conch in local Virgin Islands National Park waters from July 1 to October 30. The take is six per day and they must be mature adults. Fines can be high. The whelk season runs October 1 through March 30. They must be more than 2-1/2 inches in diameter.

It is against the law to take or bother sea turtles or their eggs. Turtle meat will not be found on the market because it is illegal to sell or import. The U.S. Fish &Wildlife Service has ruled that even if it is grown in captivity, it still is on the endangered species list. Lobsters must measure 3-1/2 inches long along the carapace and you can take an unlimited number from local waters. Within the boundaries of the Virgin Islands National Park waters, you can take two but they must be captured in ways that will not injure them, whether by hand, trap or noose. Females with eggs cannot be taken at any time. The DPNR environmental enforcement division issues commercial fishing licenses for the skipper and each crew member at $5 a year. Each commercial fisherman chooses a color code patch for his boat, traps and other gear to assist in identification and enforcement.

Spearfishing

Spearfishing is popular everywhere but prohibited within the waters of the Virgin Islands National Park. Virgin Islanders hold about 30 world records including: speedy prey such as mackerel, kingfish, snapper, pompano, and sharks over 200 pounds!

Golf

On St. Croix, residents and visitors can play at the Buccaneer Hotel Golf Course, the Carambola Golf and Tennis Club or the Reef Condominium Golf Course. The uphill third hole overlooking the ocean at the Buccaneer Course offers a real challenge. This 18-hole course and provides rental equipment and carts. Stop by the 19th Hole bar for post-game refreshments. Call their Pro Shop at 773-2100 for reservations. Nestled among the lush hills of the rain forest, Carambola Golf and Tennis Club is home to an 18-hole Robert Trent Jones world-class championship course You might find a well known golfer teeing off, since it is a popular tournament spot and hosts an annual LPGA Tournament in the Spring. Its facilities include a pro shop with equipment rentals and fashions, a restaurant, and an after-golf bar overlooking a spectacular view. For tee times call 778-5638.

On St. Croix's East End, the nine-holed Reef Golf Course is a nice warm-

Carambola Golf and Tennis Club

up for spot for pros or a fine course for the less ambitious golfer, as its 568-yard, par-five, 5th hole can be a challenge. Call 773-8844 to reserve. Also on the East End, check out The Links Miniature Golf Course by Divi Resorts.

In St. Thomas, set amid a beautiful valley and coastal cliffs, the Mahogany Run Golf Course is tough, particularly at Devile's Triangle, three Hellish seaside holes where golfballs frequently sail over the edge. The golf course has a pro shop with equipment rentals and lessons. Visit Mr. Bogie's 19th hole bar. Call 777-6006 to make the required reservations. The University of the Virgin Islands in St.Thomas has a nine-hole golf course situated alongside the road that runs through the campus. It is mainly a practice course, with no amenities and golfers can play any time.

Hiking

There is good hiking on all three islands. In St. Croix, you can hike through the rain forest, Salt River National Park, or along many beautiful beaches. You can also walk along specifically marked trails on Buck Island. In St. John, the Virgin Islands National Park has many maintained trails winding through the vegetation and ruins of old plantations. In St. Thomas you can hike along the north side and to the beach for spectacular views. Views looking north and east are the best. Read "A Walking Guide to the Caribbean" by Leonard M. Adkins for some tips. Here are some numbers to call for information. The National Parks service., St. Croix - 773-1460 St. or the Virgin Islands National Park, St. Thomas/ St. John 776-6201.

Tennis

In planning a tennis match remember it is hotter at midday. Most people like to play early morning, or later in the afternoon after work. Most major hotels in the territory have tennis courts. There are fees for playing and for lessons. Hotels charge around $18 per court per hour, daytime, and $22 per court per hour at night for guests, and $9 per person per hour daytime, and $11 per person per hour at night for non-guests. Lessons are about $70 an hour and $36 for a half hour. Check with local hotels, or their pro shop to sign up. In St. Croix at the Buccaneer Hotel call Don de Wilde at 773-3036. The Buccaneer has annual memberships at $295 single, $525 family. (Fees quoted above are from The Buccaneer).

The local government's Parks and Recreation Department operates public courts in St. Croix at the D.C. Canegata Ball Park, call 773-3850; and at the Isaac Boynes Park, Sion Farm Park, and Stoney Ground Park near the old fort in Frederiksted. The public courts are on a first-come, first-serve basis. In St. John, the Parks and Recreation Department operates public courts across from the Fire Station in Cruz Bay, on a first-come, first serve basis.

In St. Thomas, the Parks and Recreation Department operates public courts at Subbase and Bordeaux on a first-come, first-service basis. Here are some numbers to help you get oriented with tennis in the Virgin Islands. The V.I. Tennis Association President William McComb can be reached at 774-8457 in St. Thomas. The association has trained junior and Davis Cup teams, and is affiliated with the United States Tennis Association, as well as the International Tennis Federation. There is a private tennis club on St Croix at 773-0055.

Baseball/Softball

From Little League for boys and girls, to softball for men, girls and women, to baseball for young men and the over 40s crowd, baseball/softball is one of the most organized and popular sports in the U.S. Virgin Islands. Major league players on vacation often conduct clinics to introduce the game to the kids on the islands. Virgin Islander Horace Clarke of New York Yankees fame and former Pittsburgh Pirates player Elmo Plaskett (since deceased) worked in St. Croix to give youths a shot at the big time. For more information call the V.I. Baseball Federation at 772-1570.

Basketball

Basketball has been a strong sport for a long time, producing such top notch players as Tim Duncan (San Antonio Spurs) and Raja Bell, helping to put the Virgin Islands on the national sports map.

Since 2000, the University of the Virgin Islands has been hosting the USVI Annual Paradise Jam, a pre-season College Basketball Tournament for women and men. Participating colleges over the years have included Duke, Rutgers, Notre Dame and Georgetown. The event is usually held in late November.

Olympics

The U.S. Virgin Islands Olympic Committee puts together a V.I. National Team for the Caribbean Central American Games, the Pan American Games and the Summer/Winter Olympics. The committee represents 22 sports federations from across the territory. While most participants compete in warm-weather sports, the Committee sends a bobsled team to the Winter Olympics. The V.I. Olympic Committee has boasted numerous medal winning athletes in Olympic games since its inception in 1966.

In 2002 the Olympic Committee sent the first black women Olympians to compete in luge events. The Virgin Islands has been sending a Winter Olympic team to events since 1988 with the first black woman skier.

In 2008 the USVI had athletes competing in the Beijing Summer Olympics in boxing, sailing, swimming, track and field, and one shooter. They competed in the Central American Games in 2010 at Mayaguez, Puerto Rico, in about 12 sports. Four local athletes qualified for the 2010 Winter Olympics in Vancouver, Canada for the Skeleton. They practiced in Austria for the Skeleton – similar to the feet-first luge, except a slightly smaller sled and head first.

Most recently, the territory has sent seven Olympians to London in the summer of 2012 to compete in laser sailing; 100, 200, and 400-meter track;100-meter freestlyle swimming; and the triple jump. For more information on Committees call Hans Lawaetz at 778-2229 or 719-VIOC or log on to: http://www.virginislandsolympics.com

Track and Field

The Virgin Islands Track and Field Federation is the governing body for the sport of track and field. The disciplines include: Track running, field events. road running, cross-country running, race walking and mountain running) in the Virgin Islands. The Federation is the Virgin Island's affiliate to the International Association of Athletic Federations (IAAF), the world governing body and the Virgin Island's Olympic Committee.

The Federation implements the development of the sport including athletes of all ages for competition on V.I. national teams in local, regional and world championships to include: the Central American and Caribbean Games, the Pan American Games and the Olympic Games. The Federation facilitates the certification of coaches, technical officials and insures the continuity of the sport in the Virgin Islands. Contact: the V.I. Track & Field Federation at 340-643-2557. Log on to: http://virginislandspace.org

Running

The Virgin Islands Pace Runners organizes over 20 road races and related running events annually. The events are for the fitness-minded, recreational and competitive runners. There are road races, track races,cross-country races and beach runs for participants of all ages and levels of fitness. Some of these events also serve as fundraisers and charity events. Distances for the events range from the mile to the marathon. V.I. Pace Runners produces an annual Virgin Islands Running Calendar. Contact V.I. Pace Runners at 340-643- 2557, 778-8255 St Croix, or 340-777-0258. St. Thomas. Log on to: http://virginislandspace.org

Government Sports Facilities

The local government runs a summer youth program which includes: baseball, basketball, track, softball, soccer, swimming, cooking and dancing. The staff also runs the sport activities at the various recreation facilities. Below is listed the recreation facilities on all three islands.

St. Croix

All parks listed can be contacted and events scheduled through the main number of Parks and Recreation 773-0271 or 773-0160 and Canegata Ball Park 773-5588 or 773-3850. All parks are open daily at 8:00 a.m., but the recreation leaders are there

Cultural Tidbit

St. Croix is home to the annual Ironman 70.3, one of the world's premiere destination triathlon's—and a virtual local holiday. Triathletes begin the course at Hotel on the Cay, where they dive into the warm, clear Caribbean for a 1.24-mile swim. Rising from the sea at Christiansed Harbor, they then begin a 56-mile bicycle course that winds through the island's north and soutshores and features a grueling steeply sloped hill known as "the beast." The cherry atop this exhausting race is a 13.1 mile run that finishes in the town of Christiansted. Top finishers can qualify for Ironman Hawaii or the Ironman 70.3 World Championship.

from 1:00 p.m. to 9:00 p.m. Cramer's Park Beach 773-9696; Issac Boynes Complex: (Grove Place) baseball, basketball, tennis, softball, tot play area, bandstand, board games, billiards, table tennis and restrooms. D.C. Canegata Complex: baseball, volleyball, softball, tennis, basketball, restrooms, lights, bleachers, tot play area. A building for games, exercise classes. (east of Christiansted); Campo Rico: Basketball and tot play area. Horace Clarke Complex: baseball, basketball, handball, tennis; Cramer Park: beach, picnic area, camping, restrooms, volleyball. Pedro Cruz Complex: (at Estate Profit), softball, bleachers, restrooms, lights, basketball and playground area 778-4369. Fort Frederik: basketball, tennis, volleyball, tot play area, lights, beach, picnic area. Estate Glynn: tot play area, picnic and basketball; Renholdt Jackson Complex: softball, volleyball, tot play area, football, basketball, field and restrooms. (Estate Whim); Paul E. Joseph Stadium: F'sted. Facilities are currently being renovated. Rudy Kriegger Complex: softball, basketball, soccer, tennis courts, handball courts, tot play area, shaded benches, picnic tables and restrooms 719-9223. (Sion Farm); LaValle Complex: softball, picnic area, tennis, jogging and basketball, upgraded Recreation Center in 2008. Terence Martin Field: softball Mon Bijou/Frangipanni rec park: softball, basketball and picnic area. Winston Mason Pool Resort (Frederiksted - west end, beach area): junior olympic salt water pool, open 9-5 playground, picnic tables, table games.

St. Thomas

Number for all Sports, Parks and Recreation: 774-0255 Joseph Aubain Ball Park (Frenchtown): softball, Little League, Ladies League, 774-9477; Bordeaux: tennis, basketball, tot play area; Emile Griffith Park (Charlotte Amalie): basketball, softball, tot play area and games, 775-6435; Frydenhoj: basketball, softball; Kirwan Terrace Complex (Lindbergh Bay): basketball, volleyball, baseball, 775-7363; Alvin McBean Complex (Tutu): softball, Little League baseball, tennis, basketball, handball and paddle ball, 775-7183; Mandahl: basketball Nadir (Bovoni): softball and basketball and horse race-track; Winston Raymo Complex (Charlotte Amalie) basketball, indoor recreation, baseball, paddleball, handball and tot area, 774-2640; Lionel Roberts Stadium (Charlotte Amalie): baseball, softball, cricket, boxing shows, high school football, soccer and concerts. Savan: basketball Lionel "Smut" Richards (Smith Bay): softball, basketball (Little League) Subbase (Charlotte Amalie): tennis, handball and paddleball.

St. John

General # for Sports, Parks & Recreation, 776-6531 Coral Bay: baseball, basketball, tot play area; Cruz Bay: tennis, basketball, softball; Little League Park (Cruz Bay): baseball and tot area; Pine Peace: basketball and volleyball Winston Wells Park (Cruz Bay): baseball and softball.

Horse Racing

The Randall "Doc" James Race Track, near the airport is home to a favorite pastime of Crucians. The track hosts monthly races and a simulcast room where thoroughbreds, greyhounds, and harness races are broadcast 365 days a year, rain or shine. (713-7228) www.stcroixracetrack.com (slots will be added for entertainment soon). On St.Thomas check out the Clinton E. Phipps Race Track (ask locals).

Firearms and Hunting

Sports Federations/Associations (All area code 340)	
Baseball: V.I. Federation, Dennis Brow	332-3827
Basketball: V.I. Basketball, Senator Usie Richards	772-9524
Bowling: V.I. Bowling Federation, Ronald Moorehead	
Boxing: St. Thomas Amateur Boxing Fed. Jose Rosario	227-3158
Cycling: V.I. Cycling Federation, Scott Fricks	513-8281
Equestrian: V.I. Equestrian, Virginia Angus	773-0289
Hiking: St. Croix Hiking Association	772-2073
Running: VI Pace Runners , Wallace Williams	643-2557
Soccer: V.I. Soccer Federation, Derrick Martin	719-0037
Softball: V.I. Softball Federation, Warren Brooks	718-7026
Swimming: V.I. Swimming Federation, Brent Mayes	773-7374
Track & Field: VI Track & Field Federation – W. Williams	643-2557
Triathlons: Ironman 70.3, other local, Scott Fricks	513-8281

To own a gun, you must have a Public Safety Department permit. In order to get this, the department will conduct a background search. To carry a gun or keep it at your business, you need an additional permit, for which must submit your business license when applying.

If you try to bring a gun into the territory with other personal effects, it will be confiscated. Weapons must be declared to the U.S.Customs inspector, who will request that you leave the gun in police custody until your permit comes through. If you plan to purchase a gun here, don't go shopping until you have your permit. Perhaps leave your gun behind with a licensed firearm dealer till you have one. He can then ship the weapon to you. Call 774-2211, ext. 5563 for information.

Hunting is allowed for mountain doves, and white-tailed deer with bag limits in season, dictated by DPNR. The season for dove and duck hunting is set by the U.S. Fish and Wildlife and is September and December. No hunting is permitted within the boundaries of the National Parks or in the Virgin Islands Wildlife Refuges.

Wild Life

While there are not many species of wildlife on isolated tropical islands, you will see a small furry, speedy critter known as the mongoose. Heavily populated on St. Croix (the mongoose capital of the world), mongoose are

about the size of a squirrel and were first imported by plantation owners years ago to keep down the rat population in the cane fields. But since the mongoose loves sunshine and rats are nocturnal, their paths seldom crossed. You might also see "shy" tiny deer in the bush. They are popular to St. Croix and St. Thomas. You might even find a variety of insect, fruit or fish-eating bats.

A variety of birds stateside keep bugs in check, but in these islands it is the lizards! There are two different groups of these. In the daytime the Anoles, like chameleons, change color from green to brown (to match their background), and prowl everywhere to nab bugs. But in the evening hours they leave this prowling to the Gecko, a chunkier lizard with fat toes effective for climbing. The Gecko's eyes are like cats eyes with a vertical pupil. These two breeds average 3 to 6 inches and are totally harmless to humans. If one happens to get inside your house, remember they are afraid of you. One of the best ways to catch one is to chase them into a pot, put the lid on it, then drop them back outside! Another type of little lizard, a striped one, the Ameiva, lives on St. Croix, mostly at Hotel on the Cay. No cats or dogs are allowed there in order to protect this endangered specie. While the lizards mentioned above live on all three islands, there seems to be more of them on St. Croix, and more iguanas on St. Thomas.

The big iguana (see photo above) still inhabits some parts of these islands. They are vegetarian and range from bright green, as a juvenile, to a grassy brown. In less populated areas, you will see them sunning themselves along roadsides midday or in trees on long heavy branches. Some hotels have a few in their ponds as pets. Do keep an eye out for them because they may try to cross the road in front of a car. Any snakes are the small harmless types that combat bug problems and are rarely seen.

Birds

The most common and visible bird here is the snowy egret. Often called the "cattle" egret, snowy egrets perch on the backs of cows or horses to feed on insects. Also very popular, and native to most islands, are the yellow and black bananaquits and green hummingbirds. To welcome bananaquits (sometimes called sugar birds) to your home, merely put out a saucer of sugar or sugar water. Related to honey-creepers, bananaquits are year-round residents. To attract hummingbirds, buy a feeder for them locally. The pearly- eyed thrashers, known as trushees by locals, are bigger pests.They resemble a dirty brown robin and might eat food off your plate if you aren't careful.

An avid birdwatcher would recognize the Mockingbird, Kestrel (called Chicken Hawks here) and Red-tailed hawks. The Lesser Antillean Bull Finch has migrated northward and now makes the U.S. Virgin Islands its home. The male is a small black bird with red under its chin and rust under the tail. The female is brown with a speck of rust under her tail. The smooth-billed big black ani resembles a parrot's profile.You will notice the slate and white kingbirds that chatter loudly from telephone wires as they grab bugs mid-air. Along roadsides you will find zenaida doves (resembling mourning doves) and smaller ground doves as they bob along the dirt in search of insects.Herons and egrets can be seen walking along the shore. The brown pelicans resting on boats or dock pilings are very entertaining as they dive bomb the waters in search of fish. Frigate birds somewhat resemble Japanese kites. They tend to hover from overhead, where they patiently wait to pounce on birds with prey in their beaks.

Life in the tropics is unique. The beautiful blue waters, the tropical vegetation, the great climate, trade winds, and multitude of experiences, provide a beautiful and wondrous playground for lovers of the outdoors.

Cutural Tidbit
by Dr. George Franklin

The Cocks Have Clocks . . . of their own: Be aware that roosters in these islands can sometimes crow "all day and all night Miss Maryann." Yes, it can be very irritating. However it seems like these rooster have a lot to crow about. Do like the locals do, show him a box with a picture of fried chicken. Hint, hint.

Sounds of The Chain Gang: At night you will hear the sounds of the crickets and the frogs "working on the chain gang." Don't worry be happy. You will soon become anesthetized to those sounds and after awhile it will grow on you . . . like everything else island.

Mongoose Dem: Do not attempt to pet the mongoose dem if you want to leave the islands with your fingers and toes connected to your body. These little critters can be very feisty.

Settler's Handbook Chapter 9

Business Climate... A Profile of Today

The official government of the United States Virgin Islands continues its territorial relationship with the government of the United States of America. While some residents desire statehood and others want greater autonomy, in the general election in October 1993, voters in the islands determined they were satisfied with their status as an un-incorporated United States Territory. The issue is expected to resurface in the future.

The general organization of the Virgin Islands government was created through the Revised Organic Act passed by the Congress in 1954 with some powers left in the hands of the Federal government. The affairs of the islands are controlled by the Governor and the Legislature.

In January 1993, the territory was given more responsibility when the courts in the islands took over jurisdiction from the Federal Government of major felonies.

The governor of the Virgin Islands has asked Congress for an increased return of excise taxes on products developed here. The move is seen as not only a way to develop more self-sufficiency for the islands but to also reduce the burden of Federal payments for services. The Federal government now returns over $72 million in excise taxes on St. Croix-made rum and this is expected to increase substantially in the next few years, not only with Cruzan Rum products but as stated earlier with Capt. Morgan Rum.

Like island nations in the Caribbean, the USVI is economically dependent on tourism. Assets, like special tax incentives, a duty-free status, foreign trade eligibility, good commercial rental rates, a marvelous climate and the security of the "Stars 'n Stripes", all add to a favorable business atmosphere,

While the economy is heavily dependent on tourism the territory seeks to diversify through further development of light to medium industry. With that in mind, the islands offer comprehensive tax benefits and a well-developed infrastructure that includes some of the finest ports, best roads and airports in the Caribbean. Furthermore, state-of-the-art telephone service enables almost instant communication with any point in the world.

And the Virgin Islands Water and Power Authority produces and distributes electricity and desalinated water from plants on all three islands.

The territory is well served by the U.S. Postal Service as well as UPS, Federal Express, and DHL Worldwide Express. Most businesses are open from 9 a.m. to 5 p.m. Monday through Friday. Retailers stay open Saturdays, and in some cases, Sundays. The local government operates from 8:00 a.m. to 5 p.m. Federal offices. U.S. Postal Service and banks close for all Federal holidays. Schools and government offices also close for all Federal and local holidays. For a comprehensive look at the business picture, contact the Economic Development Commission at 773-6499.

Tourism

As winter grasps North America, Virgin Islanders hope that tourists will flock here for island warmth and beauty. Seventy-eight percent of the hotel guests and 65 percent of cruise ship visitors come from the U.S. mainland. However, many come from all over the world.

A government bond issue was passed to address the specifics of revitalizing St. Croix as a tourist destination. The Bond issues identify several main areas for consideration: airport modernization, construction of a shopping area, King's Alley, and a Boardwalk, both on Christiansted Harbor are now complete, as is the airport. This also included renovation of Government House in Christiansted, and the renovation of Frederiksted as an authentic Danish West Indian town. The St. Croix Community Foundation in Christiansted receives block grants and Federal funding for renovation projects and has undertaken a lot of old building renovation in Christiansted. The Frederiksted Economic Development Authority, the PFA (Public Finance Authority) and Our Town Frederiksted have assisted with the revitalization of the Frederiksted and it's waterfront.

In a 1994 referendum, St. Croix voters, the only island interested, indicated they wanted casino gambling on their island to see if it would assist in the development of hotels and create jobs. While casino gambling will bring some tourists, most of them will likely view the pastime as an additional amenity like fine dining or fun shopping to go along with their day at the beach or the golf course. The first casino in the Virgin Islands, Divi Carina Bay Resort and Casino opened on St. Croix March of 2000, and a few more investors have applied for their licenses.

In an effort to improve its marketing strategy as a tourist destination, the V.I. government has recently started marketing each of the three islands for their own uniqueness and personality. The highly developed world class water sports industry namely boating and scuba diving and the number of quality hotels and restaurants combine to make the Virgin Islands an attractive destination. The government's promotional plan is to market and capitalize on each of these three islands' specific specialties.

St. Thomas, with its deep-water harbor, is the number one cruise ship destination in the world, with over a million passengers a year looking for great duty-free shopping. Tour companies are ready to whisk the passenger off for an island tour, beach tours, air tours, harbor tours, or Scuba diving. Its many beautiful hotels attract almost half a million visitors a year to enjoy the beaches and bargains in designer name shopping. You can find great prices in liquor, linens, electronics and jewelry. St. Thomas has upscale tourist attractions like Coral World with its Aquarium, and a tramway which runs above Charlotte Amalie. A must see is St. Peter's Great House, a renovated old estate house built on the side of a mountain, with a spectacular view and beautiful tropical gardens. It is available for tours and functions.

There are about 15 major hotels, 35 smaller hotels and guesthouses and some of the best world-class restaurants located on St.Thomas. A network of private homes and villas entices visitors to stay a week or several months during the winter. Check with the U.S. Virgin Islands Hotel & Tourism Association at 774-6835.

St. Croix's uniqueness exists in its old-world charm and the blending of the historical culture of seven different nations who governed her. Mix that charm and culture with the quaintness of Frederiksted's waterfront park, cosmopolitan Christiansted, the charming boutiques, the talented local craftsmen and artists, an array of outdoor activities (diving, sailing, kayaking, horseback riding, hiking, golfing), with a smothering of friendliness and relaxation, and you could discover an island like no other. St. Croix is known for its light industry, some agriculture, cozy bed & breakfasts, small hotels, nice beaches, top-notch restaurants, its culture heritage, its heritage trails and recently, a rekindling of the jazz spirit with the Blue Bay Jazz Festival in November held every few years. Call Landmarks Society at 772-0598 for its Heritage Trail Map.

St. John is three-quarter national park and boasts some of the most beautiful beaches in the world. Tourists visit St. John for its scenic beauty. It has two major hotels, the Westin and Caneel Bay, as well as a handful of small budget guesthouses and about 250 private luxury homes for rent. Two campgrounds, both within the Virgin Islands National Park, have covered campsites and nature-trail hiking. Cruise ships may stop at its west end town of Cruz Bay (en route to St. Thomas). Passengers are tendered in from the big ships to shop, dine and tour. At its east end, Coral Bay has blossomed with home construction and new settlers, creating a need for services. Make your first stop at Connections in Cruz Bay for the latest island happenings. They also have a store in Coral Bay.

Duty Free Status

The territory's free port status, a provision of the treaty between Denmark and the United States which accompanied the 1917 sale of the islands, is still in effect. This means the territory lies outside the U.S. Customs' zone, allowing goods to enter tax free regardless of where they originated. Otherwise, most countries, including the United States, impose import tariffs, or quotas to protect local industries. The islands are almost a true free port in that goods manufactured in the U.S. or its possessions enter duty free, while those from elsewhere are charged a low uniform rate of six percent. It is not the brand name which determines an object's duty-free status, but its country of origin. Comparable to other parts of the world, the Virgin Islands is a shopper's paradise with the duty-free prices available. However, pricing benefits for the consumer under this free port status are not as meaningful as they once were. Today's merchants and suppliers have to pay various taxes to the government on imports, excise taxes and gross receipt taxes, as well as take into consideration the cost of goods imported for resale and shipping costs. While there is no sales tax, these charges and expenses are included in the retail price of the goods. Thanks to U.S. Customs laws, residents and visitors returning to the U.S. can bring, or mail, $1,600 worth of goods per person duty-free. A family of four can bring $4,800 duty-free. That's a rate twice as high as the $800 allowed duty-free from other Caribbean countries and four times higher than the $400 allowed from most other countries. If you exceed the $1,600, you pay a flat rate of five percent on the next $1,000. For those who travel back and forth between the mainland and the U.S. Virgin Islands, remember that the $1,600 duty-free allowance can only be used once in a 30-day period. You can send as many gifts as you want to friends and relatives as long as you don't spend more than $100 a day for any one address. These do not have to be declared. U.S. citizens over 21 can enter the States with four litres of liquor as part of their $1,600 duty-free allowance; one extra if they are brands such as Cruzan Rum, which is produced in the U.S. Virgin Islands. U.S. citizens can also take home five cartons of cigarettes and 100 non-Cuban cigars per person.

Be sure to keep your sales slips or invoices for items purchased. Even though you have declared items you are shipping, when you re-enter the States, you will need proof of value for each package when your articles arrive. It would be wise to check with your local U.S. Customs office if you are planning to mail goods. All articles must be strictly for your personal use and not for re-sale. Goods made in the U.S. Virgin Islands are not included in the $1,600 allowance, but if any item is worth more than $25, you must fill out a Certificate of Origin form 3229 which is available where you purchased the items. You can take back those gorgeous Anthuriums you bought along the road, but check in advance with the U.S. Department of Agriculture to find out about the other flowers and vegetables you may have discovered during your visit.

There are also specific rules and regulations for importing animals. Here are the addresses for finding out what's allowed from FAPHIS (Federal Animal and Plant Health Inspection Service) regarding plant protection and animal quarantine. Henry E. Rohlsen Airport, St. Croix, VI 00820, 778-1696. Cyril E. King Airport, St. Thomas, VI 00801, 774-5719, Federal Bldg., Charlotte Amalie, St. Thomas 00801, 776-2787. *For the "ins" and "outs" of shopping, ask the U.S. Customs office where you live for a copy of "Know Before You Go" handbook.*

The Light and Heavy Industrial Scene

The Economic Development Authority oversees activities at industrial parks on both St. Croix and St. Thomas. Located one mile from the Henry E. Rohlsen Airport, and Southshore Port facility, the St. Croix Industrial Park has 150,000 square feet of space.

With acres of flat land and specific tax incentives for businesses, St. Croix is ripe for the development of light industry. The Authority is actively seeking and encouraging new light, non-polluting industries. HOVENSA, now an oil storage facility, had until early 2012 operated a refinery on the south shore of St. Croix which included a new Catalytic Cracking Unit constructed to manufacture reformulated gasoline to meet the requirements of the Federal Clean Air Act. An alumina processing plant in the same area, was opened by Harvey Aluminum in 1965, was later purchased by Martin Marietta, then the VI Aluminum Company (VIALCO), and finally Alcoa Aluminum. aluminum production ceased in December 2000, due to a downturn in that industry. As stated earlier, the property was purchased by The Renaissance Park to develop it for light industry and renewable resources. The Renaissance Group is currently seeking tenants who would benefit from the infrastructure and facilities on the south shore.

St. Croix is also home to several watch companies. They receive a wage subsidy plus duty-free entry into the United States for watches made in the U.S. Virgin Islands. Watches assembled here with foreign parts may enter the United States duty free. Export limits are allocated among the watch companies. In St. Croix, small manufacturers produce; soda, electronics, garments and boats. St. John has few light industries other than one or two person entrepreneurial ventures. They include fiberglass cistern construction, herbs and spices and artistic ventures.

The St. Thomas Industrial Park at Subbase, with an area of 20,000 square feet, is close to shipping docks and the airport. There are few light manufacturing companies in St. Thomas with the exception of fragrance manufacturers and artistic ventures.

The Economic Development Authority

The US Virgin Islands is unique and offers many benefits. Besides the beautiful setting,th territory offers the stability of U.S. currency and the protection of the U.S. flag and U.S. court. Manufacturers have duty-free, quota-free access to the U.S. mainland with "made in the USA" labels on many items. The USVI offers a business-friendly environment; an educated work force; easy air access; world-class telecommunications; shipping advantages; and prime rental space. Our Economic Development Commission helps qualified companies reduce taxes and increase profits.

The Virgin Islands Economic Development Authority (EDA) is semi-autonomous and is responsible for promoting and enhancing the economic development in the USVI. Its five major components are: the Government Development Bank, The Economic Development Commission, the Industrial Park Development Corporation, the Small Business Development Agency and the Enterprise Zone program.

To expand its economic base, and create jobs for residents, the federal and local government enacted a series of incentives to create tax benefits for eligible businesses. By locating your business, or part of your business, to the USVI, you may be eligible to apply for tax benefits and receive substantial reduction in, or exemption from, your business and personal taxes. Companies that qualify receive either a substantial reduction, or an exemption from many of the standard business taxes. The list of some types of companies that could qualify would be: raw materials processing, financial services sector, assembly operations (i.e. jewelry), hotels/guest houses, certain services/businesses that provide goods and services to customers both inside and outside the territory, transportation and telecommunications, high tech businesses. (see EDA website www.usvieda.org). Since the tax incentive program is industry or sector non-specific, various other companies or organizations may be eligible if they prove beneficial to the territory's economic well-being.

Incentives and benefits for new businesses include: 90% exemption on local income taxes; 90% exemption on local income taxes paid by resident stockholders on dividends and interest received from the company, a maximum reduction from 6% to 1% on custom duties; 100% exemption on property and gross receipts taxes; 100% exemption on Excise taxes. The IRS has imposed source-income requirements, which make the benefits offered by the EDC tax-incentive programs to those businesses operating "wholly" in the V.I. and who ship their commodities (hard manufactured (hard manufactured goods) to places outside the mainland. These requirements fall under the Federal Jobs Creation Act. The EDC is looking at international markets for those companies who are smaller high-tech manufacturers, software developers and investment bankers to encourage economic development in the U.S. Virgin Islands.

EDC tax exemptions are offered for 10 to 30 years, depending upon the location of the business and industry in the territory. Companies may start the benefits package at any point in the first five years of business operations. These benefits may be extended in five to ten-year increments. The basic qualification is an investment of $100,000, exclusive of inventory, in an approved industry that the EDC has determined will advance the economic well being of the VI and its people, and employment of at least ten employees on a full-time basis, of which 80% have resided in the USVI at least one year. Requirements do change, so for more information see the EDA website at www.usvieda.org.

Cultural Tidbit

*W*hether visiting or moving to the Virgin Islands, one way to invest in the local economy is to buy rum, Cruzan or Captain Morgan's. Here's a simple, yet fantastic, tropical rum punch recipe that'll keep you cool in the island heat.

Ingredients:
3 oz pineapple juice
2 oz dark rum
3 oz orange juice
Splash of cranberry juice
Pineapple pieces
Splash of grenadine

Preparation
Pour rum, pineapple juice, orange juice in a shaker. Pour in glass with ice. Top off with a splash of cranberry juice and grenadine. Enjoy. Cheers! And for the sake of our economy, please have another.

For **Small Business Financing** the EDA administers business development programs through its "Lending Unit" consisting of the **Government Development Bank** of the VI (GDB) and the **VI Small Business Development Agency (SBDA).** They provide access to capital for small and medium-sized businesses to be used to start a business, expand a business, purchase an existing one, purchase inventory, machinery, equipment, supplies, furniture, fixtures employment, etc.). Loans are issued at competitive interest rates with competitive terms.

Residence requirements may apply. The applicant must own 50% of the business and be active in the management *(see site for in-depth details or call 714-1700 St. Thomas or 773-6499 St. Croix).* The **Industrial Park Development Corporation's**, established in Chapter 17 of Title 9 of the VI Code, basic function is to provide rental space for EDC beneficiaries as restricted by the agreement between the Federal Government and the IPDC.

The **Enterprise Zone** on September 14, 1999 Act No.6294, mandated that blighted areas that are historical in nature with many buildings over 150 years old, and having had some of the oldest families in the VI from these areas, be revitalized. Many of the oldest families in the VI are from these areas, but a lot of these buildings have fallen into disrepair. This applies to areas in Christiansted and Frederiksted in St. Croix, and Savan in St. Thomas. The law provides for tax incentives and calls for public, private and non-profit organizations to develop these areas.

Capital Project Financing:

The VI Government recently enacted Tax Increment Financing (TIF) to stimulate economic growth and public infrastructure. It can be used for affordable housing and schools, demolition, utilities and planning costs. The funding comes from USVI with the use of real property tax increment revenues and gross receipts tax increment to pay for, or finance the cost, or portion of capital improvements to those areas designated as TIF by the Authority and approved by the Legislature. (all info available on their web at www.usvieda.org). For further information call 340-773-6499 St. Croix and 340-774-8104 on St. Thomas, or 1-877-432-USVI.

Offshore Companies

Act 6490, Bill No. 24-0187 passed in December 2001, changed FSC's (Foreign Sales Corporations) to the VIFSC (Virgin Islands Foreign Sales Corporations. The franchise tax shall be $300. The registration requirements are: Articles of Incorporation and a Consent of Agent Form. The registration fee is a minimum of $400 as written in Title 13 Chapter 14 of the VI Code. Exempt companies may request a contract stating the benefits of Chapter 14. The cost of this is $100. Once the Lieutenant Governor's office has received and approved this paperwork the foreign-owned company can register here as an exempt company for a $1,000 annual franchise fee. For a copy of the VI Code visit www.michie.com. For further information call the Lieutenant Governor's office at 776-8515.

Marine Industry

With hundreds of boats throughout the Virgins, the marine industry accounts for 10 percent of the territory's economy. Several large charter companies rent boats to sailors. Crewed yachts provide luxury vacations for less intrepid vacationers and fuel a myriad of other businesses including grocery stores, marine parts and service companies, to mention a few. The local government in 1994 canceled a tax on boats and parts, so marine industries pay no tax on that portion of their business.

St. Thomas is the center of marine activity in the Virgin Islands. Boasting numerous marinas and boatyards, it is the hub of the charter yacht industry of the USVI. Basing their operations at Yacht Haven, is the Virgin Islands Charter Yacht League (VICL). The VICL, www.vicl.org, holds two boat shows annually for the vessels under their umbrella, one in the spring and a larger one in the fall. The fall show has about 100 vessels for charter brokers to meet the captain and crew and inspect the vessels before booking clients. Call them at 774-3944 for further info.

The two primary marinas on St. Thomas are Crown Bay Marina, located in Sub Base next to the cruise ship docks, and American Yacht Harbor on the east end of the island. American Yacht Harbor serves as the gateway to St. John and the BVI's. Famed for its annual Boy Scout Fishing Tournament in July or August, AYH is the fishing Mecca of the USVI due to its close proximity to the famed "North Drop." Anglers and vessels come from all over the world for the opportunity to catch a "trophy" Blue Marlin, although these days most vessels are strictly catch and release, a picture and measurements will get you an artificial replica of the monster you landed. For American Yacht Harbor call 775-6454. Crown Bay Marina, www.crownbay.com primarily caters to Mega Yachts during the busy winter season. Crown Bay Marina is capable of berthing vessels up to 200' long and has a 315' fuel dock with dispensers that fuel at a rate of 150 gallons per minute! Both marinas cater to the cruising sailboat enthusiast during the busy winter season. Other marinas include the Sapphire Beach Marina, Independent Boat Yard, Yacht Haven and Compass Point Marina, among others. Enjoy all that the Virgin Islands marine industry has to offer. There is plenty of fishing, diving, daily boat rentals, day sails and overnight charters available. Just go to one of the marinas and ask! Also, be sure to visit the Yacht Haven Grande Marina in the Charlotte Amalie Harbor to the east side of the harbor and just past the Havensight Cruise ship docks, for provisioning, restaurants and shopping.

Film Industry

Crystal clear water, white beaches, lush mountains and everyday sunshine set the stage for the territory's film industry. From the box-office hit, "Weekend at Bernie's II," to segments of the soap opera "The Young and Restless", with nearly, 1,000 commercial shots (including the Pepsi beach shots) in between, and reality shows such as "The Bachelor," hundreds of filmmakers have shot miles of footage here. The territory has some full-service production companies and a handful of supporting companies who offer complete facilities including casting, lighting, grip equipment, trucks, motor homes, generators, helicopters with special mounts, underwater camera housing and video editing suites. Companies can hire members of the Screen Actors Guild for many "extras" as they need them. Call the Department of Tourism at 774-8784, and their Film Promotion Office.

Agriculture

Although land suitable for commercial agriculture on St. Thomas and St. John is limited, St. Croix's plains and rolling hills support beef, dairy cattle, sheep and goats. The government maintains agriculture stations on all three islands to help small farmers. On St. Croix, small farmers sell fruit, vegetables and root crops at roadside stands and in the Agriculture Department's farmers' market. Two companies producing beef for local consumption sell to local grocery chains and at Annaly Farms. The companies also breed and export Senepol cattle, which has global demand. The cattle, developed in St. Croix, were successfully and specifically bred for use in warm tropical climates.

A St. Croix company farming the freshwater fish "Tilapia", in conjunction with hydroponic gardening, opened in the last few years. A Tilapia fish farm is part of the Fisheries studies at UVI. In St. Thomas, success has come through the growth of herbs and spices sold to island supermarkets, at roadside stands, and the government's market at Market Square in Charlotte Amalie. Exports of bush tea products to the mainland, used locally for medicinal purposes, are increasing. Farmers also grow root and garden crops for sale at open markets.

Finding a Job

Life in the tropics is more than palm trees and pina coladas, so you will need a few dollars for necessities. If you have decided to live out your dream, plan on enough money, depending upon your standard of living, to see you through until you are settled. Taking a temporary job is a good idea until you have been here long enough to know if you like island living. Unless you are recruited from the mainland, employers will want to make sure you will stay awhile before they invest in you.

USVI law requires that all job openings be posted through the Departmet of Labor. The Labor Department matches the local labor supply with jobs, providing placement, referral, training, information and counseling services. Jobs for accountants, mechanics, bakers, bartenders, bookkeepers, carpenters, chefs, cooks, electricians, pastry chefs, plumbers, secretaries, and servers are always available. (See www.vidol.gov)

Another free and easy way to seek employment is job postings on Career.VI. Many well-known VI employers post their openings through www.career.vi. and consider it as one of their main recruiting platforms.

The website offers hundreds of job listings from across the Virgin Islands and opportunities for employers to provide applicants with feedback. Like in the mainland craigslist (http://virgin.craigslist.org) is also a main source for employment classifieds.

If you have just arrived, jobless and anxious to get started, look to smaller restaurants, tour companies or charter boats for instant jobs, particularly in the busy winter season. Real estate brokers, barbers, beauticians, plumbers, electricians, construction contractors, and draftsmen, need a license from the Department of Licensing and Consumer Affairs (774-3130, St. Thomas or 773-2226, St. Croix).The Department of Health (774-0117 St.T, 713-9924 St.C) will issue licenses for doctors, dentists, nurses and pharmacists. They will also issue health cards for workers who are employed in a food service position.Attitude counts. If you are a self-starter, you may find yourself in your home-based business with an opportunity to grow.

If you are already here, check the Department of Labor, the government's Personnel office, the local newspapers, and in St. John, the bulletin boards placed around town. Though it is difficult to find a job from off-island, you may try requesting a local phone book from Innovative Communications, call 779-9999 or go to www.viphonebook.com. The same book covers all three islands, and you can get a start in employment research. You will probably have to pay your own way here if you manage to land a job in advance of your arrival. If you get a key position, you might be able to negotiate relocation costs with your company.

The Work Force

Halfway through the fiscal year of 2012, 43,119 persons were employed compared to 43,859 during the same period in FY 2011—about 1.7 percent less or 740 fewer jobs. One in ten of those jobs were in the goods sector, while 90 percent were in the service sector. In December 2012, the most updated information we could attain following the Hovensa closure, there were 23,848 eligible to work in St. Croix and 19,795 were employed-- a 17% unemployment rate for the month. In the St. Thomas/St. John district26,497 were eligible to work in December 2012 and 23,878 were employed; a 9.9% unemployment rate. By comparison, the national unemployment rate for the same month was 7.8%.

As of press time, the territory's average unemployment rate for 2012 was 11.7 percent (this represents January-through-December rates, which were highly driven by St. Croix's numbers following the HOVENSA refinery closure). By comparison, the territory's average unemployment rate for 2011 was 8.9 percent. For the same twelve-month period, St. Thomas' average unemployment rate was 9.6%.

The current unemployment insurance tax rate for new employers is 3 percent of the taxable wage base, which is subject to change yearly. In 2009, the wage base was $21,800. Rates for existing businesses vary. It s based on how often they laid off workers in the previous twelve quarters. Employees can collect when they are laid off or unfairly fired.

The local government, and the service industry are the largest employers in the territory, with others in construction, manufacturing, finance, insurance, real estate, transportation, communications, public utilities, and in the wholesale business. The Labor Department matches the local labor supply with jobs. It provides placement, referral, training, information and counseling services. Jobs for accountants, auto mechanics, bakers,

bartenders, bookkeepers, Maintenance carpenters, chefs, cooks, electricians, sports instructors, Maintenance mechanics, pastry chefs, plumbers, secretaries, cocktail waiters and waitresses are always available. (See www.vidol.gov)

A roadside vendor cuts a coconut and serves it up for drinking.

Training

The Virgin Islands has a well-educated work force. Most residents complete high school. Many continue their education at The University of the Virgin Islands or travel to mainland colleges. The Labor Department oversees federally-subsidized training for interested citizens through the Workforce Development Act. The program repays employers up to 50 percent for on-the-job training and will, in some cases, offer classroom programs and financial stipends. The Department works closely with private industry to custom tailor training programs that meet their needs. Call them at 776-3700 ext. 2081.

Federal Unemployment Tax

All employers pay a federal unemployment tax called FUTA and pay 0.8 percent of the first $7,000 paid to employees. They must fill out Form 940 and then file with the Federal Internal Revenue Bureau in Philadelphia.

Wages

Overall, wages here are lower than on the mainland. The minimum wage for most jobs is $7.25 per hour. Tipped employees must earn at least $7.25 an hour, as long as tips bring it up to that.

Benefits

Although a comprehensive benefits package is not required in the private sector, most businesses provide a minimum of health insurance. Larger businesses also offer pension plans.

Worker's Compensation

Workers compensation insurance is mandatory for all businesses with premium rates varying by job. Workers compensation insurance is available only through the Department of Labor

Social Security

Businesses contribute to the employee's social security at the same rate as in the States. They pay 7.65 percent (1.45% Medicare and 6.20% is for old-age) and the employee pays 7.65 percent on wages up to $113,700 (2013). Self-employed residents pay 15.3 percent (consisting of a12.4% component for component for old-age, survivors, and disability insurance, and a 2.9% component for Medicare on wages up to $113,700 (2013). However, they must fill out form 1040 SS, rather than the usual 1040 SE, Form 1040 SS and the payment is filed with the Internal Revenue Service in Austin, Texas. All benefits are the same as on the mainland except there is no supple- mental security income. In summary, Social Security taxes are still paid to the United States Treasury, while withholding is paid to the U.S. Virgin Islands Government.

Financial Help

If your business needs financial help, check with your bank, the Federal Government's Small Business Administration at 774-8530, or with the local government's Small Business Development Agency at 714-1700. The three organizations offer counseling and financial assistance. The Small Business Development Center at the University of the Virgin Islands offers counseling, research and technical assistance to eligible businesses. Call 776-3206 on St Thomas, and 692-5270 on St. Croix for more information.

Business Insurance

For business insurance purposes, local agents can arrange for coverage of your needs with various packages and can often finance your premiums. Rates depend on business gross receipts or other type of exposure.

Bonding

U.S. Customs, bid and performance, fidelity and surety, and court bonds are available to those who qualify, but the process is slow. Only a few agents offer this service. Whenever possible, have a certified financial statement prepared and confer with your agent long in advance of need.

Getting a Business License

Once you have evaluated the local economy, the labor market and the territory as a whole, and you decided you want to do business here, you need a business license. The fee schedule varies with a range of $1.00 for commercial farming license, $50 for an itinerant vendor, $100 for retail shops, $200 for restaurants with more than 25 seats, $300 for business and management consultants, and $400 for hotels and guest-houses over 100 rooms. Businesses are responsible for renewals since the department does not send notices. Those who plan branches on more than one island must file separate applications. Also if you have two different businesses and two different names, you must file two applications. *Call the Licensing department in St. Thomas at 774-3130, for St. Croix call 718-2226. www.dlca.gov.vi*

Business Taxes Corporate Income Taxes

In addition to the usual income taxes, corporations registered in the U.S. Virgin Islands pay a 10 percent surcharge due to a 1985 act passed by the local Legislature. It is paid with your quarterly tax return.

Corporate Franchise Tax

Every incorporated business, whether domestic or foreign must pay tax on the amount of capital used in the business. The tax is $1.50 for every $1,000 of capital stock. The minimum tax is $150. A penalty of 20%, or $50, whichever is greater, for failure to pay by June 30th, and 1% interest compounded annually for each month beyond June 30th is imposed.

Gross Receipts Tax

Businesses pay a five percent gross receipts tax on all money earned from all transactions including services and may not deduct expenses. If you earn under $120,000 a year you must file annually at the Internal Revenue Bureau. If you earn more than $120,000 you must also file monthly. Businesses that earn under $225,000 per year are entitled to a $9,000 per month exemption.

Entertainment Tax

A five percent tax is levied on the gross receipts for performances or entertainment, including, motion pictures, shows, boxing matches, circuses and concerts where admission is charged unless the performance is sponsored by a recognized non-profit organization.

Excise Tax

Pretty much anyone doing business in the Virgin Islands, except those that are specifically exempt, must pay excise tax on all goods, merchandise, or commodities manufactured in or brought into the Virgin Islands for business purposes. The excise tax is based on the invoice value of such merchandise, plus a mark-up of five percent. Rates of tax depend upon the applicable category, and range from two percent to twenty-five percent.

The following rates apply to the following categories of goods: Drugs, medicine, and clothing, 2% percent; tires, 5%; self-propelled vehicles, firearms, ammunition and bicycles, 10%; U.S. beers, $1.55 per case; foreign beers, $2.08 per case; liquor, $6.00 per case; wine, $2.50 per gallon; tobacco (exclusive of cigars), 20%. More info on rates is available in the *Tax Structure of the U.S. Virgin Islands* booklet, available at viirb.com.

Hotel Room Tax

Those who stay in hotels, guest houses, apartments, condominiums, or residences for less than 90 days are charged a Hotel Room Tax. The rate is 10% of the gross room rate, which is the total sum charged to a guest for room use plus additional charges, such as an energy surcharge or a maintenance fee, but not charges for food, beverages, and gratuities.

Business Organizations

The Chambers of Commerce in St. Croix and St. Thomas/St. John work hard to improve the business climate and overall community. Membership is open to business and non-business people. Both Chambers have small staffs guided by a board of directors. Feel free to call them with questions. Staff members will either know the answers or tell you where to find them. Both Chambers provide and publish information packets, newsletters, business notifications, membership guides, and directories. The Chamber groups also have monthly luncheons and "Business-After-Hours" meetings for members and the public. To contact the St. Croix Chamber of Commerce, call 718-1435, (fax) 718-8172, www.stxchamber.org. Write to them at: 3009 Orange Grove, #12, Christiansted, St. Croix, VI 00820, e-mail: info@stxchamber.org. The St. Thomas-St. John Chamber of Commerce is located at 6-7 Dronningens Gade, or write to: P.O. Box 324, St. Thomas, VI 00804-0324, 776-0100, (fax) 776-0588, www.usvichamber.com, e-mail: chamber@islands.vi.

Other Professional Organizations

Advertising Club of the Virgin Islands: 774-8478
American Institute of Architects:(St.C) 772-5904; (STT), 777-1600
Christiansted Retailers/Restaurant Association: 773-2148
St. Croix Hotel & Tourism Association: 773-7117
St. Thomas - St. John Hotel Association: 774-6835
St. Croix Board of Realtors: 334-5618
St. Thomas Board of Realtors: 866-598-1440 ext 234
V.I. Territorial Association of Realtors: 773-1855
V.I. Taxi Association: 774-4550
V.I. Bar Association, vibar@viaccess.net, 778-7497

Labor Associations

American Federation of Teachers: (STC) 778-4414; (STT) 776-1825
Our Virgin Labor Union   St. Croix 719-1464
Police Benevolent Association (STC) 778-2211; (STT) 774-2211
United Industrial Workers of S.I.U.:(STC) 773-6055; (STT) 774-3895
United Steel Workers of America: (STC) 778-5906; (STT) 774-8510
V.I. Workers Union, (STC) 773-3131

Settler's Handbook Chapter 10

You and the Government...

The U.S. Virgin Islands is governed by the Revised Organic Act passed by the United States Congress in 1954. In this document, U.S. Congress defined the three branches of the territorial government, set debt limits, and spelled out voting rights. It includes a bill of rights that substantially extends the same rights enjoyed by U.S. mainlanders to the islands. Under the U.S. Constitution, the Federal government reserves any powers not expressly granted to the States and the people. In this unincorporated territory, the government has only such powers as Congress may give or take away. While autonomy has increased over the years, residents first elected a governor in 1970, but voted in a 1993 referendum that they wanted no change in their status. The referendum options ranged from independence to statehood.

There have been four attempts to pass a Virgin Islands Constitution, the last one in 1981, but the Virgin Islands electorate each time has turned down the measure in the hopes that the next draft will be perfected to meet the majority's acceptance. In 2009 another Committee to redraft a new Constitution was formed and it is still on-going.

The Federal government maintains a presence here through various agencies. A Federal Inspector General, appointed by the Interior Department keeps watch over local use of Federal government revenues and expenditures.

Income Taxes

Islanders use familiar federal forms to pay income taxes. The rate is the same as in the states,but the funds remain in the U.S. Virgin Islands. When income is earned here, on the mainland, or anywhere else in the world, taxes are paid where the taxpayer declares his bona fide residence on December of that year. If you reside here, but earn money elsewhere you pay your entire tax on any world-wide income to the U.S. Virgin Islands, but you need to report it on a 1040-SS information form. If you are a U.S. resident with some island income, complete Form 1040 and Form 8689 to determine your tax liability to the U.S. Virgin Islands. This means you allocate taxes between both jurisdictions. File by April 15. Be aware that a local holiday may mean that the filing date is different than that on the mainland.

All tax forms are available at local Internal Revenue Bureau offices located at Estate Diamond, Lot 7B, Christiansted, St. Croix, VI 00820, 773-1040. Administrator's Office; The Battery, Cruz Bay, St. John, 00830, 776-6485, and Mandela Circle, 9601 Estate Thomas, St. Thomas 00802, 774-5865.

Social Security

Social security taxes are deducted from all paychecks. Self-employed residents pay their social security tax at the same rate as mainlanders, but unlike residents of other U.S. territories, use form 1040-SS.

Other Taxes

All U.S. citizens who move here from the U.S. mainland are subject to Federal estate tax laws no matter where the assets come from, whether it be England or Kansas. Since usual stateside exemptions apply here, most people who inherit small estates pay no taxes. If you are born here or naturalized in the U.S. Virgin Islands, Puerto Rico, or other U.S. territory, your assets on the U.S. mainland are taxed but not those here or elsewhere in the world. The taxes are payable to the U.S. Treasury Department. A 2% stamp tax is paid on real property transfer. That would be 2% on value up to $350,000; from $350,001 to $1 million it is 2.5%, and from $1 million to $5 million it is 3%. Anything over $5 million is 3.5%. Contact the Recorder of Deeds in St. Thomas/ St. John at 774-9906 and in St. Croix at 773-6449.

Voting

U.S. Virgin Islanders cannot vote for the President and Vice-President of the U.S. However, the local Republican and Democratic parties are active with their respective national committees. While these islands cannot vote for the President and Vice President, we do however vote for our Delegate to Congress every two years here in the territory. This position does have an office in Washington and does serve on various house committees. There is an office in St. Croix and St. Thomas for this office. Residents elect the Governor and Lieutenant Governor to four-year terms and Senators to two-year terms. We vote for seven senators on St. Croix, seven on St. Thomas, and one "at-large' senator from St. John. Members of the Board of Education and Election Board are also elected. To register bring passport, birth certificate, or naturalization certificate PLUS your social security card.

Years ago, the individual islands had more autonomy through municipal councils, but now the reins of government rest with the territorial government. While there are no elected mayors or other municipal officials, periodically residents in St. John and St. Croix push for more home rule. Register to vote at Elections Board offices at: St. Croix: 93 Sunny Isle Annex, 773-1021. Mail to: 1499 Kingshill, VI 00851, St. John: The Battery, Cruz Bay, St. John, VI 00801 776-6535 (open Tuesday/Thursday). St. Thomas: 212 Crystal Gade, Charlotte Amalie, St. Thomas 00802, 774-3107, Mail to: P.O. Box 6038, St. Thomas, VI 00801-6038.

Executive Branch

The Governor and Lieutenant Governor, elected to four-year terms, may serve two terms. The Lieutenant Governor acts in the Governor's stead when he is off-island. When both are temporarily out of the territory, the Finance Commissioner is next in line. The Attorney General, Budget Director, Education Commissioner, Public Works Commissioner, Housing Commissioner, and Police Commissioner follow. Should the Governor and Lieutenant Governor permanently leave office, the Legislature's president and vice president are next in the line of succession. They are followed by the same line of government officials as when the Governor and Lieutenant Governor are temporarily absent.

The Government's cabinet consists of Commissioners from each of the executive branch's many departments. The Lieutenant Governor's office has the responsibility for tax assessors' offices, recorder of deeds offices, regulates the banking and insurance industries and is the repository for all official documents. Administrators on each island are the Governor's representatives.

Government Officials

Governor: St. Thomas 21-22 Kongens Gade, Charlotte Amalie, VI 00802, 774-0001
Legislative Bldg.,St. Croix: No. 2, Lagoon St. Complex, F'sted, 772-1000 Govt. House, St. Croix: King St., Christiansted, 00820, 773-1404
St. John: The Battery, - Cruz Bay, Box 488, 00830 776-6484
Lieutenant Governor: St. Thomas -18 Kongens Gade, Charlotte Amalie, 00802, 774-2991 St. Croix 1131 King Street, Christiansted, 00820, 773-6449, www.ltg.gov.vi
Office of the Lieutenant Governor, Divisions:

Banking & Insurance:	773-6459 *St. Croix*	774-7166 *St. Thomas*
Corporations & Trademarks:	773-6449 *St. Croix*	776-8515 *St. Thomas*
Passport Office:	773-6449 *St. Croix*	774-4024 *St. Thomas*

Recorder of Deeds: Office records property deeds – St.Croix: King Street, Christiansted, 773-6449 : St.Thomas - Kongens Gade, Charlotte Amalie, 774-9906

Tax Assessor: Office responsible for appraising property value:
St. Croix - King St., C'sted, 773-6449 ; No. l Lagoon St., F'sted, 772-3115
St. John - The Battery,Cruz Bay, VI 00830, 776-6737
St. Thomas - No. 18 Kongens Gade, Charlotte Amalie, VI 00802 776-8505,
Cadastral (office that houses property maps) St. Croix 773-6549
St. Thomas 776-8505
V.I. Medicare/ State Health Insurance Program (SHIP),
772-7368, St. Croix   St. Thomas; 714-4354
Administrators' Offices: Government House, St. Croix: King St., Christiansted, 00820, 773-1404
St.Thomas: Government House, Charlotte Amalie, 00802, 774-0001

Legislative Branch

The territory has a unicameral, 15-member Legislature with all the members elected to two-year terms every two years. Elections are held in even-numbered years. Senators take office the second Monday in January of the following year. The territory is grouped into two districts: St. Thomas/St. John and St. Croix. Voters in those districts elect seven senators each. Voters on all three islands elect a senator-at-large, who by law must be a resident of St. John.

The Legislature meets throughout the year for committee meetings or sessions. The Governor or the Legislature's President can call specific sessions so Senators may address specific issues. While the main Legislature offices are in Charlotte Amalie, where all sessions are held, Senators may also have offices and hold committee meetings in St. Croix and St. John.

The Senate has nine standing committees that deal with issues and pending legislation related to the government's various departments. It also has final approval on all zoning and variance changes and trust land permits. Bills are passed by majority vote. They become law when the Governor signs, or if he fails to sign, within 10 working days.While he can veto bills, the Legislature may override his veto with a two-thirds vote.

U.S. Virgin Islands Legislature

St. Croix: Lagoon St. Complex, Frederiksted, 00840 Mail: Box 4800, Christiansted, 00822, 773-2424
St. John: #9 Enighed, Cruz Bay, St. John, 00831 Mail: Box 1690, Charlotte Amalie, St. Thomas 00801, 776-6285
St. Thomas: Old Barracks Yard, Charlotte Amalie, St. Thomas 00801 Mail: Box 1690,Charlotte Amalie, St. Thomas, 00801 774-0880

153

Judicial Branch

The U.S. Virgin Islands has two judicial levels, the local and Federal judiciaries. Most of the cases go to the Superior Court, which handles all criminal and civil matters from litter to murder. There are five judges in St. Thomas and four in St. Croix. A judge visits St. John for traffic, litter, family, and small claims cases. The judges are appointed by the Governor and confirmed by the Legislature. U.S. District Court tries federal crimes and may elect to try serious local crimes including murder. Assaults on Virgin Islands National Park officers and crimes involving interstate transfer of funds are among those tried by a federal court. The judges are appointed by the President and confirmed by the U.S. Congress. There are two judges and two magistrates sitting here with mainland judges assigned when the case load is more than the sitting judges can handle. A federal grand jury hands down indictments. Appeals from the Superior Court are heard by a three-member appeals panel consisting of one territorial and two federal judges. Cases from the appeals panel are heard by the 3rd Circuit Court of Appeals, Philadelphia. The U.S. Supreme Court is the last step in the appeals process. Defendants who can't afford an attorney are represented by a public defender or a court-appointed attorney in both Superior and U.S.District Court cases. All the territory's attorneys are on a list. When their name is at the top, they get the next case.

Legal Services of the Virgin Islands Inc.: This non-profit agency handles many civil and immigration matters for those who need legal advice and cannot afford the cost. Call St. Croix at 718-2626, or in St. Thomas at 774-6720.

Traffic tickets can be paid by mail or in St. Croix and St. Thomas at Superior Court. In St. John, they are payable at the Police Department's motor vehicle inspection lane.

Superior Court locations: Alexander Farrelly Justice Center, Veteran's Drive, or Box 70, Charlotte Amalie, St. Thomas 00804, 774-6680. Hall of Justice, Box 929, Christiansted, St. Croix 00821, 778-9750

Superior Court Public Defenders: Company St., Christiansted, St. Croix 00820, 773-6312. Subbase, P.O. Box 6040, St.Thomas, 00841, 774-8181

U.S. District Court locations: Federal Building, 5500 Veterans Drive, Ste.3110, Charlotte Amalie, St.Thomas, 00802, 774-0640. Federal Building, 3013 Estate Golden Rock, Lot 13, Christiansted, St. Croix 00820-4355, 773-1130

Federal Public Defender: Box 1327, St. Thomas 00804, 774-4449. Box 3450, Christiansted, St. Croix 00822, 773-3585

Useful Federal and Local Government Addresses and Telephones: There are many Federal agencies and local government departments and commissions with offices on both St. Croix, St. Thomas and infrequently, St. John. Most local department Commissioners are based in St. Thomas.

V.I. Department of Agriculture: This local department sells plants and assists farmers with their plants and livestock, provides veterinary services, heavy farming equipment and builds farm ponds. Estate Lower Love, Kingshill, St. Croix, 00850, 778-0997 Estate Carolina, Coral Bay, St. John 00830, 776-6274, 7944 Estate Dorothea, St. Thomas, 00802, 774-5182

U.S. Department of Agriculture: Federal agency oversees various Federal programs and enforces Federal agricultural laws. Agricultural Research Service, Box 3008, Kingshill, St. Croix 00850, 778-1312.Animal and Plant Health Inspection Service, Box 8119, St. Thomas, 00801, 776-2787. Plant Protection & Quarantine, Henry E. Rohlsen Airport, St. Croix, VI 00820, 778-1696. Cyril E. King Airport, St.Thomas, 00802, 774-5719.Waterfront, St. Thomas 00802, 774-2561. Natural Resources Conservation Service, Federal Experiment Station, P.O. Box 4399, Kingshill, St. Croix 00851, 778-1312

U.S. Coast Guard: Federal agency patrols the territory's waters, works in drug interdiction, U.S. maritime laws, marine safety. Inspection Office— Frederiksted, St. Croix, 772-5557. Cutter Point Ledge, Charlotte Amalie, St. Thomas 00802. Marine Safety Detachment — Waterfront, Charlotte Amalie, St. Thomas 00802, 776-3497 Search and Rescue Coordination Center, San Juan, P.R., 1-787-729-6770

VI Council on the Arts: Reports to the Governor and disburses grants, promotes arts and holds exhibits. Strand St., Christiansted, St. Croix 00820, St. Thomas 774-5984 / St. Croix 773-3075

Delegate to U.S. Congress: Represents the U.S. Virgin Islands in the House of Representatives as a non-voting Delegate. Sunny Isle Shopping Center, St. Croix, VI 00823, 778-5900. Federal Building, Charlotte Amalie, St. Thomas 00801, 774-4408. Longworth House Office Building, Washington, D.C., 20515-5501, [1-202-225-1790]

U.S. Department of Defense: Federal agency recruits armed forces members and runs support centers. Army Recruiter, Nisky Center, St. Thomas 008022, 714-3027. Recruiter St. Croix, Sunny Isle Mall 719-9077

V.I. Education Department: Oversees Federal and local money that funds the public school system. Each island's Board of Education and insular superintendent implements policy, planning and operation for each public school system. 2133 Hospital St. Christiansted, St. Croix, 00820, 773-1095. No. 44-46 Kongsbergite, St. Thomas, 00802, 774-0100

V.I. Energy Office: Promotes energy-saving programs, provides information to residents and publishes a newsletter for residents. Located at Mars Hill in Frederiksted, St. Croix 00840, 772-2626 or 713-8436; St. Thomas 714-8436. Visit their website at www.vinenergy.org for energy related matters and information. The site offers many ways that residents can conserve gasoline by driving more efficiently and tips to lower water and power (WAPA) bills. Speakers are available to discuss subjects such as: energy efficiency, renewable energy applications to include: solar power, wind energy, and net metering; global warming, rebate incentives, and building an energy efficient home to catch the sun and wind for huge energy savings. With the recent surge in energy rates, the VIEO has seen increase activities in both the public and private sector to incorporate alternative energy solutions in daily living. The VIEO is a division of the Office of the Governor and they are serving you to save energy dollars!

Farmers Home Administration (USDA): Federal agency finances loans for first-time home owners and makes farm loans. Room 14B, Ville La Reine, Kingshill, St. Croix 00850, 778-5224

Federal Aviation Administration: This agency controls the airport tower and maintains navigational equipment on St. Thomas Cyril E. King Airport, Box 302120, St. Thomas 00803, 774-1836. The airport in St. Croix is privatized on a contract basis. Henry E. Rohlsen Airport, Rt 1, Airport, Kingshill, St. Croix 00820, 778-4826

St. Thomas Legislative Building

Federal Bureau of Investigation: Investigates Federal and major local crimes. Federal Bldg., 3013 Estate Golden Rock, Christiansted, St. Croix 00820, 773-7922. Al Cohen Plaza, Charlotte Amalie, St. Thomas 00802, 777-3363. If no answer call San Juan, Puerto Rico: 1-787-754-6000

Federal Highway Administration: Federal department funds road construction programs and highway and bicycle safety. 84 Kronprindsens Gade, Charlotte Amalie, St. Thomas 00821, 776-5820. Lagoon Street Complex, Frederiksted, St. Croix 00840, 772-3025

V.I. Department of Finance: This local department oversees accounting, treasury, data processing, government payroll, and insurance fund activities. 4008 Estate Diamond, Lot 7B, Christiansted, St. Croix 00820, 773-1105, 75 Kronprindsens Gade, St. Thomas 00802, 774-4750

V.I. Fire Services: Responsible for putting out fires and issuing burning, blasting, and fireworks permits. It also conducts business license inspections, public fire education, and arson investigations. To report a fire call 911. Here are the numbers for the fire stations:

St. Thomas: 774-7610; Charlotte Amalie 774-1211 ; Dorothea 774-5156 Tutu 775-0205

St. Croix: 773-8050 , Richmond 773-1211, Cotton Valley 773-9670 Grove Place, 692-2410; Frederiksted, 772-0213

St. John: Cruz Bay 776-6333; Coral Bay 776-6365

General Services Administration: Federal agency manages all Federal buildings and leases space for Federal agencies. Federal Building 5500 Veterans' Drive, Rm.107, Charlotte Amalie, St. Thomas 00802 714-1367. Federal Building, Rt. 75 Northside Road, Golden Rock, St. Croix, 00820-4355, 773-4636

Human Services Department: Federal agency manages all Federal health and social services programs. Social Security Administration, Federal Building, Charlotte Amalie, St. Thomas 00802, 774-0930, Sunny Isle Shopping Center, Professional Building, Christiansted, St. Croix 00820-4423, 773-2323 (Social Security office). Disability Programs, Federal Building, 5500 Veterans' Drive, Charlotte Amalie, St. Thomas, VI 00802, 774-7375

Housing Authority: This local department operates low-income housing units. LBJ Gardens, Christiansted, St. Croix 00820, 778-8442. Building l, Room 206, Subbase, St. Thomas 00801, 777-8442. George Simmons Terrace, Cruz Bay, St. John 00830, 776-6830

V.I. Health Department & Clinics: Operates local clinics, extensive outpatient services, alcoholism and drug treatment centers, public health services, environmental health, mental health, family planning, maternal and child health and crippled children's services.The Myrah Keating Smith

157

Community Health Center on St. John, 693-8900, is operated by the Hospital on St. Thomas. Community Health Clinic—774-7477. Department of Health, Commissioners offices, Sugar Estate, St. Thomas 00802, 774-0117. St. Croix: Charles Harwood Medical Complex 718-1311

V.I. Department of Human Services: Administers federal and local welfare and food stamp programs. Oversees various youth, adult and senior citizen programs. 20A Strand & 5BB Smith St., Christiansted, St. Croix 00820, 773-2980 and 773-2323. St. John (mail goes to St. Thomas address), 776-6334. Knud Hansen Complex, Building A, Hospital Ground, St. Thomas 00820, 774-0930

U.S. Homeland Security/Immigration: Federal agency is responsible for enforcement of immigration laws and naturalization. Sunny Isle Shopping Center, Box 1468, St. Croix, VI 00823, 778-6559. Nisky Center, St. Thomas, 774-1390, T. S. A. Transportation, Security, Administration 715-2271 St. Thomas

U.S. Department of the Interior: Inspector General's Office: St. Thomas, 774-8300s St. Croix 778-9012

V.I. Department of Justice: Headed by the territory's Attorney General, this local department prosecutes most of the territory's criminal and civil cases. It oversees appeals, administration law, ethics, conflicts of interest and general litigation. It is responsible for the territory's jails and prisons, the Criminal Justice Complex, the Medical Examiner and the Civil Rights Commission. 6040 Estate Castle Coakley, Christiansted, St. Croix 00820 773-0295. 48B-50C Kronprindsens Gade, GERS Building, Charlotte Amalie, St. Thomas, VI 00802, 774-5666

V.I. Department of Labor: This local department can help you find a job and pay you unemployment compensation if you are laid off or unfairly fired. It also deals with training, youth employment, labor relations, wage and hour management, occupational safety and health, workers' compensation, and fair employment practices. St. Croix 773-1994, St. Thomas, 776-3700

The Bureau of Labor Statistics: provides an in-depth and graphic picture of the local labor picture. Church Street, Christiansted, St. Croix 00820, 773-1994. Box 2606, Charlotte Amalie, St. Thomas 00803 776-3700

V.I. Department of Licensing and Consumer Affairs: Reviews, issues and enforces all matters pertaining to licensing, weights and measures and consumer protection. It oversees the Public Services Commission, Taxi and Real Estate Commission and Architects and Engineers, Electricians, Plumbing, Alcohol Control, Contractors, and Barbers and Beauticians boards. Golden Rock Shopping Center, Christiansted, St. Croix, VI 00820, 718-2226. No. 1 Sub Base, Rm. 205, St. Thomas, VI 00802, 774-3130

V.I. Office of Management & Budget: This local office is responsible for the territory's budget. It parcels out money from the local and federal revenues. St. Thomas, 774-0750. St. Croix, 778-8925.

V.I. National Guard: The territory's National Guard is called out in case of disaster. Run by the adjutant general who also oversees the territory's civil defense operation, the Virgin Islands Territorial Emergency Management Agency unit has about 800 members on both St. Croix and St. Thomas. 774-5919 Adjutant General, 4031 La Grande Princesse, Lot 1B, Christiansted, St. Croix 00820-4353, 712-7711. VITEMA, Leonard B. Francis Armory, St. Thomas, 774-2244 ; St. Croix 773-2244

U.S. National Park Service: There are parks run by the Federal Government on all three islands. On St. Croix, the park oversees Christiansted Historic site, Buck Island Reef National Monument, and Salt River Bay National Historic Park and Ecological Preserve. On St. John, Virgin Islands National Park has a camp-ground, visitor's center, biosphere reserve, and about 12,000 acres of land and sea. On St. Thomas, the park has a visitor's center at Red Hook and oversees Hassel Island, a historic cay in Charlotte Amalie Harbor. The superintendent's office is at the Red Hook visitor's center. The mailing address is: P.O. Box 7789, Charlotte Amalie, St. Thomas, 00801

St. Croix: Fort Christianvaern, 773-1460

St. John: Cruz Bay Visitor Center, 776-6201, Cinnamon Bay Campground information, 776-6330. For reservations, call 1-800-539-9998, Biosphere Reserve (U.S. Geological Survey), 693-8950

Sports, Parks & Recreation: This local department runs local parks and recreation programs. LBJ Gardens, Christiansted, St. Croix, VI 00820, 773-0160 / 773-0271, Box 122, Cruz Bay, St. John, VI 00831, 775-6531, Sub Base, Bldg. No. 1, Rm. 206, St. Thomas, VI 00802, 774-0255

V.I. Division of Personnel: This local department administers, recruits, classifies, trains and keeps the records on all government employees. Orange Grove, Christiansted, St. Croix 00820, 773-0341 48B-50C Kronprindsens Gade, St. Thomas 00802, 774-8588

V.I. Department of Planning & Natural Resources: (known as DPNR) is responsible for coastal zone planning, capital development, historic preservation and archaeology, issuance of construction permits, libraries, archives and museums, environmental protection, fish and wildlife, boating and mooring permits. 6003 Anna's Hope, Christiansted, St. Croix,VI 00820, 773-1082. Cyril E. King Airport, St. Thomas, VI 00802, 774-3320

DPNR - Enforcement Division: 6003 Anna's Hope, Christiansted, VI 00820, 773-5774. Cyril E. King Airport, St. Thomas 00802, 774-3320

Fish &Wildlife Division: 45 Mars Hill, Frederiksted, St. Croix, 00840,

772-1955. Estate Nazareth, St. Thomas, VI 00802, 775-6762
Coastal Zone Management Program: Anna's Hope, Christiansted, St. Croix, VI 00820, 773-3450, Cyril E. King Airport, St. Thomas,VI 00802, 774-3320

V.I. Dept. of Public Safety (Police Department): Responsible for all anti-crime activities, including drug interdiction, Special Operations Bureau as well as the Motor Vehicle Department. Call 911 for all emergencies. If you are using a cell phone, for emergencies call 772-9111.

CRIME STOPPERS – to report anonymously a crime or lead, call: **1-800-222-TIPS (8477)**

VI Police Department: The territory's prime law enforcement body has offices on all three islands. St. Croix 45 Mars Hill, Frederiksted 778-2211, Wilbur Francis Command, Frederiksted 772-3566, Anselmo Marshall Command, Christiansted   (Basin Triangle) 773-2530. St. John Leander Jurgen Command, Cruz Bay 693-8880. St. Thomas Richard Callwood Command, Norre Gade, Charlotte Amalie 774-2310 Bassanio David Command at Lindberg Bay 775-3445 :

Bureau of Motor Vehicles: This office is responsible for managing most matters related to the acquisition or renewal of driver's licenses and vehicle registrations. www.usvibmv.org, St. Croix, Golden Grove 713-4268 St. John, Cruz Bay 776-6262; St. Thomas, Subbase 774-5765

Offices: St. Croix, 45 Mars Hill, Frederiksted 778-2211
St.John Leander Jurgen Command, Cruz Bay 693-8880

VI Territorial Emergency Management Agency (VITEMA): The agency with primary responsibility for ensuring the territory's resilience to disasters. VITEMA partners with federal, state and local government agencies, and with the private sector to assess, prepare, and ensure effective responses to disasters. St. Croix 773-2424; St. John 776-6444; St. Thomas 774-2244 Alexander A. Farrelly Criminal Justice Complex, Charlotte Amalie, St. Thomas 00802 774-2211 (commissioner's office)

VI Port Authority: This entity develops and operates public air and marine ports. It is a major engine of economic growth and helps maintain the Virgin Islands' position as a major tourism destination. Persons interested in learning more, leasing VIPA's facilities, or doing business with VIPA may contact (340) 774-1629 or info@viport, or www.viport.com.

Box 1134, Christiansted, St. Croix 00821	778-1012
Box 1707, St. Thomas 00803	774-1629
Manager, Cyril E. King Airport, St. Thomas	774-5100
Marine Manager, St. Croix	778-3131
Marine Manager, St. Thomas	774-2250

V.I. Department of Property & Procurement: Purchases, warehouses, controls inventory, distributes materials used in all government lepartments, and executes contracts and leases; runs the central motor pool, government mail service, printing plant and administers the Federal surplus property program. Suppliers can ask to be on the mailing list for bid notices. Bidding practices favor USVI enterprises that meet the qualifications. St. Croix 773-0370; St. Thomas 774-0828.

Public Services Commission: Regulates telephone, electric and cable television rates. Complain to them when you have a problem with the telephone, electric or cable television companies. Barbel Plaza, P.O. Box 40, Charlotte Amalie, VI 00804 776-1291. On St. Croix call 778-6010

V.I. Public Works Department: Oversees activities concerning roads, solid waste, utilities, signals, and bus routes. 6002 Estate Hope, Christiansted, VI 00820, 773-1290 #6 Suzannaberg, St. John, VI 00830, 776-6346, 8244 Sub Base, St. Thomas, VI 00802-5805, 776-4844

Small Business Administration: This Federal agency makes loans to small businesses. Sunny Isle Professional Bldg., Suites 5&6, Christiansted, VI 00820, 778-5380, 3800 Crown Bay, St. Thomas, VI 00802, 774-8530 Sunshine Mall lower level, St. Croix, 692-5270

Small Business Development Center: Assists with the set up and development of businesses, and runs courses to assist new business owners. Sunshine Mall lower level, St. Croix, 692-5270, 8000 Nisky Center, Ste. 720, St. Thomas, VI 00802, 776-3206

V.I. Department of Tourism: This local department oversees all activities concerning tourism, domestic and foreign offices. King Street, Christiansted, St. Croix (Government House) 773-0495 Strand Street, Frederiksted, St. Croix, 772-0357, Cruz Bay, St. John, VI 00830, 776-6450 Waterfront, P.O. Box 6400, St. Thomas, VI 00801, 774-8784

Offshore Offices:

Washington DC, 444 North Capitol Street NW, Suite 305 Washington, DC 20001• (T) 202-624-3590 • (F) 202 624 3594 • (E) lbertrand@usvitourism.vi

Massachusets, P.O. Box 812247 Wellesley, MA 02482• T 508-507-8097 • F 770-745-2757 • E usvi@judithakerman.com

Miami, 18495 South Dixie Highway, #160 Miami, FL 33157-6817 • T 305-322-2740 • F 770 7452757 E jhodge@usvitourism.vi

Chicago 4100 N. Marine Drive, Suite 14-F Chicago, IL 60613 • T 312 -670 3784 • F 312-670-8788 • E awartenberg@usvitourism.vi

Atlanta 3961 Floyd Road, Suite 300-391Austell, GA30106 • T 404-688 0906 • F 770-7452757• E kmilliner@usvitourism.vi

U.S. Attorney: This office prosecutes all Federal crimes. King Street, Box 3239, Christiansted, St. Croix 00822, 773-3920 Federal Building, 5500 Veterans' Drive, Charlotte Amalie, St. Thomas 00802-6424 774-5757

U.S. Customs and Border Protection: An arm of the Federal Treasury Department which enforces U.S. Customs regulations. Old Post Office Building, 1 Church St., Christiansted, VI 00820, 773-5650, The Creek, Cruz Bay, St. John, VI 00830, 776-6741, Federal Building, 5500 Veterans' Drive, Charlotte Amalie, St. Thomas, VI 00801, 774-2510

U.S. Department of Justice: This Federal office provides Federal court security, transports Federal prisoners, administers warrants and subpoenas. Federal Building, 3013 Estate Golden Rock, Lot 13, Christiansted, St. Croix, VI 00820, 778-2051 U.S. Marshal's office, 773-1072, Federal Building, 5500 Veterans' Drive, St. Thomas, VI 00801, 714-1761 U.S. Marshall's office, 774-5999

Water and Power Authority (WAPA): This semiautonomous agency, called WAPA by locals, provides electricity and desalinated water. P.O. Box 1009, Christiansted, VI 00820, 773-2250, Cruz Bay, St. John, VI 00830, 776-6446, Box 1450, Charlotte Amalie, St. Thomas, VI 00804, 774-3552

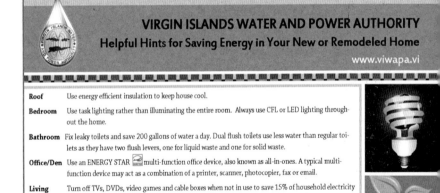

VIRGIN ISLANDS WATER AND POWER AUTHORITY
Helpful Hints for Saving Energy in Your New or Remodeled Home
www.viwapa.vi

Roof	Use energy efficient insulation to keep house cool.
Bedroom	Use task lighting rather than illuminating the entire room. Always use CFL or LED lighting throughout the home.
Bathroom	Fix leaky toilets and save 200 gallons of water a day. Dual flush toilets use less water than regular toilets as they have two flush levers, one for liquid waste and one for solid waste.
Office/Den	Use an ENERGY STAR multi-function office device, also known as all-in-ones. A typical multi-function device may act as a combination of a printer, scanner, photocopier, fax or email.
Living	Turn off TVs, DVDs, video games and cable boxes when not in use to save 15% of household electricity use.
Kitchen	Use the right sized pot on stove burners and save 40% of the burner's heat. Develop the "lids on" habit to lower temperature settings.
Dining	Install a programmable thermostat to automatically adjust air conditioner. When weather is mild turn off A/C and open windows.
Laundry	A full-sized ENERGY STAR certified clothes washer uses 15 gallons of water per load, compared to the 23 gallons used by a standard machine.
Car Port	Install a solar water heater or use a timer. Keeping the door leading into the house closed can help to keep the house cool.
Exterior	Shade windows on the sunny side of the home with film or trees. Using motion sensor lighting outside your home saves energy because they only turn on when needed.

Vienergize
Energy Revolution...We Are the Solution

PARTNER
EDIN-USVI
Energy Development in Island Nations

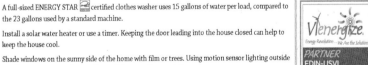

LIKE US ON
facebook

SERVICES DIRECTORY

17th Edition
of the
Settler's Handbook
for the
U.S. Virgin Islands

This Services Directory is but
a small sampling of the professional
organizations and local businesses
who offer goods and services
commonly needed by newcomers, visitors, investors,
or potential residents to the USVI.

Please support OUR advertisers if
you have any questions or need
their services.

This section is divided by islands:
St. Croix, St. John, St. Thomas, and,
there are some who service all three of these islands.
Ask when you call.

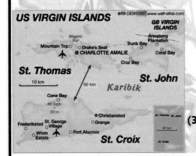

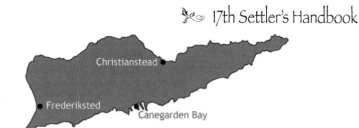

Services Directory for ST. CROIX, U.S. Virgin Islands (All area codes 340)

ACCOUNTANTS/CPA

AIR AMBULANCE

SkyMed AirAmbulance - membership plans (see display ad page 182)

ATTORNEY

ILP+McChain Miller Nissman- provides high quality legal representation in many fields. We combine in-house expertise with strategic alliances with leading legal experts throughout the country to ensure our clients are well served in the unique Virgin Islands legal environment. (See display ad BELOW).

BANKS

Bank of St. Croix - Your local, full-service, community bank. Our service makes the difference! P O Box 24240, Christiansted, VI 00824. Gallows Bay 773-8500, and Peters Rest 713-8500, Fax 773-8508 Visit our website at www.bankofstcroix.com

Banco Popular- all branches 693-2777
FirstBank -(see branch listings pages 77-78 and display ad page178

Scotiabank- Estate Diamond (near Sunny Isle), 778-5350

COMMUNICATIONS

Choice Communications - Peter's Rest Mall 340-778-8864
Innovative Communication Corporation - (see display ad page 179)

DISTILLERIES

ST. CROIX

Diageo/ Captain Morgans- See display ad on next page.

Captain Morgan®

VISITOR CENTER
ST. CROIX USVI

Join us for a legendary experience! Individual or group tours available. Learn about the history of the U.S. Virgin Islands and the process behind our Captain Morgan brand.
Tour Hours: Sun-Fri, 9am-5pm except major holidays.
For details call 340-713-5654.

DRINK RESPONSIBLY, CAPTAIN'S ORDERS!

EMPLOYMENT

Career.vi- visit *career.vi.com*

ST. CROIX

HOME DECORATING AND INTERIOR DESIGN

Patalidis Designs- Furnishing homes and offices on St. Croix for over 34 years, 126 Gallows Bay Christiansted, St. Croix VI 00820. Phone 778-6560 • Fax 772-5205.

HURRICANE SHUTTERS

Centerline Corporation- Hanna's Rest, 772-0030

INSURANCE PROVIDERS

American Medical Plans of the V.I., Inc. - Specializing in group and individual health, life, disability plans and air medical services for over 20 years. Our friendly staff is dedicated to providing you with the best in service and a plan designed for your specific needs. Call or e-mail Mary, Liz, Ann or Terrie at 773-8658 or email ampagencyvi@live.com, P.O. Box 24389, Christiansted, VI 00824.

Inter-Ocean Insurance- See Display ad inside back cover

SETTLERSHANDBOOK.COM

MOVING, VISITING OR INVESTING?
WE'VE
GOT
YOU
COVERED!

INTERNET SERVICE PROVIDERS
Broadband VI - See page 73 and display ad, page 164
Choice Communications - Peter's Rest Mall, 340-778-8864
Innovative Communication Corporation - see display ad, page 179

LAND SURVEYOR
Survey Services Company, LLC - Gary Bourdon, President.
Providing professional land surveys. * Boundary *Topographic* As built
* Subdivisions * Consultations
*Tel. 340-713-4555 * Fax 340-692-0998
* Email: garybourdonpls@gmail.com
*website:www.surveyservicescompany.com
*Address 27-28 King Cross Street, Christiansted, VI 00820

LAND SALE DEVELOPMENT
Jay-Ro-Mar Development, LLC - See display ad on outside back cover

MARINAS
St. Croix Marine- Gallows Bay, 773-0829

MARKETING

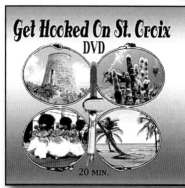

ST. CROIX

MOVERS, SHIPPERS AND FREIGHT FORWARDERS

Bob Lynch Moving & Storage - (see display ad, page 173)
Brandon Transfer - (see display ad page 166)
Caribtrans Inc.- Subbase, 776-8660
Ferrol Trucking- trucking, trailer, forklift, container rental and sales, 778-9602

O'Neale's Transport- 778-1111

MOVERS, SHIPPERS AND FREIGHT FORWARDERS CONT.

VI Cargo- See display ad inside front cover

Water Spirit Freight Services– Shipping cargo from Puerto Rico to St. Croix and St. Thomas, 773-0441

PRIVATE SCHOOLS

WE MOVE YOU IN SO MANY WAYS.

Bob Lynch Moving & Storatge
St. Thomas
340-774-5782
St. Croix
340-778-1813
www.boblynchmovers.com

Moving is one of life's great challenges and moving to the Caribbean island is a new venture for most of us. But it doesn't have to be a hassle if you do your homework and seek out the right company to handle your move.

What you need is a company with years of experiene who will take good care of you from your old residence to your new home. You need a company who know the island, the people, the regulations and systems. Bob Lynch started his business in St. Thomas in 1972. Now it's regarded as the "go to" company to handle your move with professional efficiency, care and concern. Bob Lynch and his team work with stateside and global professionals and are authorized agents for Allied & North American, United & Mayflower, Atlas & Redball, Belkins Worldwide, Graebel Movers International, Global Worldwide and many more. Together they partner to ensure that your move is on schedule from start to final delivery.

They will handle customs clearance, arrange for delivery to the new location, and, if necessary, hold your effects in storage. As Bob Lynch promises, "we will take good care of you, we know how to do it and we've been doing it for years." Just ask their hundreds of satisfied customers.

ST. CROIX

REAL ESTATE

REAL ESTATE CONT.
Seaglass Properties- Located on all three island. See display, page 185

Team San Martin
Teamwork Makes Dreams Work.

Call us and make
your real estate dreams come true

St. Croix's 1st Buyer's Agent
Selling St. Croix since 1984

www.teamsanmartin.com
340-773-1048
RE/MAX St. Croix
5 Company St.
Christiansted VI 00820
joe@teamsanmartin.com

RE/MAX
Above the Crowd!

REAL ESTATE APPRAISERS
Caribbean Engineering Associates - Call 718-1936, fax 718-3193,
Noreen Dunn - 139 Castle Coakley • 773-6666

REAL ESTATE HOME INSPECTIONS
St. Croix Home Inspections - 201-4078, email stxinspections@gmail.com
SOLAR HEATERS
J & O Solar Heaters and More - Specializing in Solar Panels,
power/Solar water heaters. For quotes contact Jorge at (340) 332-9516/
(340) 332-9583   email: omairaconcepcion @yahoo.com

TELEVISION
Innovative Cable TV - (see display ad page 179)

VISETTLERSHANDBOOK.COM

VETERINARIANS

Island Animal Clinic - Dr. Paul Hess — Dr. Paul Hess has been taking care of St. Croix's pets and exotics for over 33 years. Dr. Hess and his staff welcome Dr. Tom House to our team of professionals. We are open 6 days a week and are available 365 days a year 24/7 for emergencies. We offer all services related to pets and we have an air conditioned boarding facility for when you have to leave island. 5 corners location • (340) 718-3106 • iac.usvi@gmail.com • P.O. Box 1640, Christiansted, VI. 00821. Contact us for any information you need regarding moving your pets to the USVI.

Sugar Mill Veterinarian – La Grande Princesse • 718-0022

www.visettlershandbook.com

WAREHOUSE RETAIL. AND OFFICE LEASING

WIESNER DEVELOPMENT COMPANY
Since 1955

OFFICE, RETAIL & WAREHOUSE LEASING

www.stcroix-usvi.com
Tel: (340) 773-1498

**42 Queen Cross Street
C'sted St. Croix U.S.V.I 00820**

WASTE MANAGEMENT

V.I. Waste Management Authority - 712-4962, www.viwma.org

WEBSITES

GoToStCroix.com - produced entirely by island residents, offers useful information, links, articles, maps, photos, and live interactive webcams to help make your time on St. Croix great! Stocked with information about relocating, schools, business services and organizations, and the most comprehensive event calendar on the web. Begin your research for St. Croix on GoToStCroix.com, locally grown, globally known!

ST. CROIX

VisitStCroix.com - One site for all your travel and relocation needs from your exploratory trip to temporary and permanent housing, moving and storage and more. Plus, information on where to eat, shop, bank, recreate, buy insurance and obtain healthcare. VisitStCroix.com features FREE videotravel guides, webcams and more. Research your new home on VisitStCroix.com, part of the VisitTheVI.com family of web sites, with links to hundreds of other helpful sites. VisitTheVI.com, home of the islands leading informational websites. (see display ad, page 186)

Service Directory for **ST. JOHN** U.S. Virgin Islands

(All Area Code 340)

ACCOUNTANTS/ CPA

Travel Tax- See display ad, page 165

AIR AMBULANCE

SkyMed- See display ad, page 182

BANKS

Merchants Commercial Bank – 481-2 Chocolate Hole 779-2696
Scotiabank- Charlotte Amalie, 774-0037

COMMUNICATION SERVICES

Choice Communications- dial 340-693-9152
Innovative Communications- see display ad page 179

ST. JOHN

COMMUNICATION SERVICES CONT.

Connections - On-island communications services: mail, internet access, postage, phones, fax, copies, notary, Western Union, day sails, fishing charters. Message service center. Two great locations: Box 37, Cruz Bay, St. John, VI 00830, 776-6922, fax 776-6902, **and** Coral Bay, 9001 Emmaus, St. John, VI 00830-9726, 779-4994, fax 776-6136, connections@islands.viwww.connectionsstjohn.com

Innovative Communication Corp. - (see display ad page 179)

EMPLOYMENT

Career.vi- visit *career.vi.com*

HEALTH

Department of Health - M.F. de Castro Clinic, 776-6400, 779-4195
Community Health Center - The Myrah Keating Smith Center offers full health care services including family practice, nutritional counseling, AIDS/HIV counseling, 24 hour emergency service, 693-8900
Chelsea Drug Store - 776-4888
Health Care Connection - in The Marketplace, has family medicine, lab services, pediatrics, dermatology and more, 693-7444

MOVERS, SHIPPERS AND FREIGHT FORWARDERS

Bob Lynch Moving - (See display ad page 173)

PRIVATE SCHOOLS

St. John Christian Academy - 26 Contant, 693-7722
St. John Montessori - located at John's Folly, 775-9594

REAL ESTATE

Seaglass properties- See display ad, page 185

St. John Properties - B.J. Harris, Broker/Owner. Established in 1983, we have years of experience pairing people with properties. Let us make your dream a reality. Start with a rental and move into land, condo, home or development property purchase. We will help you every step of the way. Friendly and professional personalized service is our trademark.
P.O. Box 700, St. John, VI 00831, 693-8485, 1-800-283-1746
bj@stjohnproperties.com • www.stjohnproperties.com

SHOPPING

Starfish Market/Starfish Gourmet & Wines- Located at The Marketplace. 779-4949.
The Marketplace- Estate Enighed, 776-6552.

TELEVISION

Innovative Cable TV - (see display ad page 179)

WASTE MANAGEMENT

V.I. Waste Management Authority - 712-4962, www.viwma.org

WEBSITES

GoToStJohn.com - produced by Virgin Islands residents, this site offers useful information, links, articles, maps, photos, and a guide to the National Park so that your stay on St. John is great! It's also kept current with ferry schedules, taxi fares, and an event calendar. Begin your research for St. John on GoToStJohn.com.

VisitStJohn.com - One site for all your travel and relocation needs from your exploratory trip to temporary and permanent housing, moving and storage and more. Plus, information on where to eat, shop , bank, recreate, buy insurance and obtain healthcare. VisitStJohn.com features FREE video travel guides, webcams and more. Research your new home on VisitStJohn.com, part of the VisitTheVI.com family of web sites, with links to hundreds of other helpful sites. VisitTheVI.com, home of the islands leading informational websites.

ST. JOHN

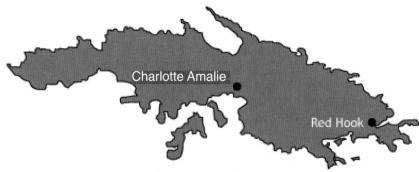

Charlotte Amalie

Red Hook

Services Directory for ST. THOMAS, U.S. Virgin Islands
(All Area Code 340)

AIR AMBULANCE

SkyMed Air Ambulance Membership Plans— A must when living in the USVI for unexpected injury, or illnesses that can't be treated here. Affordable competitive rates to: Puerto Rico, Florida or City of Choice. Air ambulances to Miami can cost $20,000. Join today!
• www.skymedusvi.com
• Direct to St Croix 1-866-349-1494 • St. Thomas 1-866-3491494.

BANKS

Banco Popular- all branches 693-2777
FirstBank - (see branch listings pp. 77-78 and display ad page 178)
Merchants Commercial Bank - Tutu Park Mall 779-2265
Scotiabank - Visit www.usvi.scotiabank.com

COMMUNICATIONS

Innovative Communications Corp.-- See diplay ad page 179
Choice Communications- Nisky Cent.-715-8282 Havensight 774-0024

EMPLOYMENT

Career.vi- visit *career.vi.com*

FINANCING

Schaffer Mortgage- See display ad, page 169

INSURANCE PROVIDERS

Inter Ocean Insurance Agency, Inc. - Your property and casualty agency. Serving the Virgin Islands for over 32 years. Contact us for your insurance needs. 9800 Buccaneer Mall Ste. 312, St. Thomas, VI 00802, 774-2999, fax 774-2899, infostt@interoceaninsurance.com (see display ad BACK COVER).

MARINAS/ MARINE STORES

Island Marine Outfitters - Crown Bay, 714-5311; Red Hook, 775-6621

MAIL SERVICES

Messages, Mail & More – 25+ years of experience in Mail Service. Mail boxes accessible 6 am -10 pm (get notifications of packages via text or email). Answering Service & Internet Access. Shipping with USPS, Fedex, UPS and DHL. Scanning, copying, packing supplies and more... 8168 Crown Bay Marina, Ste. 310, St. Thomas VI 00802-5819, 776-4324 (fax) 776-0020 www.mmmvi.com

MOVERS, SHIPPERS AND FREIGHT FORWARDERS

Bob Lynch Moving & Storage - (see display ad page 173)
Carib Trans- 129-131 Subbase, 776-8660

Water Spirit Freight Services – Shipping cargo from Puerto Rico to St. Croix and St. Thomas, 773-0441

PRIVATE SCHOOLS

Antilles School- See display ad on page 183.
VI Montessori School & International Academy and IB World School - (340) 775-6360, St. Thomas.

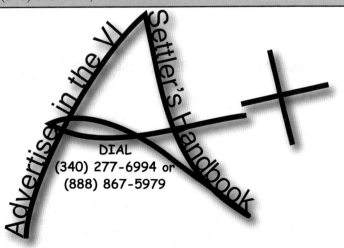

Advertise in the VI Settler's Handbook

DIAL
(340) 277-6994 or
(888) 867-5979

SHOPPING

Tutu Park Mall - Charlotte Amalie 775-4658

TELEVISION

Innovative Cable TV - (see display ad page 179)

WASTE MANAGEMENT

V.I. Waste Management Authority - 712-4962, www.viwma.org

WEBSITES

GoToStThomas.com- produced by Virgin Islands residents, this site offers useful information, links, articles, maps, photos and two beautiful live webcams (one from famous Magen's Bay!). It's also kept current with ferry schedules, taxi fares, and an event calendar. Begin your St. Thomas research with GoToStThomas.com

VisitStThomas.com- One site for all your travel and relocation needs from your exploratory trip to temporary and permanent housing, moving and storage and more. Plus, information on where to eat, shop, bank, recreate, buy insurance and buy healthcare. VisitStThomas.com features FREE video travel guides, webcams and more. Research your new home on VisitSt.Thomas.com, part of the VisitTheVI.com familyof websites, with links to hundreds of other helpful sites. VisitTheVI.com, home of the islands leading informational websites. (See diplay ad below)

Services Directory Index

Services Directory Index (continued)

Services Directory Index (continued)

Index by Subject

Index by Subject (continued)

Index by Subject (continued)

Index by Subject (continued)

St. Thomas

POINTS OF INTEREST
A. University of the Virgin Islands and Reichhold Center
B. Cyril E. King Airport
C. Sub Base/Crown Bay Dock
D. Frenchtown
E. Sugar Estate Post Office
F. Havensight/Cruise Ship Dock
G. National Park Dock
H. Red Hook/St. John Ferry
I. Coral World
J. Mahogany Run Golf Course
K. Magens Bay Beach
L. Mountain Top
M. Ag. Experiment Station

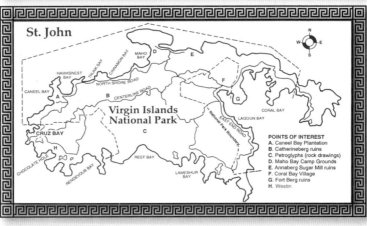

St. John

Virgin Islands National Park

POINTS OF INTEREST
A. Caneel Bay Plantation
B. Catherineberg ruins
C. Petroglyphs (rock drawings)
D. Maho Bay Camp Grounds
E. Annaberg Sugar Mill ruins
F. Coral Bay Village
G. Fort Berg ruins
H. Westin

St. Croix

POINTS OF INTEREST
A-Rain Forest
B-Estate Whim Plantation
C-Botanical Gardens
D-Cruzan Rum Factory
E-Carambola Golf Club
F-Henry E. Rohlsen Airport
G-Salt River National Park
H-Renaissance Group
I-Hovensa
J-Sunny Isle
K-Island Center
L-Buck Island National Park
M-Point Udall

Notes

Notes